A Diminished
ROAR

WINNIPEG
PUBLIC LIBRARY

A Diminished ROAR
Winnipeg in the 1920s

JIM BLANCHARD

UNIVERSITY OF MANITOBA PRESS

To my grandson, Mathias Foss Mitchell

A Diminished Roar: Winnipeg in the 1920s
© Jim Blanchard 2019

23   22   21   20   19   1   2   3   4   5

All rights reserved. No part of this publication may be reproduced
or transmitted in any form or by any means, or stored in a database
and retrieval system in Canada, without the prior written permission
of the publisher, or, in the case of photocopying or any other
reprographic copying, a licence from Access Copyright,
www.accesscopyright.ca, 1-800-893-5777.

University of Manitoba Press
Winnipeg, Manitoba, Canada
Treaty 1 Territory
uofmpress.ca

Cataloguing data available from Library and Archives Canada
ISBN 978-0-88755-839-9 (PAPER)
ISBN 978-0-88755-581-7 (PDF)
ISBN 978-0-88755-579-4 (EPUB)

Cover design by Frank Reimer
Interior design by Karen Armstrong

Printed in Canada

The University of Manitoba Press acknowledges the financial support for
its publication program provided by the Government of Canada through
the Canada Book Fund, the Canada Council for the Arts, the Manitoba
Department of Sport, Culture, and Heritage, the Manitoba Arts Council,
and the Manitoba Book Publishing Tax Credit.

Funded by the Government of Canada | Canadä

CONTENTS

Unidentified woman walking down Portage Avenue, 1922. Photo by Peter McAdam. Archives of Manitoba, McAdam fonds 4, N17772.

Preface

The decade described in Jim Blanchard's *A Diminished Roar: Winnipeg in the 1920s* is one in which the city began a slow shift away from the political and social structures dominant during its first fifty years. Something of a watershed moment, the city's sixth decade is notable for the emergence of new voices in the public sphere, as well as for the difficult impact that broad global trends had on Winnipeg's economy and its prospects for the future. For Blanchard, the decade of the 1920s is a natural extension of his earlier work on Winnipeg: *Winnipeg's Great War: A City Comes of Age* and *Winnipeg 1912*. To tell the story of these tumultuous years—in particular, issues around employment for returned soldiers, unemployment generally, political trends, and the growing presence of women in public life—he consulted a wide range of sources, including the relatively untapped archive of the City of Winnipeg itself.

As a corporate body, as a political and social force, as a collective of individuals engaged in civic life, Winnipeg has generated a considerable body of records. While these records document the role of municipal government in piecing together the services that define urban life, they also serve as evidence of a critical point of intersection between citizens and their elected representatives. For example, just prior to the March 3, 1919, meeting of City Council, the city clerk received a letter from a citizen suggesting that the mayor "go into the matter of getting our business men to let the Thousands of Married Women go home and look after their homes and make a place for our returned

Boys who are forced to be out of work on account of these women being held in jobs which should be at once left open."[1] Indeed, Council minutes reference many letters that ask the city to cooperate by finding work for returning men. Most of these letters were referred to the Standing Committee on Finance, which at the time had authority to "appoint, engage, and employ"[2] all city staff. When the issue surfaced again in 1924, Council appointed a special committee to enquire into the employment of married women, and required that all city departments prepare lists showing "every employee and their residences, also a list of all married women and what their husbands are employed at."[3] The thirty reports received by the special committee contain the names of every person then employed by the city, including their home addresses, and, in the case of women, their marital status and information on their husbands' employment. While only fourteen of 1,932 employees were married women, the special committee recommended a policy of not engaging married women if they were not dependent on their work to manage their affairs, and of not engaging anyone who lived outside the city itself. A motion to this effect was passed by Council in September of 1924. Details regarding the application of this policy can be found in city records until its repeal in 1953—decades after the particular concerns and pressures that led to its implementation had long passed.

Tracing the effect of this one letter reveals much about the nature and tone of civic politics and life in Winnipeg, about civic processes and actions that derive from public engagement, and about the sluggish pace of change within institutions as closely tied to their constituents as are civic government and administration—all themes that Blanchard explores and enriches through his use of newspaper accounts and records held in other archives. In bringing together these sources, voices, and perspectives, Blanchard reveals the fluid nature of the social, political, economic, and cultural conventions that frame our lives. This contingency—our innate capacity to make and remake our shared lives—is perhaps the defining storyline of this engaging look at Winnipeg's past.

—Jody Baltessen
Archivist, City of Winnipeg

A Diminished
ROAR

Golden boy statue being hoisted atop Manitoba Legislative Building, 21 November 1919. University of Manitoba Archives, Winnipeg Tribune *fonds.*

Introduction

The year 1920 was the fiftieth anniversary of Manitoba's entry into Confederation and of the beginning of the crazy half-century of growth of Winnipeg. It was also the year in which the Legislative Building was officially opened. Manitoba's magnificent government building is the quintessential symbol of the ambitious, striving boomtown of 1913, the year construction began. Now, seven years later, it was ready at last.

It was July 15, 1920, a perfect summer day in Winnipeg—sunny with a high of 18 degrees Celsius. At 3:00 p.m., Lieutenant-Governor Sir James Aikins stood on the steps, dressed in his court uniform, complete with cocked hat and ostrich plumes, and declared the building officially open. He reminded the crowd of the building's great importance: "This building in its beauty, its strength and its useful purpose is a manifestation and expression of our present Canadian Christian civilization. Dedicated to the legislative and executive government of Manitoba, in stately silence it proclaims to all the right and power of a free people to make and maintain such laws as they think best for their own guidance, the performance of duties and the preservation of their rights."[1]

Behind him loomed what was arguably the most beautiful parliament building in Canada, and the most beautiful building in Winnipeg. Above all, it was a symbol of the democracy that Canadians valued and had fought for in the recent war: the symbol of a free people. The sheer size of the building and the quality of the interior surfaces and furniture may also have reminded

Manitoba Lieutenant-Governor Sir James Aikins with family, Government House, 3 October 1926. Photo by L.B. Foote. Archives of Manitoba, L.B. Foote fonds, 10155.

some in the crowd of the heady days of a decade ago when the Legislature was just one of many ambitious buildings going up in a city confident that growth and success would continue far into the future. In the Winnipeg of 1920 there was little enough of that old confidence. The recent past had made it difficult to be optimistic.

Liberal Premier Tobias Norris had introduced the lieutenant-governor, saying it was appropriate that he be the one to open the new building since his father, also a Manitoba lieutenant-governor, had dedicated the old Legislative Building nearby on Kennedy Street in 1884. Aikins had been Norris's political rival in 1915 when Aikins led the Conservative Party to its worst defeat ever in the aftermath of the legislative scandal. But they had been working together since Aikins's appointment as lieutenant-governor by Robert Borden in 1916.

In his own remarks the premier said the old Legislative Building, still standing to the east of the new one, was like a homesteader's first cabin on the corner of a farmyard now graced with a modern clapboard house and barn. This comparison would have resonated with many in the audience—people from homesteader families like the premier's. The "new" is always better, and the "old" served mainly as a benchmark to demonstrate how far hard work had brought the pioneer. Premier Norris took his audience through the various periods during the past half-century. The future was likely something Norris preferred to ignore, since the recent provincial election had left him with a minority government and an uncertain grip on power.

Of course, the premier did not mention the area's Indigenous people, whose history stretched back thousands of years. Their gifts, in the Selkirk Treaty and Treaty 1, of the land the city stood upon or of the water from Shoal Lake that Winnipeggers had been enjoying since the completion of the aqueduct the previous year, were not acknowledged. Neither was the destruction of their lands along the Winnipeg River that resulted from the building of the hydro dams that powered the city. Non-Indigenous Manitobans would continue to forget or ignore these and other contributions, without which Winnipeg would not exist, for many years to come.

On this day, the government played host to the people, serving refreshments until 11:00 p.m. The crowd eagerly explored the building, climbing up the spiral stairs to the dome and peering into all the rooms and the Legislative Chamber. The Winnipeg Grenadiers regimental band played during the afternoon. For the evening, a thirty-three-piece ensemble had been organized, consisting of local musicians and conducted by Maurice Genser, who had been the leader of the Walker Theatre Orchestra.[2] They played inside the entrance near the

Full front view (south) of the Manitoba Legislative Building, n.d. University of Manitoba Archives, Winnipeg Tribune fonds.

staircase, and people danced on the polished marble floors or simply listened, sitting on the steps or standing on the second-floor balconies. A visiting opera company had been engaged to perform famous arias and choruses.

The architect, Frank Simon, was present at the opening, and the newspapers said that the many architects and artists who had come to Winnipeg to view the new building paid him lavish compliments. In spite of the celebratory atmosphere, it was likely difficult for some in the crowd not to see the new building as a sort of reminder of the city's ambitious past. The future was very much a question mark in people's minds.

❖

This book is about Winnipeg during the ten years from 1920 to 1930. It is a decade that may appear to be uneventful compared with the tumultuous fifty years that preceded it, but the 1920s in Winnipeg were a period during which its people and institutions were faced with problems, challenges, and adjustments more profound than any they had seen before, as the city attempted to come to terms with its changed situation.

Winnipeg had experienced major challenges in the years leading up to the 1920s. War, the General Strike, the growth of other western cities, the post-war depression, and other influences caused the West's oldest city to lose the pre-eminent position it had occupied in the region. The Great War brought European immigration to an end and, with that, a major source of the city's prosperity. The General Strike, a fully justified work stoppage, could be said to have failed. The result was demoralizing for the Labour movement. Union membership had grown toward the end of the war as workers suffered from the effects of inflation. Then, postwar depression and unemployment set in, and, with no unemployment insurance, many families were forced to rely on the inadequate relief available from the city. But the strike did have some positive results. People who had participated in the strike remembered it as a time when they stood up for their rights. Unions took pride in the organizational ability they had demonstrated. The One Big Union (OBU) maintained the loyalty of many of its members as a place in which to express that they were not beaten. The Ukrainian Labour Temple, built with volunteer labour shortly before the strike, still stands as a symbol of the confidence and determination felt by the Winnipeg Labour movement at the time. Labour politicians emerged from the strike—some emerged from prison—determined to establish themselves as a permanent and effective group on City Council and in the provincial Legislature. However, the nationwide postwar depression, itself a result of the end of the war, acted as a check on Winnipeg's growth and development. It resulted in the weakening of some of the city's main economic engines and created a massive unemployment problem in Winnipeg.

All these things meant that the people of Winnipeg were faced with an enormous task: coping with the unfavourable economic situation. The boom years seemed to be over, and the city would no longer be the "commercial centre of the Canadian west," the "bull's-eye of the Dominion," or the "Chicago of the North," to quote just three of the slogans formerly applied to Winnipeg. In the past the expansion going on in the West poured money into Winnipeg, and a cohesive business community and Board of Trade usually called the shots. New policies and strategies were needed to solve the problems that existed in the 1920s, but there were many competing points of view about which actions to take.

The story of the phenomenal growth of the previous half-century, from the little village of wooden buildings in 1870 to the status of third-largest city in Canada, was a source of pride for Winnipeggers. The people who built Winnipeg in the early decades had believed in its future, its potential to become a great metropolis. The city was seen as a place where a person could make their fortune, and people flocked there hoping to become rich. Many had indeed made fortunes, and the main streets of the 1920s were lined with beautiful commercial buildings, and there were magnificent homes in the leafy suburbs, large public parks, and well-built schools, all reminders of the prosperity of the boom years.

Winnipeg's great success was, however, blemished by the way in which groups like the Metis were elbowed aside, dispossessed, and deprived of the lands promised to them in the Manitoba Act at the time of Confederation. First Nations people were no longer seen in the city, restricted as they were to their allotted reserves.

The boom years had also left behind poor districts, like the one immediately north of the Canadian Pacific Railway (CPR) yards, characterized by poorly built and inadequate housing, outdoor privies, and outbreaks of diseases such as typhus and tuberculosis. Infant mortality was still unacceptably high in the North End wards. On the outskirts there were shantytowns like the one that would eventually be called Rooster Town, south of the city. Here, people built their own houses out of scrap lumber, tarpaper, and pieces of discarded tin. Rooster Town was home to many Metis families and others whom the boom had passed by, people for whom the frantic growth of Winnipeg had resulted only in loss and exclusion in an area where they had once been the majority.

For the "winners" who had gained control of Winnipeg and made it a symbol of success, the 1920s were characterized by a sense of gloom over the city's future and anxiety that the good times would not return.

Winnipeggers of different generations and backgrounds came forward to fight for the city. The city leadership had a wider range of viewpoints than in the past, a situation that meant that compromise and working together were more important than they had been. Unfortunately, the atmosphere in the city made compromise and working together difficult. Different political groups struggled over how to manage the city and solve its problems. The Board of Trade and their allies continued to have influence and were able to sponsor initiatives that could be said to favour the return of the old Winnipeg. But their control was no longer as complete as it had been, and the Independent Labour Party (ILP) and their sympathizers were strong and adept enough to achieve some of their objectives and push the city in new directions. There were also a few non-aligned politicians who occasionally exerted their influence.

This book does not present a simple narrative that moves chronologically from year to year, but rather presents a sampling of representative events and trends in order to describe what the city was like. The book has four parts. The first part looks at the effects of the Great War, postwar depression, and the General Strike on the city, as well as the impact of the personal fortunes amassed by some leaders of the business community. The second part focuses on city politics and public utilities. The third part examines some of the social changes that were taking place in the 1920s in Canada and how these changes played out in Winnipeg. The fourth part looks at two ambitious projects of the 1920s: the construction of Memorial Boulevard and the renewal of the neighbourhood around it; and the sustained but ultimately unsuccessful campaign to revive the city's annual Industrial Exhibition.

❖

PART 1

After the Great War and
the General Strike

❖

Mounted police charge strikers, Main Street in front of City Hall, 21 June 1919. Photo by L.B. Foote. Archives of Manitoba, N2757-1.

CHAPTER 1

Hope against Despair

The great war of 1914 had blown the roof off nineteenth century civilization. The walls and foundations still stood, cracked but erect, and the inhabitants of the western world lived on bravely in them until they too tumbled down in 1931. . . . All the great myths of the 19th century: stability in progress, truth despite contradiction, hope against despair, all were still alive. In the west people still believed in growth, immigration, new farms, new production and filling the wilderness with the prosperous and the comfortable homes of a simple democratic people.—W.L. Morton[1]

Many of the soldiers returning to Winnipeg after the Great War were shaken in just the way historian W.L. Morton describes. They were in a mood to question pre-war truths, assumptions, and ways of doing things, and had expectations that their suffering and sacrifice during the fighting would lead to some undefined new and better world. Writer and professor Douglas Durkin, himself a veteran, captured this sense in his book *The Magpie: A Novel of Postwar Disillusionment*, published in 1923. Durkin wrote about the return to civilian life of his protagonist, Craig Forrester. As a successful member of the Winnipeg Grain Exchange before enlisting, he had enjoyed a good income and married the daughter of a wealthy family. But on returning from the war, he rejected attempts by the government and business leaders like his father-in-law to "restore the order of things that prevailed before the war." "In other words," says Craig, "they want to restore the order out of which the war grew. When we went to the front to fight, it was with the idea that we were fighting to bring in a new order." The Allies beat the German war machine "not with

Douglas Durkin fishing on Grass River, n.d. Archives of Manitoba, John A. Campbell Series IV, #17.

a machine of our own but by something else—something that we knew only as . . . the Cause. . . . The strange thing now is that we hear nothing about the Cause for which we fought." He asks if the preachers and politicians lied to the men who joined up. He concludes, "Either there must be a lot of poor fools in the world or there must be a lot of damn liars."[2]

Craig goes through a good deal of soul searching, and decides to leave his old life and separate from his wife. She does not sympathize with his self-doubt, preferring the confidence of one of Craig's colleagues who is focused on making money. Craig meets people who are Labour sympathizers with a leftist analysis of the situation, and, in the end, he finds peace by returning to past traditions, farming, his birth family, and the land.

The Magpie is a novel. The reality of what faced many troops as they arrived home in 1919 was grimmer than the experience of Craig Forrester. On March 17, 1919, the *Winnipeg Tribune* published an article by Mary Speechly, writing on behalf of a combined committee of women's groups about the return of demobilized soldiers and the growing crisis they faced, because the "number of returning men arriving with their families becomes increasingly greater every week."[3]

Speechly was born in England and studied at the universities of Liverpool and Cambridge. She came to Canada with her husband, a doctor, and lived in Pilot Mound and later in Winnipeg. She was an advocate of home economics education and of birth control. She helped found the Manitoba Family Planning Association, and was for many years a member of the University of Manitoba Board of Governors.

The various women's groups working to help returned men and their families had already sent a joint resolution to the prime minister, Manitoba members of parliament, and local councils, recommending that all the government money being made available for housing should go to returned men who originally came from Manitoba and were now married. In the cover letter signed by Speechly, she wrote that the daily contact the groups had with returning men, and their wives and children, convinced them that "conditions are already becoming serious." She argued that "the welfare of the returned man is very closely bound up with the question of homes. If they know that efforts are being made to secure homes it will have a reassuring and stabilizing effect not only for the men but the whole community."[4] The knowledge that the city was not doing much to assist them undoubtedly contributed to the radicalization of many of the soldiers during the General Strike.

The volunteer groups supported returning soldiers in a variety of ways. The Returned Soldiers Association still met the trains bringing men home from the Front, as they had been doing since 1915, when the first casualties started to return to Winnipeg. They offered food and hot tea as the men arrived, answered questions, and arranged what help they could for the men. The Manitoba Red Cross also met all troop trains and helped any sick men or family members to get to hospital. The Winnipeg Young Women's Christian Association (YWCA) helped to arrange accommodation for a night or two if needed. The day following the arrival of the soldiers, the YWCA would put them in touch with the Patriotic Fund for financial help. Sometimes the Imperial Order Daughters of the Empire (IODE), which had operated a military hospital in the Immigration Building at the CPR station, also stepped in to provide hot meals and temporary accommodation for families with no local contacts. The Salvation Army provided accommodation for single men, as did the Young Men's Christian Association (YMCA). War brides arriving alone or with children could stay at the YWCA building, and the YWCA had also rented the entire Stock Exchange Hotel at Logan Avenue and Arlington Street to accommodate families. This gave the exhausted travellers some breathing space while they searched for more permanent accommodation. In her *Tribune* article Speechly wrote that, "in spite of all efforts made by the combined committee to get houses, or even rooms, it is often several days before any kind of place can be found. If there is this difficulty in the early stages, it is hard to say what will happen in the future."

The returning soldiers may have believed all the rhetoric about how grateful the nation was for their sacrifices during the war, but a letter written by a returned soldier in spring 1919 to the *Tribune* revealed the kinds of real, everyday problems they faced when they arrived in the city, and how little help they were likely to get. The soldier wrote that he was engaged to be married to a woman still in England. He asked if there were housing loans and business loans available. Could people like his fiancée get a reduced fare to Winnipeg? Did returned men receive any preference in housing? The answers printed by the paper were that the federal housing loans were "still up in the air," but something should be known in a few weeks; and, as for the other issues, there was no help locally, but he was encouraged to write to the Secretary of the Repatriation Committee in Ottawa. There were funds available to bring his fiancée to Canada, but it may well have seemed to him that the nation's gratitude was not producing much of real value.

In addition to Speechly and her women's organizations, many prominent business leaders in the city had their own ideas of what would help to turn around the issues created by the war.

James Aikins

James Aikins is a good example of what the city's establishment was thinking as the 1920s began. He was the lieutenant-governor from 1916 to 1926, and he was also the head of a large, successful law firm, and the founder and president of the Canadian Bar Association. In August 1919, just weeks after the end of the General Strike, Aikins delivered his presidential address to the Bar Association at its meeting in Winnipeg. He talked about the aftermath of both the war and the General Strike. He spoke about the sacrifice of 60,000 Canadian lives during the war. He also mentioned what he considered the positive things that had come from the fighting: the fact that, for the most part, Canada had financed its own war debt, and that the bravery and fighting skill of its soldiers had led Canada's "astonished foes and admiring allies to realize that a new power had entered the lists."[5] Then, referring to psychological effects similar to those mentioned by Morton and Durkin, he talked about how the war had created "an intellectual, temperamental and spiritual ferment." Everything, from mathematics and physics to the theories of Adam Smith and John Stuart Mill, was now being challenged, he said. The claim was being made that "there are no definite absolute rights."

Then he specifically addressed the General Strike, saying that friction was natural in industry when there was so much change happening. Canadian industry was being retooled to suit postwar conditions. In such times, he told his audience of lawyers, their role was to create new laws and rules for public conduct to encompass new situations. The laws should be written with basic principles in mind, the most important being that every advance in the civilization they enjoyed and the laws to express it should be gradual and "not attained by revolution." Referring to labour unrest in Winnipeg and across the country, Aikins said that lately the power of corporations and labour unions had been used to the detriment of each other and of the general public. It was necessary, he argued, to make compulsory arbitration the method of solving disputes in order to avoid strikes and lockouts, an idea that was not popular with labour unions who were working for collective bargaining.

He regretted that, at the moment, "in politics strong agitation is made for collectivism and enslavement to system in substitution of individual liberty and for group and class control in lieu of popular democracy and for Bolshevism instead of settled national government by the people, of the people and for the people." He argued that "the essential unit of Democracy is the individual upon the proper development and use of whose capacities and powers depend Canada's safety and progress, whose due regard for the rights of others means a nation's internal quietness and whose right to possess the fruits of his labour is fundamental to the prosperity and comfort of the whole."[6]

Aikins's defence of liberal democracy was moving and articulate. But it ignored the point of view of gradualist Social Democrats, like many of the General Strike leaders, who were not opposed to the basic political system in Canada but wanted to make sure it benefited everyone. During their trials in the early months of 1920, the strike leaders and their lawyers would argue, often eloquently, that they believed strongly in individual liberty and democracy. They attempted to demonstrate to the juries that they were merely exercising their rights as free British subjects during the strike. Two of the accused, Frederick J. Dixon and Abraham A. Heaps, were acquitted, partly because of the brilliance of their statements to the court.

Frederick J. Dixon

Frederick Dixon, in his address on February 13 and 14, 1920, to the jury at his trial for seditious libel, said: "I want to emphasize the fact again that so far as liberty of opinion is concerned, that is what is on trial, I contend. Liberty of speech and the press have been secured by the fearless action of British juries and Canadian juries, and they can only be preserved by the same method."

Later he read into the record a speech he had made that was used against him by the prosecution. He quoted: "The imprisonment of those who hold unpopular opinions is the negation of democracy. While these men are in jail not one of us is really free. It

Frederick J. Dixon, one of the General Strike leaders who enjoyed political success during the 1920s. Archives of Manitoba, Legislative Assembly, 1921.

was their turn yesterday. It may be ours tomorrow. It is easy to stand for free speech for those who think as we do—the Czar or the Kaiser would go that far—but the acid test of our faith in democracy is that we insist on free speech for those whose ideas are contrary to our own, and that is the only safe course to pursue if we would preserve our own freedom for who knows when he may want to say something that is unpopular."[7]

Dixon was a Social Democrat, and he argued in favour of the very type of individual freedom that James Aikins spoke of in his speech to the Bar Association. Social Democrats like Dixon began to enjoy political success during the 1920s, elected as democratic politicians to City Council, the provincial Legislature, and the House of Commons. Their success can be seen as one of the results of the strike. In the future their voices would always be part of political debate.

In Britain, the Labour Party would soon become the Official Opposition and in 1924 would form the first Labour government. Winnipeg would elect two socialist mayors and many Labour and Communist aldermen during the 1920s and 1930s. These individuals proved to be dedicated and skilled politicians who claimed a role for themselves and made significant contributions in solving the city's problems.

Judge Hugh Robson and James Winning

Judge Hugh Robson was appointed by the provincial government to carry out a Royal Commission investigation into the General Strike. Judge Robson's Royal Commission "Report" of November 6, 1919, is of great interest for what it can reveal about the aftermath of the strike. Robson laid out the details of the dispute over collective bargaining that led to the strike. He gave prominence to the testimony of James Winning, the president of the Trades and Labour Council and a member of the General Strike committee. Beyond the basic issue of the establishment of collective bargaining, Winning spoke about the range of problems faced by working-class people that made them willing to walk off the job. They were, he said, distressed by the high cost of living and the resulting difficulties they were experiencing by the end of the war. Winning spoke of the "long hours people were expected to work, low wages and undesirable working conditions, profiteering and the growing awareness on the part of the working class of the economic inequalities in modern society, the refusal of some employers to recognize the right of workers to organize and the refusal to recognize the right of collective bargaining."[8] Even those workers whose wages had risen during the war were struggling because inflation was pushing the cost of everyday necessities out of reach.

It was often impossible to survive on the wages people were being paid. Winning gave the example of a man who had testified before the commission that he was working seven days a week for twenty dollars to feed his family. Thomas Flye, who had been a member of the Strike Committee and would be a city alderman for many years, testified at the Royal Commission hearings that at the end of the war he was earning sixty-eight cents an hour and had to watch his children go hungry because he could not afford to feed them properly.

Winning described unemployment as "the greatest 'nightmare'" of the working class because unemployed working-class families were forced into debt. "A man's children can't have shoes and clothes and his wife can't see a doctor if she is sick. Eventually, when you get far enough behind with the rent, you are put out of your apartment," he testified. The problem of unemployment and the inadequacy of unemployment relief would continue through the 1920s and into the 1930s in

Judge Hugh Robson (c. 1915). He led the investigation into the General Strike. Archives of Manitoba, N32305.

Winnipeg. It would be 1940 before the first unemployment insurance system was put in place by the federal government, ending two long decades during which the only recourse for unemployed people was the humiliation of asking for relief. Winnipeg Labour Member of Parliament (MP) A.A. Heaps would play a leading role in drafting and arguing the case for the unemployment insurance legislation.

In his final report, Robson wrote: "Labour takes the view that as a fundamental part of the producing force of the country it should never suffer a want that is not shared by the element that benefits from its labour, and if a time of hardship arises, means should be taken to see that there is such an application of wealth that labour will in an honourable way, and as a right and not by grace have the means to tide itself over until normal periods return." Furthermore, he recommended, "in addition to the provision of subsistence in the period of distress that is likely to arise this winter," that government provide "medical services and medicinal necessaries."[9]

Robson also quoted Winning on how labouring people can see that "the other elements of the community never seem to be in want, neither in the matter of food, clothing, suitable residence, education, medical and other professional attention, or even recreation, yet labour is not only never assured but is very often deprived of the essentials of these things."

Robson showed some sympathy with Winning's views: "Winnipeg unfortunately presents a prominent example of these extremes. There has been, and there is now, an increasing display of carefree, idle luxury and extravagance on the one hand, while on the other is intensified deprivation. The general cold indifference of the one section to the condition of the other and the display of luxury aggravate this feeling of social disparity into one of active antagonism by the one class against the other." He called for something like a welfare state: "If capital does not provide enough to assure labour a contented existence with a full enjoyment of the opportunities of the times for human improvement, then the Government might find it necessary to step in and let the state do these things at the expense of capital."[10]

He pointed out that the children of working-class families cannot afford to go to university and that this was a "waste of human capital." He called for a taxation system that would provide for things like medical care, noting that mothers often had to forgo medical treatment for their children because they could not afford the doctor's bills.

Like many other middle-class people, Robson differentiated between the activities of those Labour leaders he saw as political radicals and those concentrating on better wages and working conditions. He was speaking the language of the Red Scare gripping Canada and the United States in 1919 when he described the threat he felt was posed by political radicals, influenced by the Russian Revolution and other developments in Europe.

One of Robson's recommendations was that an arbitration system should be established by proclaiming the Industrial Conditions Act, passed by the Legislature in March 1919, but not made law. The Joint Council of Industry provided for in the Act would then be appointed. The council was to have one general, two business, and two Labour members. This sort of arbitration body was favoured by employers, but workers and their unions were working toward collective bargaining between unions and employers as the standard method of negotiation. No Labour representatives were appointed at first. But, in March 1920, the Act was officially made law and the Joint Council began to operate. In the event, it did not have the power to impose a solution in a dispute. It could arbitrate, but the union members were still free to strike and the employers could lock out their employees. The council had settled thirty-two of thirty-four cases heard in 1921–22. It operated until September 1923 when Premier Bracken abolished it, arguing that this would save $10,000 a year.

Workmen having their lunch on Main Street, 1922. Photo by Peter McAdam. Archives of Manitoba, McAdam fonds 5, N17740.

CHAPTER 2

The Postwar Depression and Its Effects

Many of the dramatic changes that Winnipeg experienced in the 1920s, as well as the ways the city adapted, were caused by the depression that took hold of most of Canada and many other combatant countries after the Great War. When the war ended the Allied nations were heavily in debt to the United States. Ten billion dollars had been loaned by the Americans to help feed and equip the Allies in their war effort. After 1919 America decided to stop making loans; this was a catastrophe for European nations trying to recover from the war and its effects would soon be felt in Canada.

The war had resulted in an expansion of the Canadian economy and of the number of available jobs for both men and women. But, in spite of the fact that many people were working and earning good wages, inflation ate into the buying power of working-class people. In 1914 and 1915 inflation sat at 1 to 2 percent. It rose to 8 percent in 1916, 23 percent in 1917, and 20 percent in 1918. Inflation continued after the end of the war. In 1919 the cost of living rose 10 to 12 percent, and in the first half of 1920 it rose 20 percent.

The end of the war did not bring a reduction in demand for goods, because European nations were now spending on foodstuffs and the many things needed to restart their economies. In the West, where the government had taken control of grain marketing, agricultural prices were kept high through 1919. Then, in the middle of 1920, prices dropped. Across Canada the country's cost of living declined 15 percent in 1920 and a further 10 percent in 1921.

People suffered in all areas.[1] In western Canada the depression began in the fall of 1920. One of the causes was that wheat prices collapsed. In summer 1920 wheat was selling for $2.85 a bushel. In the fall the price dropped and by 1921 it was at 81 cents a bushel. Prices remained low until 1924.[2]

Western farmers had invested in land and equipment during the war to produce the large quantities of wheat the Allies required, and government intervention kept prices high. Many farmers had taken mortgages on additional land and borrowed to buy tractors and other farm machinery. In the fall of 1920 the government closed down the Wheat Board, which had been controlling prices, and the Winnipeg Grain Exchange resumed its role as the market for western wheat. Because this coincided with the drop in price, farmers demanded a return to government control. This did not happen.

Although wheat prices were down, the farmers' costs remained high. Many farmers were not bringing in enough income to make loan payments, pay taxes and freight for their grain, and buy the necessities of life. Many lost their farms and, without farm income, the whole economy of the West slowed down. Wholesale and other businesses in Winnipeg also began to fail or lay off employees. Merchants found themselves with inventories for which they had paid high prices and which they now had to sell at a large discount. In Canada as a whole, 1920 saw 2,451 business failures and in 1922 the total was 3,695. Banks and companies that had made loans to farmers also suffered as their customers defaulted on mortgages and other debts. There were a number of bank failures and mergers of smaller banks with larger ones. In 1910 Canada had thirty chartered banks and by 1928 only ten were in business.[3] Smaller banks were simply not as able as larger banks to absorb the losses resulting from the depression, and, in some cases, resulting from business mistakes and miscalculations. They took the route of selling out to one of the larger banks. The Union Bank was one such bank that did not survive.

Union Bank

The postwar depression of 1920 to 1925 was the worst Canada has ever seen, with the exception of the 1930s. For the agricultural economy of western Canada, the fall of grain prices and poor crops contributed to high unemployment and dramatically reduced economic activity in Winnipeg. One result of this depression was the disappearance of a number of smaller and medium-sized banks, because farmers and other customers were unable to pay back loans taken out during the Great War. The Union Bank, with headquarters in Winnipeg and a great many Winnipeg shareholders, was one such bank.

Most of these banks merged with larger institutions such as the Royal Bank, the Bank of Commerce, and the Bank of Montreal. Minister of Finance Sir Henry Drayton, speaking about the Home Bank, another failed bank, later said: "Under no circumstances would I have allowed a bank to fail during the period in question. . . . If it had appeared to me that the bank was not able to meet its public obligations, I should have taken steps to have it taken over by some other bank or banks." He said that if insolvency "with a consequent loss to the depositors" was the only alternative, he would press for a merger.[4]

In Winnipeg's boom period before the First World War, the Union Bank had been one of the symbols of the city's success. For the Winnipeg directors of the Union Bank, moving the head office from Quebec City in 1912 demonstrated the city's progress toward becoming the metropolis of western Canada. Most other Canadian banks had their western headquarters in the city, but the Union Bank was a Winnipeg institution with the majority of shares owned locally. The Winnipeg banking industry profited from financing the massive growth that occurred in the West before the war.

In January 1922, in the second year of the depression, the Union Bank had seemed to be coping well with the economic situation. At its annual meeting that month, Winnipegger William R. Allan was elected president, replacing George Galt, who was too ill to travel to Winnipeg from Victoria where he now lived. Harold B. Shaw, who had been general manager, was now a vice-president. Allan, a partner in Allan, Killam and McKay Real Estate and Insurance, and George Galt, partner with his cousin in a large grocery wholesale company, were members of the founding group of Winnipeg business leaders. Like many of their contemporaries, they were connected to wealthy eastern families. Allan was the son of Hugh Allan of the Allan Shipping Lines, and Galt was a member of a family that included a Father of Confederation and was now involved in business enterprises across the country. Galt's last presidential address was read by Allan. The general situation was grim: prices were down, trade was disorganized and uncertain, and manufacturers had fewer customers. But Galt's message was confident, stressing that the bank had been very cautious and as a result it had finished 1921 in good shape.

Two years later, on March 7, 1923, the situation had changed. It was announced by Allan that Shaw, the bank's vice-president, was leaving due to "differences of opinion between the directors and him with regard to matters of administration." This cryptic announcement is partly explained by Winnipeg businessman Robert T. Riley, who had been on the board for many years and wrote in his memoirs about this incident. He said that Shaw was a very "energetic, resourceful man, but I was so impressed with the fact that he was ignoring the authority of his board and doing so many things first and getting them confirmed afterwards that I became alarmed, retired from the board and sold my holdings." Canadian Finance, the local financial newspaper, stated that the bank had lost money due to "the problems created by some unauthorized speculation in London."[5] It seemed that Shaw had been speculating in foreign currencies and had lost a good deal of the bank's money.

The bank's directors decided to draw down its reserves and pay all its obligations off so that it could continue to operate. Then, Riley reports in his memoirs, he was asked by the president of the Bank of Montreal and the minister of finance to rejoin the directorate of the bank, and was assured that if he did they would give any assistance required. Riley was a well-known and well-respected city businessman. He purchased enough shares to qualify and became the chairman of the executive committee. A sum of $4 million was transferred from reserves to cover the losses, and the shareholders watched nervously as the value of shares fell.

By February of 1924 it seemed that the crisis was over. The bank's annual report stated reassuringly that the bank had successfully dealt with the problems of 1923. Both President Allan and the new general manager, James W. Hamilton, spoke about how well the bank had weathered the storm and how it was now the fifth-largest bank in Canada. In January 1925 the Union Bank again reported a good year. They had paid four dividends and their liquid assets were 52 percent of the bank's liabilities, up from 49 percent. Reserves and undivided profits totalled $2 million. The annual report struck an optimistic tone: the dead wood had been thrown overboard and the bank was unimpaired in its capital.

Then one day, wrote Riley, "like a bolt from the blue," an offer came from the Royal Bank to buy the Union Bank. This was an "exceedingly good bargain, because, whilst the Royal Bank shares that we were paid with were valued at the time at two hundred and fifty, today [he was writing in 1928] they are worth over four hundred and are paying a dividend at the rate of sixteen percent. The Union Bank shareholders were exceptionally well satisfied with the transaction."[6]

The Royal Bank was the largest bank in Canada. In the decade from 1910 to 1920, it had merged with four smaller Canadian banks, including the Northern Crown Bank of Winnipeg. The merger brought the Royal Bank's 327 western branches and $115 million in deposits. It was the largest bank amalgamation in Canadian history up to that time.

This 1928 Main Street scene shows the Union Bank (left) renamed after the merger and amalgamation with the Royal Bank of Canada. Archives of Manitoba, N21159.

Why, if the Union Bank was, in fact, no longer in crisis, would the board and shareholders be willing to sell? It is likely that many shareholders had been shaken by the drop in the share price the year before and, given the general situation, were not anxious to take risks. There were special meetings of both the Royal Bank and the Union Bank shareholders to approve the acquisition of the Union Bank.[7] In the fall of 1925, at the Union Bank meeting, Allan recommended the merger, telling the shareholders, "From the sentimental side the change is one to be regretted, but it was realized by all that it was in the best interests of the shareholders of the Union Bank." They voted unanimously in favour of the change. In September, Allan and Riley became members of the Royal Bank board and of a committee that met in Winnipeg to make policy decisions about the West.

The ease with which the shareholders gave up Winnipeg's only bank headquarters is evidence of how the city's old ambitions were beginning to slip away. People were no longer in a confident, expansive mood. The shareholders voted for the safety of acquiring Royal Bank shares, and ownership of the Union Bank with its western branch network passed to Toronto. Almost immediately some staff were let go and some of the Union Bank branches were closed.

Other major banks began to reduce their operations in Winnipeg. For example, in October 1921 Vere Brown, who had for some years been the superintendent of the Bank of Commerce for western Canada, left Winnipeg to take a job with National City Bank in New York. Brown had been an active and prominent member of Winnipeg's business community. With his departure the bank divided the western territory, and Alberta and Peace River were supervised from Calgary while Winnipeg was responsible only for Manitoba and Saskatchewan. The growth of the populations in the provinces further west meant that in banking, as in so much else, no longer would everything be managed from Winnipeg.

The Board of Trade

The Board of Trade was another Winnipeg institution affected by the economic and political conditions in Winnipeg. Beginning in the 1880s, the board had played an important role in the city's development. City Council and the Board of Trade worked in tandem and shared many members. If the board was in favour of a policy, it was likely that Council would also support it. In 1920, his first year as mayor, Edward Parnell was also president of the Board of Trade, but this was the last time in the 1920s that the two offices were held by the same person at the same time. As businesses failed or downsized in the early 1920s, the membership of the Board of Trade shrank and it was no longer able to get its ideas accepted and put into action as easily as in the past. The board, which had created the Citizens' Committee of 1000, had played a central role in causing the General Strike to fail, but there were few signs that people took much satisfaction from the victory. Many spoke of a pall hanging over the city. The confident boosterism of the boom years evaporated, replaced by pessimism about the city's future. In the business community there were often expressed worries that no one would want to invest in a city that had been the scene of such massive labour strife, or that elected a Labour mayor.

Travers Sweatman, in his farewell speech after five years as president of the Board of Trade in 1925, spoke of the difficulties the Board had been experiencing: "Winnipeg has been passing through a critical period in her history when she very much lacked leadership. . . . one problem is that the brightest and most energetic young businessmen . . . were tending to join the various service clubs and were devoting their energies to . . . the social and charitable activities of these clubs and neglect the larger sphere of promoting the commercial and business prosperity of the city." He said the city lacked the kind of leadership that had been supplied in the past "by those old stalwarts who put Winnipeg

Board of Trade Building, 1919. During the General Strike it was the headquarters of the Citizens' Committee of 1000. Archives of Manitoba, L.B. Foote fonds, N2755.

on the map and took part in the great development that culminated in 1912." These people had retired, died, or moved to some other part of the world, and "during the past 10 years it has been impossible for the younger men to come forward to take their places."[8]

One sign of the Board of Trade's changed status was that it moved its offices in fall 1925, leaving the iconic Industrial Bureau building on Main Street and Water Avenue and taking over rented space on the ground floor of the Confederation Life building. The move was necessitated by the dilapidated state of the Industrial Bureau building, which, although it was only thirteen years old, had deteriorated badly. The building was supposed to be a showplace for Winnipeg products and encourage investment, but it needed repairs and upgrading that the board could not afford. The bureau's auditorium, a 3,000-seat venue for public events and conventions, had been closed by the city because it was no longer in compliance with the fire code. That the board was short of money is illustrated by the fact that the membership were canvassed for donations to help pay for the move.

The Board of Trade was, then, no longer as powerful as it had been. The animosities and rancour of the General Strike may also have discouraged business people from becoming involved in civic affairs that were now marked by more controversy than in the past. The new reality was that the board and the people who had been its members were no longer accepted as the unquestioned leaders of the city.

The Winnipeg Grain Trade

Similar to the Board of Trade, the Winnipeg Grain Exchange, since its founding in 1887, had been one of the most important engines of the city's economy. During the 1880s the Winnipeg Board of Trade had successfully gained control of the grading and inspection of western wheat from the Toronto Board of Trade. Canada's grain-grading system allows the sorting of a crop into wheat of different qualities and therefore prices. Before the West began to develop as a wheat-exporting area, the Toronto Board of Trade and the Montreal Board of Trade administered the grading system for the country. In the 1880s Winnipeg began to play a larger role and eventually became the centre of the western grain industry. In 1883 Winnipeg's Board of Trade was authorized to appoint a Board of Grain Examiners, whose job was to examine candidates for the position of grain inspector and license those who passed the examination. This Board of Examiners also would send representatives to the annual meetings in Toronto where the standards for each grade of grain were established for the year. Just two years later, in 1885, a Dominion order-in-council established that inspection and other arrangements for grain handling in the West were entrusted to the Winnipeg Board of Trade. The names and grades of Manitoba wheat were to be included in the Canadian Inspection Act. After 1888, the standards for western grades of wheat became the responsibility of a separate Western Standards Board with representatives from all western boards of trade. This Western Standards Board met once a year and established standards for grades of all wheat grown west of Lake Superior. Because the grade of a shipment of wheat is the key factor in determining the price the farmer receives and the price the buyer pays, disputes over grades are part of the system. Disputes had been sent to Toronto for arbitration, but after 1890 there was a Western Board of Arbitrators to make decisions on disputes.

The Winnipeg Grain Exchange operated within this regulatory framework as a market where prices could be determined and the ever-growing flood of western grain could be efficiently moved from the prairies to the seaboard for export. The small group of Winnipeggers who founded the exchange created it from scratch, developing a language of trading terms, and creating their own internal dispute mechanisms and methods of keeping track of trades. From 1887, the exchange was connected by telegraph to the great grain markets in Chicago, Minneapolis, and Liverpool, so that prices in these places could be used as a basis for the Winnipeg prices. The exchange became the heart of the western Canadian grain industry, interconnected and interacting with Winnipeg-based elevator companies, insurance and banking services, and government agencies. Its massive office building on Lombard Avenue housed the exchange but it was also home to most of the important entities of the industry.

By the time of the Great War, the Winnipeg Grain Exchange had grown to be one of the continent's largest wheat markets. On the floor of the exchange, sellers and buyers traded on their own behalf or as the agents of others who wanted western Canadian grain or had grain to sell. Trading took place using the open outcry method. Buyers and sellers used hand signals and shouted bids in trading sessions that moved the crops of the Canadian prairies along to markets in the East and Great Britain and Europe.

The exchange had 463 members in the 1920s. Seats on the exchange were officially priced at $50,000, but the actual price a prospective member might have to pay could be much lower, depending on the circumstances. Only 343 members were actually engaged in grain handling or buying and selling grain, the two branches of the industry. Commission agents and cash grain brokers collected per-bushel fees for the specialized services they provided to the sellers and buyers of wheat, oats, and barley. Given the volume of grain traded, these commissions provided a good living. During the first decades of the twentieth century, many of the wealthiest families in Winnipeg were involved in the grain trade. Bankers, shippers, insurance brokers, and representatives of the milling and malting industries and of the various grain companies also had seats on the exchange. The capital amassed by grain merchants was invested locally in such ventures as Great-West Life, and members of the exchange were on the boards of most local financial and manufacturing companies.

Grain companies maintained lines of country elevators in prairie towns, as well as large terminal elevators at the heads of the Great Lakes and, beginning in the 1920s, at Vancouver. The elevators were key components in the infrastructure needed to move the crop to export, collecting storage and handling fees for doing it. The standard or line elevators that became the iconic symbol of the prairies were built to a design favoured by the CPR. In fact, William Van Horne of the CPR mandated that only these elevators would be built at the company's stations. They made the storing of grain and the loading of

Grain Exchange Building, c.1920. Archives of Manitoba, L.B. Foote fonds, N2755.

grain cars more efficient than the older, flat warehouses in which grain was handled in sacks. Van Horne's policy had been extremely controversial around the turn of the century, but by the 1920s standard elevators lined all the railway lines. And, of course, the railroads charged shipping fees, and the banks whose western headquarters were clustered around Portage Avenue and Main Street provided the millions of dollars in short-term loans needed to keep the grain moving from the country elevator to market. The Bank of Montreal branch at Portage and Main still has a solid-gold wheat sheaf on its wall as a reminder of the wealth the bank earned financing the trade.

Grain farmers on the whole did not believe the grain traders when they were told that the Grain Exchange was an essential part of the industry. There was a great deal of suspicion of the exchange, which was seen as a "combine with a gambling hell thrown in" by farm leaders like Edward Partridge, one of the founders of the farmer-owned United Grain Growers. The Grain Exchange and the railroads were viewed by many farmers as adversaries that were "bleeding us."[9]

Before the turn of the century it was true that producers were sometimes not treated fairly by the industry. But grain farmers, as a group that provided the country with its largest export commodity and represented a large block of votes, succeeded in having the federal government create an effective regulatory structure to ensure fairness in grading, weighing, and shipping of grain. This structure was based on the Canada Grain Act and other legislation administered by the regulatory agency called the Board of Grain Commissioners, founded in 1912. But in the marketing area, farmers still had to rely on the exchange to sell their grain. That was about to change.

The strong position of the Grain Exchange as the sole market for western grain was undermined during the Great War. In fall of 1915, during which the largest wheat crop in Canadian history was harvested in western Canada, food shortages were looming in the Allied countries and there was a threat of inflated food prices. To ensure Britain and her allies would have adequate supplies at reasonable prices, Sir George Foster, the federal minister of trade and commerce, commandeered 15 million bushels of wheat at the Lakehead and eastern points for sale at a fixed price to the British Wheat Export Company. Again in 1917 and 1918 the government intervened in disposing of the wheat crop because of concern over rising prices and speculation. A special agency, the Board of Grain Supervisors, was created to take control of the crop, set the prices, and decide on grain allocation between domestic users and the Wheat Export Company. Robert Magill, secretary of the Winnipeg Grain Exchange, served on the Board of Grain Supervisors and the members of the exchange supported its activities, saying it was their patriotic duty to do so. In 1917 the price the Grain Supervisors set for No. 1 Northern, the highest grade of western wheat, was $2.21 a bushel for grain delivered at Fort William. In 1918 the price was $2.24 a bushel. These were excellent prices that ensured farmers would make money and stay in the business of growing wheat. Farmers' sons were exempt from military service and, in 1918, from conscription, so that they would stay on the land and produce food for the Allies and the military.

For one more year, in 1919, the government maintained a monopoly in the marketing of the western Canadian wheat crop, this time through the agency called the Canadian Wheat Board.

The Wheat Board purchased grain from farmers at a fixed price. The farmer delivering his grain was also given a certificate entitling him to a second payment, his share of any profits the Wheat Board had made by the end of the year. In 1919 farmers received a total of $2.63 a bushel for No. 1 Northern wheat. The prices were stable and high, and many farmers decided that they much preferred government-controlled marketing to the free market of the Grain Exchange.

In August 1920 government intervention ended and the Grain Exchange began to operate once more. Prices fell from $2.74 a bushel in August to below $2.00 in December. The general downward trend continued until December 1923 when the price reached ninety-three cents a bushel and then began to slowly recover. Canadian wheat prices were hit hard by a complex of factors, including the postwar re-emergence of Australia, Argentina, and other wheat exporters. Because of the danger of submarines and the high cost of insuring shipping during the war, these countries had been virtually eliminated as competitors. The inability of Canada's former customers in Europe to afford wheat imports was another factor. In some parts of the prairies, the dreaded leaf stem rust disease and drought added to farmers' problems.

Wheat prices fell but farm costs and farm debts remained the same or rose. Some farmers simply gave up and walked away from their land. The fall in prices was seen by farmers as proof that the Grain Exchange did not work to their benefit and that the traders were once more stealing their profits. The government in Ottawa responded, predictably, with a Royal Commission on Grain Marketing that reported in early 1925.[10] While the commissioners made numerous suggestions for revisions to the Canada Grain Act, they found no proof of wrongdoing on the part of the grain trade. The findings of the commission had little influence on farmers' opinions, and agitation to re-establish the Wheat Board on a permanent basis continued. When attempts to do so failed, a new strategy emerged. Economist Harold S. Patton wrote that "in 1923, when the futility of the campaign for the re-establishment of government marketing became conclusive, the western farmer's organizations turned their efforts from the direction of government compulsion and monopoly to voluntary and cooperative action."[11]

This voluntary and cooperative action came in the form of the wheat pool movement. The first pool was established in Alberta in 1923, followed by Saskatchewan and Manitoba. In a wheat pool the members contracted to sell their wheat through a central selling agency, receiving an initial price and a final payment that was a share of the net profit at the end of the year. Farmers were free to join the pool system or not, but once they were members they had to contract to deliver all their wheat to the wheat pool for a period of years in order to ensure a dependable supply of grain. By 1924 the wheat pools created a central selling agency in Winnipeg to handle the marketing of pool grain.

Interior of the Grain Exchange Building, sixth-floor trading room, 1921. Archives of Manitoba, L.B. Foote fonds, N2036.

The agency had seats on the Grain Exchange and used its facilities to sell their grain, although the agency also sold increasing quantities directly to customers.

From 1924 to 1928 western farmers enjoyed stronger prices and a period of good crops, culminating in the record 1928 wheat harvest, which, although large, was of lower quality. Wheat exports grew steadily and in the 1928–29 crop year earned $429 million, 40 percent of all Canadian export earnings. The pools were credited by many farmers with the improved economic situation, and by the end of the decade the three prairie wheat pools were selling around half of the western Canadian crop. The pools and the farmer-owned United Grain Growers, between them, controlled 38 percent of the country elevators in western Canada and a good deal of the terminal storage space in Vancouver and at the Lakehead. The private grain companies competed for what was left.

A war of words raged between representatives of the Grain Exchange and the pools through the 1920s and for many years after. The central question was whether the prices the central selling agency was able to get for pool members' grain were greater than those obtainable on the Grain Exchange. There never has been a satisfactory conclusion to this debate.[12]

An example of the sorts of arguments made is found in Winnipeg Grain Exchange President James Richardson's address to the 22 December 1924 annual meeting. He was critical of the pools, pointing out that the price paid for Alberta wheat was set by managers based in Fort William, whereas a large portion of the Alberta crop went out through Vancouver. He mentioned the administration expenses of the pool that had to be paid out of the money owed to pool members. Alberta farmers who sold on the open market received as much as $1.50 per bushel while the pool price was $1.02. "We still tend to the belief," Richardson said, "that the free play of opinion of farmers, merchants, millers and exporters and importers the world over, year in and year out, will record in the future, as it has in the past, a wheat price that has an uncanny way of reflecting true conditions and reflecting them much better than any body of men can possibly forecast them."

In 1929, the year after a record harvest in western Canada, it was clear that all the other major wheat-producing countries were also enjoying bumper crops. In Canada the price declined, reaching a disastrous fifty-eight cents a bushel in 1930. This produced a crisis for the wheat pools. In 1929 they had made an initial payment of one dollar per bushel, and when prices fell below that figure, it seemed they would be bankrupted. When there was no improvement in 1930, they appealed to the provincial governments to guarantee their loans with the banks. On February 27, the Manitoba Legislature responded with a bill that committed Manitoba to guarantee the advances made by the pool; Saskatchewan and Alberta had already done the same.

These bailouts were not popular with the private trade that had been making important changes to deal with the decline in their share of the business. To quote Charles Anderson, an historian of the grain trade: "To the private firms the answer to this new threat seemed clear; if they were to survive and prosper then they must look for ways to combine together to match the efficiencies of large-scale, centralized management and administration then being realized by the cooperatives."[13]

There were a number of mergers of smaller companies. For example, in 1928 six companies with a total of 223 licensed elevators amalgamated to form the Western Grain Company. It was incorporated in 1929 as a public company with issues of bonds and preferred shares. It became the fourth-largest private company after Alberta Pacific, Federal Grain, and Searle Grain. The pools said this was a plot to build public support for the private trade: an editorial in the February 1929 *Scoop Shovel*, the newspaper of the pools, warned pool members not to invest in the company's bonds and once again accused the private trade of making profits on the backs of farmers.

Another example of the mergers of that time was when, in 1929, Augustus Searle amalgamated his family firm with a number of smaller firms like the Liberty and Home grain companies to form Searle Grain Ltd., a company owned privately by the family.

Federal Grain, another new entity, which resulted from the amalgamation of eight smaller companies, also incorporated in 1929. Three men—James Stewart, John C. Gage, and Henry E. Sellars—between them owned a majority of the shares in the constituent companies and they became the president and vice-presidents, respectively. In 1929 Stewart, one of the wealthiest of the Winnipeg grain merchants, made the same mistake as the central selling agency of the pools and assumed that the price of grain would rise. He bought a good deal of grain but did not follow the normal practice of hedging it in the futures market. As a result, when the price began to fall in 1929, he suffered enormous losses. Sellars's son George later remembered the incident:

> The market went down instead of up, and, like the guy going to the races Stewart kept doubling up to make up. Ultimately, on a Sunday, he asked Gage and my father if they would come over to his house, and they went over and he told them they were virtually

Aerial photograph showing Main Street with the Fort Garry Hotel on the left, c. 1920s. University of Manitoba Archives.

> bankrupt. This was quite a shock of course. Stewart was about the biggest grain man in Canada . . . but despite that, out of all this debacle he didn't get any money personally. There was no intended fraud on his part; on the other hand he had no business doing what he did without the directors' or his partners' knowledge.[14]

Stewart sold everything including his house to cover his losses. Gage died soon after, leaving Sellars in charge of Federal Grain, in financial difficulties at the opening of the Depression. Thanks to careful management he survived and so did the company.

The other large organization in the private grain trade, the companies belonging to the Richardson family, took a slightly different course at the end of the 1920s. James A. Richardson diversified his business enterprises, establishing Western Canada Airways in 1926. He had a great deal of success with the airline, winning the first airmail contracts and playing a strong supporting role in the opening of the North. Piloted by ex-military fliers, his planes carried the mail and transported prospectors and anyone else who had business in the North. By the end of the 1920s Richardson's airline was one of the largest in the British Empire. James Richardson himself was now on the boards of a wide range of national companies including the CPR, as well as being the chancellor of his alma mater, Queen's University. He and his wife had become leading figures in the world of Winnipeg charities and the city's social life. In the late 1920s Richardson was also heavily involved in the investment and securities business through the stock brokerage section he established for James Richardson and Sons. Richardson did not escape the damage inflicted by the stock market crash. In 1929 work had begun on the basement of a new headquarters of the Richardson companies at Portage Avenue and Main Street, but when it became clear that he was faced with heavy losses, Richardson ordered the basement filled in and put his new building on hold.

The positions of the Grain Exchange and the private grain companies, formerly two important engines of the Winnipeg economy, were undermined by the controlled marketing imposed during the Great War and by the growth of the prairie wheat pools. Another heavy blow to the fortunes of private companies would be struck in 1936 with the establishment of a new Wheat Board that would, before long, have a monopoly over the marketing of wheat for human consumption.

Freight Rates

In addition to the grain trade, the city's establishment as a wholesale, distribution, and transportation hub for the region drove the phenomenal growth of Winnipeg between 1870 and 1912. The city's business class had worked tirelessly to achieve this status, building a Red River bridge for the CPR and competing successfully to be the railroad's administrative and maintenance centre. The Winnipeg Board of Trade worked to attract the other key institutions of the grain trade and to create the conditions that made the city dominant in the warehousing and wholesale business in the West.

Freight-rate concessions made by the railroads had helped establish Winnipeg as a distribution and shipping centre, but by the 1920s these concessions were being withdrawn due to demands from rival western cities such as Regina, Saskatoon, and Calgary. Winnipeg had developed in a vacuum, without competitors, but now the city was forced to fight to preserve its special advantages. It was a fight the city ultimately lost.

Rail freight rates were, of course, a major cost for anyone wanting to export agricultural produce or import goods and raw materials for manufacturing, and in Canada, where vast distances often separate producers and consumers, rail freight rates were a perennial topic for argument and negotiation. Cabinet was the ultimate authority over rates until the establishment of the Board of Railway Commissioners in 1904. Of course, political involvement did not end with the appointment of the Railway Commissioners, but existed to a lesser degree.

The Crow's Nest Pass Agreement of 1897 contained freight-rate concessions important to Winnipeg, and its abolition became an important political issue in the early 1920s. Winnipeg's Board of Trade took a leading role on the prairies during the struggle over the agreement's abolition. The Crow rate issue came to a head in 1922, although it was not finally settled until 1925. At the same time other special freight-rate agreements favourable to Winnipeg that had been entered into by the railroads over the years were challenged and the Board of Trade worked to defend those as well.

The Crow's Nest Pass in the Kootenay region of southeastern British Columbia attracted attention in the 1890s when rich mineral discoveries were being developed in the area. Silver, gold, and copper deposits dotted the area and the vast Crow's Nest coal field stretched east of Fernie. The Rocky Mountains virtually sealed the area off from the rest of Canada; at the same time there was relatively easy north-south access from American rail centres such as Spokane. American railroads were beginning take advantage of this easier access, and the Canadian Pacific hoped to block them by building a line through Crow's Nest Pass, the only route connecting Nelson, British Columbia, with Lethbridge, Alberta.

In September 1897 the Crow's Nest Pass Agreement was signed between the federal government and the Canadian Pacific Railway. The government undertook to pay the railroad a subsidy of $11,000 per mile up to a maximum of $3.63 million for a 531-kilometre rail line running from Lethbridge to a point near Nelson. The CPR promised to adhere to a number of conditions contained in sections 9 to 13 of the agreement. Of most interest to western farmers was the stipulation that from Fort William and all points west of Fort William to all points east of Fort William on the company's main line, rates on grain and flour would be reduced below the standard rate by three cents per 100 pounds. The lower rates for grain and flour would, for farmers, become "the Crow rate" and would be the part of the agreement that would survive in one form or another until 1996, when it was finally abolished under the Western Grain Transportation Act.

Freight rates were also reduced on a specified list of items called "settler's effects" shipped from Fort William and all points east of Fort William along the CPR's main line. Rate reductions ranged from a high of 33.3 percent for "green and fresh fruits" to a 10 percent reduction for a large group of items, including iron, agricultural implements, and livestock. The goods on the list were of interest to Winnipeg firms that imported such items and forwarded them on to points on the prairies, a business Winnipeggers had been involved in since the 1870s. During the 1920s, rates for shipping grain as well as the items on this list were the subject of prolonged disagreements between the railroads and their customers.

In addition to the Crow rate, there were other special shipping rates that benefited Winnipeg. The Winnipeg Board of Trade had played a role in establishing special treatment for the city. Early in 1897, for example, the board sent James Ashdown, chair of its Freight Rates Committee, to Ottawa to lobby the CPR and the federal Cabinet. Winnipeg economic historian Ruben Bellan described Ashdown's accomplishment: "The CPR introduced a new tariff (tariff 490) . . . that resulted in a 15% reduction in freight rates for Winnipeg wholesalers. The enormous warehouses of Winnipeg's Exchange District owe their existence in part to these favorable rates. One result was to enable Winnipeg wholesale firms to stock larger inventories so that their western customers were able to find more of what they wanted in Winnipeg. Winnipeg companies soon replaced eastern wholesale firms in handling the largest part of the western trade."[15]

In 1901 Manitoba won another concession when Premier Roblin negotiated what is known as the Manitoba Agreement with the Canadian Northern Railway. The Canadian Northern was just beginning a long period of expansion by building a line from Winnipeg to Fort William–Port Arthur, and in return for the province's guaranteeing the railway's bonds, Manitoba wholesalers received a 15 percent reduction in rates from the Lakehead to Winnipeg and the Manitoba government gained the right to set the rates for shipping grain. The CPR was forced to match the lower rates of the Canadian Northern. Roblin considered this agreement one of his most important accomplishments for farmers.

Isaac Pitblado, the Winnipeg lawyer who helped negotiate Winnipeg's advantageous freight rates. This 1950 photo by Walter Christopherson belongs to the Winnipeg Tribune *collection at University of Manitoba Archives.*

Beginning in 1907, western cities such as Portage la Prairie, ambitious to establish their own distributing businesses, began appealing to the Board of Railroad Commissioners, complaining about rates that discriminated in favour of Winnipeg. In 1909 the Board of Railroad Commissioners ordered the railroads to completely eliminate the special advantages Winnipeg enjoyed. The railroads opposed this order, arguing that Manitoba had earned its freight-rate advantage by guaranteeing railroad bonds. They subsequently introduced a new tariff that established Winnipeg's distance from the Lakehead for the purpose of calculating freight rates as 250 miles (402 kilometres) instead of the actual 420 miles (676 kilometres).

The Board of Trade fought the erosion of Winnipeg's special position by arguing that local businesses had made large investments in warehouses and shipping terminals on the basis of the old tariffs. They also argued that because of the great distance from the West to the potential markets for western goods, fairness demanded some form of subsidy. They complained that rates were lower in the East. The answer to this was that the railroads had competition from water transport in the East and therefore needed to charge less. This argument was made for British Columbia as well, where the railroads faced competition from ocean-going carriers.

The Board of Trade not only worked to protect Winnipeg's interests in competition with other cities in the West, but it acted to counter the attempts of other cities to gain freight-rate advantages. For example, the Board of Trade hired Winnipeg lawyer Isaac Pitblado in November 1921 to argue before the Board of Railroad Commissioners, at their sittings in Winnipeg, that the special higher rates for shipping goods through the mountains should be left in place. Vancouver merchants and manufacturers argued that the rates—based on the railroads' claim that it cost more to build and operate rail lines in mountainous country—made it impossible to develop new markets on the prairies and they wanted them lowered.

In the 1920s, the City of Vancouver became a major rival of Winnipeg. The opening of the Panama Canal enabled Vancouver to develop its port because of the increasing volume of material shipped into and out of the city. As Vancouver built additional storage space for grain, its participation in the grain trade increased dramatically. In 1920–21, 700,000 bushels were shipped through Vancouver; in 1921–22 this increased to 7 million bushels; in 1922–23, 19 million bushels were shipped; and in 1923–24, 25 million bushels. The grain moved to Vancouver from Alberta and western Saskatchewan, formerly territory serviced by Winnipeg. Vancouver was also becoming a warehousing and distribution centre for incoming goods. *Canadian Finance* acknowledged the effect of the Panama Canal on this growth, "though its effect was not noticeable until after the war." Another key factor in the shipment of grain was the number of freighters available in the port, which had risen from 82 in 1921 to 200 in 1923.[16]

Pitblado made all the same arguments that the smaller prairie cities made against Winnipeg. He said that removing the higher rates, or equalizing the rates, would destroy industry in Manitoba. Winnipeg was "no mean manufacturing center," but equalizing rates would allow Vancouver firms to "snatch" customers in the prairie region who were rightfully Winnipeg's. He said that Vancouver merchants thought only of themselves and ignored the result the change would have on other cities. Pitblado said Vancouver used the "development argument" that the rates were standing in the way of their firms' growing and opening new markets. And yet their businesses had grown and prospered during the period of higher mountain rates.[17] Pitblado was successful in having the higher rates left in place for the immediate future.

The railroads made a compelling case in favour of higher rates. They had experienced huge cost increases during the inflationary war years. The CPR was still a profitable corporation, but increases in the costs of equipment, coal, wages, and every other input meant the railroad was faced with lower profits and lower dividends. The Canadian Northern and the Grand Trunk railroads had both boldly set out to build transcontinental lines in the boom years. Both companies ran into serious financial difficulties during the war because of rising costs and the unavailability of capital to pay interest charges and complete their lines. Both railroads were taken over by the government and amalgamated to become Canadian National Railways (CNR).

The Board of Transport Commissioners and the Supreme Court to which the transport commissioners' decisions could be appealed both agreed that a crisis faced the railroads. As the country's largest corporations, their difficulties had national implications, and the transport commissioners generally issued decisions that supported them in rates disputes.[18]

In 1919 the Board of Transport Commissioners suspended, until 1922, special freight rates like those in the Crow's Nest Pass Agreement and Roblin's Manitoba Agreement. In addition, in September 1920, after a long series of hearings, the board granted the railroads freight-rate increases of 40 percent in the East and 35 percent in the West, as well as a 20 percent increase in passenger fares.

In 1922 the matter came to a head as the suspension expired. The Board Transport Commissioners held hearings across the country. The Crow rate was a political issue of some importance for William Lyon Mackenzie King, whose Liberal government was dependent upon Progressive Party support in the House. The Progressives, the voice of Canadian farmers, wanted the Crow rate on grain restored. The railroads wanted it permanently abolished. The Conservatives favoured placing the rates under the Board of Railway Commissioners, with the freedom to make changes as they saw fit.

Each camp had lawyers to argue their case. Herbert J. Symington, KC, of Winnipeg was engaged by the Board of Trade and represented the three prairie provinces in arguing that the Crow's Nest Pass Agreement rate for grain should be restored. (Symington was a Liberal and a friend of John W. Dafoe and Progressive Party leader Thomas A. Crerar. He would be named to the board of the CNR in 1936 and served as the president of Trans Canada Airlines later in his career.) Prime Minister Mackenzie King decided to set up a committee to look at the issue. It recommended restoring the lower Crow rate for grain and flour but ruled that the other rates in the agreement, covering such things as building materials, should remain in suspension until July 6, 1924.

As the end of the rate-suspension period approached in July 1924, the railroads circulated a letter suggesting that they be abolished altogether. The Winnipeg Board of Trade again fought hard on the issue, lobbying, writing letters, and convening protest meetings where the premier, the mayor of Winnipeg, and local MPs as well as representatives from other prairie cities passed motions calling for the restoration of the non-grain special rates.

In the end, the King government moved to end the controversy by passing a new Railroad Act on June 18, 1925. The new Act left the Crow rate on grain and flour shipped out of the West alone, establishing them at the 1899 level for all western points. All other freight rates in the old agreement were now the province of the Board of Railway Commissioners. The board proceeded to hold a cross-country series of fifty-nine public hearings on freight rates between January 1926 and August 1927, after which they handed down decisions in 311 cases of alleged discrimination. One of these decisions eliminated the non-grain parts of the Crow's Nest Pass Agreement.

The cancellation of the Manitoba Agreement of Premier Roblin was referred to the Supreme Court, and the court ruled against Manitoba in 1924. In spite of a great deal of effort, the Board of Trade ultimately had failed to restore Winnipeg's advantageous freight-rate position. Winnipeg lost its position as the primary large warehousing and distributing centre in the West, although that business and organizations like Eaton's catalogue operations continued to employ large numbers in the city. The 1920s saw the city turn to the Winnipeg manufacturing sector as a replacement for the wholesale business. This particular change was symbolized by a number of large warehouses being taken over by garment industry firms for use as factories.

Augustus Nanton, c. 1924. Archives of Manitoba, N23250.

CHAPTER 3

Twenty-One Millionaires

There is no doubt that by the end of the pre-war boom in Winnipeg, in 1912, the city had many wealthy citizens. One might imagine that the fortunes amassed by people before the war would play some part in mitigating the decline of the city in the postwar recession. If some of the old sources of wealth were disappearing, did private wealth provide investment funds to create new enterprises, new jobs, new bulwarks for the city's economy? In the histories of many cities, family fortunes were passed down to the next generation and reinvested and expanded, benefiting not only the family but the city in general. Did this happen in Winnipeg? A partial answer to that question can be found by looking at the wills of some representative citizens to see if and how they passed their wealth along.

In 1910 the *Winnipeg Telegram* published a list of twenty-one residents of Winnipeg who had assets of $1 million.[1] Almost immediately there were tongue-in-cheek articles in other papers listing millionaires that the *Telegram* had missed. The "twenty-one millionaires" article is well known and is often cited by historians as a symbolic measure of the city's prosperity during the pre-war boom.

On August 1, 1928, the *Canadian Finance* newspaper printed an item reporting that there were 272 millionaires living in Canada, and Winnipeg was home to twenty-one of them.[2] In Winnipeg, the article reported, there were also 37 individuals worth $500,000, 79 worth $250,000, 230 worth $100,000,

647 worth $50,000, and 3,222 people worth in the range of $5,000 to $50,000. So around 4,500 people had a total net worth totalling over $100 million, or about $1 billion in 2016 dollars.[3]

What role did the twenty-one millionaires and other wealthy citizens play in the economic life of 1920s Winnipeg? Did their fortunes provide venture capital for future growth? When they died, were their estates large enough to enable their families to continue to produce wealth and jobs for the city? The answer is, in some cases, yes. There had also been failures of businesses that caused enormous damage in the city.

By looking at the wills and in some cases the business records of a sampling of wealthy people who passed away in the 1920s, we get a sense of how their fortunes did or did not contribute to future growth and prosperity.

Andrew R. McNichol

In 1926 local businessman Andrew R. McNichol gave a number of gifts of money amounting to $875,000. McNichol died in 1931 but his 1926 gifts constituted a sort of will with bequests. He donated $250,000 to the Winnipeg General Hospital; $100,000 each to the Children's Hospital, the Children's Home, and the Margaret Scott Mission; and $50,000 to the Knowles Home for Boys. He gave $25,000 each to the Jewish Orphanage, the Convalescent Hospital, the YWCA, the YMCA, the Salvation Army, St. Joseph's Orphanage, the Great War Veterans Association, and the Victorian Order of Nurses.

McNichol was a Conservative, belonged to the Congregationalist Church, and loved to golf. He never married. Born at Beverley, Ontario, he opened a general store at the age of sixteen at Clyde, only a few miles from his birthplace. He sold this business after a few years and moved to Winnipeg, where he began working in the real estate and insurance business. He had a very successful career, and a few years later he was made manager and treasurer for western Canada of the Mutual Reserve Fund Life Association of New York (later Mutual Reserve Life). A few years later McNichol was promoted to the position of general manager and treasurer of the northwestern department of this company, with a staff of over 6,000 agents. After his retirement, the firm of A.R. McNichol Limited was established on January 1, 1924. All his assets, including extensive real estate holdings throughout Winnipeg (he had the highest tax bill in the city), were taken into the firm for the purpose of consolidating his interests.

McNichol did not own a business that might have continued to operate after his death. Although his bequests were charitable and helped support the many institutions to which he donated money, his money did not benefit the city in the long term by providing jobs or generating profits in the years after his death.

Augustus Nanton

Augustus Nanton, at the time of his death on April 24, 1925, was one of a small group of leaders of Winnipeg's business elite. He was a partner in the Toronto Osler, Hammond and Nanton banking and investment firm, and was head of the Winnipeg branch of the firm, with its headquarters located at Portage Avenue and Main Street.

Nanton came to Winnipeg in the 1880s at the same time as a number of other young men from Ontario. Unlike the homesteaders who were beginning to come from Ontario to claim their lands in Manitoba, or the waves of immigrants who came later after the turn of the century, these men came as the representatives of firms headquartered in the East—in Toronto, Montreal, or some of the smaller cities such as Hamilton. They intended to be in on the ground floor, to provide the capital, equipment, and supplies that the settlers needed. Nanton, like many of these immigrants, came from a wealthy background. His father had been a law partner of Alexander Galt, one of the Fathers of Confederation. Galt's son and nephew also arrived in Winnipeg at this time, founding a wholesale grocery business and creating the Blue Ribbon food brand that still exists today.

Nanton's mother was the daughter of William Jarvis, who was the sheriff of Toronto and whose estate, Rosedale, later became the site of the exclusive Toronto district of the same name. Augustus Nanton's father died in his early forties from the effects of alcoholism, leaving his family destitute. His wife operated a private girls' school in order to support herself and her children.

Augustus was educated at Upper Canada College, but at the age of fourteen he went to work to help his mother. He paid for his brother to attend the Royal Military College and took care of his mother's debts. He worked first for Henry Pellat's brokerage firm and then for the firm of Osler and Hammond. In 1883, while still in his twenties, he was sent by this firm to reconnoitre in the West. He arrived immediately after the collapse of the great western land boom that followed the announcement that the CPR main line would be built through Winnipeg.

Many investors who had seen a chance to make quick money through speculation during the land boom had suffered losses when land prices collapsed in 1882. After that experience, many Easterners were unwilling to risk their funds in the West. Nanton's firm, however, was interested in the long term. Making a first tour of the West, he travelled as far as he could on the CPR and then explored on horseback and by buggy, sleeping under the open sky. He would be responsible for investing other people's money in the development of the prairies and so he wanted to develop a good knowledge of the land and its character. Nanton concluded that the West had enormous potential. His balanced, intelligent reports sent back to Toronto earned him the role of the firm's western representative and he moved permanently to Winnipeg in 1884 to establish the company there.

As a young bachelor he lived in a house nicknamed the "Shanty" on Roslyn Road. Walter T. Kirby of Oldfield Kirby and Gardner; lawyer George W. Allan; lawyer Heber Archibald; and William R. Allan of Allan, Killam and McKay, a Winnipeg insurance firm, all lived in the house as well when they were young. In William Allan's obituary, the *Tribune* recorded that the "Shanty was a great center of social activity in the old days, and the great room which served as living and dining room during the daytime was the scene of many a merry dance when night fell."[4] This shared experience created close bonds among the men, all of whom became prominent in the city in the years ahead.

Nanton was successful in bringing Scottish, English, and eastern Canadian capital to the West and offering sound conservative advice on its use. He made many people rich and became rich himself. He also gave money away, supporting charities in his adopted city and, during the Great War, donating enormous amounts of money—some sources say half his assets—and time to such causes as the Patriotic Fund, established to support the wives and families of soldiers who had gone overseas. He headed several prairie campaigns for the sale of Victory Bonds, an enormous undertaking that raised millions of dollars for the war effort. He also took a personal responsibility for people, which taxed his time and energy. One story typical of that time was how Nanton got up in the night to drive the pregnant wife of a soldier serving in France to the hospital because she had no one else to help her. By the 1920s he was on many national corporate boards, including those of the CPR, the Hudson's Bay Company, and Winnipeg concerns such as the Winnipeg Electric Company. His business interests connected Winnipeg to enterprises all across the country.

In 1924, when the death of his partner Edmund Osler left the position vacant, he moved to Toronto to become president of the Dominion Bank. When they left Winnipeg, the Nantons were honoured with several dinners at which there was much talk about his many accomplishments and contributions to the city. Nanton was still exhausted from his war work and he seemed unwell, giving only short responses at the official events. He settled into the work in Toronto but soon he became seriously ill with Bright's Disease, a kidney disease that

Lady Ethel Nanton and friends, in the garden of her five-acre estate "Kilmorie" on Roslyn Road, 1924. Photo by L.B. Foote. Archives of Manitoba, N2330.

would today be called nephritis. There was no cure, and he died in Toronto on April 24, 1925, at the relatively early age of sixty-five. Nanton was buried four days later in Winnipeg, in St. John's churchyard, after a funeral service in St. Luke's Church, where he had been a parishioner.

His funeral attracted enormous crowds, an indication of his stature in Winnipeg. His body was brought to St. Luke's Church at 10:00 a.m., and from then until the funeral started at 2:30 p.m., a constant stream of people passed by the casket. Robert Fletcher, the deputy minister of education, played the organ in the church, which was completely filled. A large overflow crowd stood in the streets outside. There were so many wreaths, from businesses and from private individuals, that they occupied the entire front of the church.

The pallbearers were friends and business associates who had worked with him over the previous forty years: Hugh John Macdonald, the former premier and son of John A. Macdonald; Walter Kirby; T.L. Peters; F.L. Patton, an old friend of Nanton's and an official of the Dominion Bank; George W. Allan; Hugh F. Osler, Nanton's partner; P.L. Naismith of Calgary; and Thomas R.

Deacon, owner of Manitoba Bridge and Iron Works. After the funeral service the casket was taken to St. John's Cathedral. Many stores closed while the procession passed and the streetcars stopped for five minutes. About 600 employees of the Winnipeg Street Railway, of which Nanton had been president, lined Nassau Street between River Avenue and Roslyn Road.

There was a sense that with the death of Nanton and many of his contemporaries during the 1920s, the old Winnipeg was also dying. People began to replace Nanton in his many positions. In Toronto, Albert Austin became president of the Dominion Bank, a bank his father had founded. Austin had also lived in Winnipeg in the 1880s and built the city's first streetcar company before returning to Toronto. Hugh Osler became president of Osler Hammond and Nanton. George W. Allan became chair of the Canadian Committee of the Hudson's Bay Company. Andrew McLimont took Nanton's place as president of Winnipeg Electric and its various subsidiaries.

According to his will and the accompanying documents, the value of Nanton's estate at the time of his death was $1,053,610. Using a calculation based on inflation, that figure would be the equivalent of $13 million today.[5] Because he had not yet established his change of residence with the Manitoba taxation department at the time of his death, his estate was taxed by Manitoba and Ontario and the federal government, and the total death duties were close to $200,000.

His estate was a reflection of his business interests. He had shares in many Winnipeg firms in addition to his own. The largest investments were in Great-West Life ($118,000), Winnipeg Electric ($13,000), Manitoba Cartage ($26,500), Manitoba Cold Storage ($11,000), and Crescent Creameries ($20,000). He also owned shares in Northern Trust, Northern Mortgage, and the Canadian Fire Insurance Company, Winnipeg firms in which many members of the elite invested. He participated in the management of some firms. He could be said to have been one of the founders of Great-West Life and served on the board. He was also on the board of Winnipeg Electric Company and had been the president for some years. Loaning mortgage money was an important part of Osler, Hammond and Nanton's business, and at the time of his death Nanton held fifty-one mortgages on farmland.

After making various bequests to relatives and employees, his will stated that he wanted the bulk of his estate to be put into a trust to provide income for his wife, who would provide for their children until they reached the age of twenty-five, when they would begin to receive the income from their part of the trust. At thirty the boys would get the capital. The daughters would continue to get only the income, and, if they married, the trust ensured that the income would be their own property and not their husbands'.

Half of Nanton's estate consisted of $500,000 in shares in Osler, Hammond and Nanton. He directed in his will that this investment should be sold five years after his death but that, if any of his sons was able to become a partner, $250,000 should be left invested for him. His son Edward did become a partner and eventually president of the firm. By leaving a bequest for his son if he wished to go into business with Osler, Hammond and Nanton, Augustus Nanton did contribute to the future development of Winnipeg and of his firm. Money from his estate that was managed as a trust might also provide investment funds for local firms.

Nanton was generous to the servants who had worked for him for decades. He had purchased a house for his chauffeur, Charles Wright, when he retired, and paid for his gardener, Charles Beavis, to return home to England when he stopped working for the Nantons. These men also received a small monthly pension from the estate.

Lady Nanton continued to live in Kilmorie, the Nantons' home on Roslyn Road, until 1935, when, in order to reduce her $3,200 tax bill, she had the house demolished. She lived in a smaller house on the property until her death in 1942.

James H. Ashdown

James Ashdown came to Winnipeg in 1868, making him one of the earliest arrivals among the city's elite. He worked at various jobs, including as part of Colonel Dennis's survey crew that Louis Riel stopped. With a loan from Colonel Dennis and money he had saved, he purchased a tinsmith shop on Main Street and opened a hardware store. He developed his business into a large retail and wholesale hardware and catalogue enterprise, serving the whole of western Canada. In the 1870s he made his father a partner in the firm. Of all the many merchants who operated businesses along Winnipeg's early Main Street, Ashdown was certainly the most successful.

He was intimately involved in the founding and development of Winnipeg, serving as mayor and stepping in at many crucial moments to support improvements like City Hydro. He was known as a hard bargainer and a strong advocate for the city. He was a Liberal, a Methodist, and a Temperance supporter.

At his death on April 5, 1924, his estate was valued at $1,451,548 after all liabilities were paid. He owned a good deal of real estate in Winnipeg, Kenora, and prairie cities such as Edmonton and Saskatoon. His real estate holdings were valued at $371,000 in 1924. He also owned $633,000 worth of stocks, of

529 Wellington Crescent, the home of James H. Ashdown, c. 1914. Archives of Manitoba. View of the parlour.

which $568,000 was Ashdown Hardware stock. He had $29,000 invested in Northern Trust, $12,000 in Northern Mortgage, $13,000 in Canadian Fire Insurance, and $20,300 in Canadian Indemnity, all locally controlled firms. His assets also included $59,000 in mortgages owed by individuals. These would have been on property the mortgagees bought from him. We know that James Ashdown, during his early years in the city, had invested in a good deal of land. Most of this property was used for his hardware business but some was held to be sold at a profit.

His will made many bequests to his family, his wife, children, and grand-children. Half of each of these were in the form of J.H. Ashdown Hardware stock, thus keeping control of the company with his family. He also left gifts, ranging from $25,000 to $100,000, for the General Hospital, Children's Hospital, the YMCA, Wesley College, and other Winnipeg institutions.

Like Nanton, close to 50 percent of Ashdown's estate consisted of shares in the company he had built. Ashdown Hardware was a public company so the assets of the company were separate from Ashdown's personal estate. By leaving company stock to his family, he ensured that the business would survive and continue contributing to the prairie economy, providing jobs and income not just in Winnipeg but in other cities where his stores were located. Ashdown Hardware continued in operation until the 1960s.

William Alloway

William Alloway came to the West in 1870 with the Wolseley Expedition. Born in Ireland, he had grown up in Montreal. His first business in Winnipeg was a tobacco store, and he then made his living hauling freight. He started out working for James McKay, the larger-than-life Metis freighter, but soon established his own shipping and forwarding business. He forwarded supplies to government and railroad survey gangs and to the Mounted Police posts on the prairies. He was one of the first to participate in this business, which became very important for Winnipeg in the years ahead.

In 1879 he and Henry Champion opened a bank that continued in operation until 1923. Alloway did not participate in the mad real estate speculation of the early 1880s, concentrating instead on buying up good farmland in Manitoba and the northwest, which he subsequently sold, lending the buyers mortgage money. Alloway and his brother Charles, like many other Winnipeggers of the time, also did a large business in buying and selling Metis scrip, the certificates handed out to Metis as a proof of their claim to land granted in the Manitoba Act. The scrip was often sold to speculators as soon as it was put in the hands of the Metis. The manner in which the promise made to the Metis in the Manitoba Act was carried out has been the object of a storm of criticism and litigation in the past decades, and the Supreme Court of Canada has ruled that the Metis were not treated fairly or honestly. Negotiations are currently underway between the federal government and the Metis people over how this historic wrong will be righted.

William Alloway provided capital to help in the founding of many local businesses, including Ogilvie Milling and Manitoba Cartage. He and his bank were thus intimately involved in the growth of the city. With the influx of European settlers that began in the 1890s, Alloway and Champion opened a Main Street branch a block from the CPR station, which provided exchange for money the new arrivals brought with them and other services such as acting as ticket agents for new Canadians bringing relatives to join them in Winnipeg.

William Alloway was one of the local business elite who was in a position to sell, not buy, real estate during the 1907 to 1913 boom years. He was able to realize considerable profits because of the rise in real estate values. He had, for example, purchased property on the south side of Portage Avenue between Main and Smith streets in 1900 for $90,000. He sold this property during the boom for a total of $500,000. In a legendary deal, Alloway had traded a buggy and two horses for the strip of land between Portage Avenue and the Assiniboine River and Maryland and Walnut streets. He sold this land during the boom for $30,000.[6]

The Alloway and Champion Bank was incorporated in 1912 with an authorized capital stock of $3 million and paid-up capital of $1,025,000, "mostly held by the original partners."[7] Theirs was for a time the largest private bank in Canada. Champion died in 1916, and Alloway sold the bank to the Bank of Commerce in 1919. He remained in the position of president until 1923 when he retired. He and his wife had one child who died in infancy so there was no one to continue the business.

Alloway had always been supportive of public institutions and served on the boards of the Winnipeg General Hospital and the Margaret Scott Mission, a

privately funded public health nursing station serving women in the North End. He gave an annual donation to the Winnipeg Federated Budget Board, the precursor of the United Way, and he made the initial donation of $100,000 to establish the Winnipeg Foundation.

When he died on February 2, 1930, William Alloway's estate was valued at $1,156,105. His assets were almost entirely securities, stocks, and bank shares, but he still owned real estate valued at $55,000, mostly located in St. Charles and St. Boniface. His trustee was Peter Lowe, long an employee of Alloway and Champion's bank and the first secretary of the Winnipeg

William Forbes Alloway, c. 1925. Campbell's studio photograph. Archives of Manitoba, N22965.

Foundation. Alloway's wife, Elizabeth, had died in 1926, so he made some personal bequests to his brother and other relatives and to some friends, and left his paintings and artworks to the Manitoba Club. The balance of the estate he gave to the Winnipeg Foundation, donating the securities rather than selling them and donating the proceeds. His wife had also donated generously to the foundation when she died. Many have followed their example in the years since. The Winnipeg Foundation is a typical Winnipeg institution in that the first donations came from the first generation of the city's elite, joining together to found the institution as they had cooperated during their lives in creating many local businesses. Since then, thousands of Winnipeggers have added to the foundation's capital. While William Alloway's fortune did not support continued economic development in the city, it was the basis of an extremely successful foundation that through its grants has done a vast amount to develop Winnipeg over the years.

Douglas C. Cameron

Douglas Cameron was born into a well-off farming family in Prescott County, Ontario. He came to the West in 1880 and went into the lumber business in 1883. He reinvested his profits in new timber limits—areas in which he had exclusive rights to harvest trees. He was therefore well positioned to profit from the great building boom of the decade before the First World War. His Rat Portage Lumber was one of a handful of large firms supplying the West. After 1906 he began to expand his business to include retail lumberyards. He had a large lumber mill and yard in St. Boniface, south of the General Hospital. He was involved in other businesses, as president of Maple Leaf Flour Mills and director of Northern Crown Bank and Manitoba Bridge.

Cameron was a Liberal and had been elected to the Ontario Legislature in the 1890s. He was knighted and became the lieutenant-governor of Manitoba in 1911. In that office he played a significant role in exposing the scandal involving the construction of the Manitoba Legislative Building in 1915.

When Douglas Cameron died on November 21, 1921, his estate was valued at $515,000, about $4 million in today's money. His wife, who by then lived in Vancouver, his daughter, Mrs. F. Homer-Dixon, who lived in Victoria, and his two sons, who were carrying on the Rat Portage Lumber company business in Vancouver, were the beneficiaries in his will. There were other assets that were not distributed, totalling $1,208,445, both in Manitoba and outside the province. Of this amount, $355,000 consisted of shares in Rat Portage Lumber that were being held waiting for a favourable market. Some of the amount was the value of real estate holdings. His assets that had been sold included his St. Charles Country Club share, a $1,000 debenture for the Manitoba Club, forty shares in Crescent Creamery, and various other shares including large holdings in Maple Leaf Flour Mills, Canada Bread, and Manitoba Bridge, and $21,000 in Victory Bonds.

Cameron had been spectacularly successful in the boom years, but at the time of his death the shares in his own company and his land holdings may not have been worth as much as the inventory attached to his will suggests. The fact that his shares in Rat Portage Lumber were being held for a favourable market may suggest they were not considered desirable stocks to buy. Cameron's portfolio also contained a number of stocks that were listed as having no value, a common thing in the wills of Winnipeggers at this time.

Douglas Cameron's family had moved away from Winnipeg and so the fortune he left did not contribute to the city's economy in the 1920s. He was one of the millionaires of 1911, but the end of the pre-war boom had reduced the value of his lumber business and his other investments. In this regard Cameron was typical of many of the Winnipeg elite.

George V. Hastings

George Hastings was born and educated in Montreal. Through his mother he was related to the Ogilvie milling family. He began working in the milling industry in the 1870s at the time a revolution in milling technology was just beginning. (Mills had begun replacing grinding stones with steel rollers to process grain. The roller mill scrapes the wheat kernel apart in several phases and uses an elaborate set of sieves to remove the bran and produce fine white flour, as opposed to the coarse brown product resulting from stone grinding.) Hastings worked for Ogilvie Mills and then formed his own company and began designing and building the new mills that would be required to house the new steel roller milling equipment. He built mills in Milwaukee, Chicago, and Niagara Falls. He came to Winnipeg in 1881 to work on the construction of the new Ogilvie flour mill in Point Douglas. In partnership with his brother and George Stephen, one of the owners of the CPR, he founded Lake of the Woods Milling Company and built a large flour mill at Keewatin. He was president of the Northern Mortgage Company and a director of Lake of the Woods Milling, the Winnipeg Electric Company, and the Canadian Fire Insurance Company. He was one of the founders of the Winnipeg Grain Exchange.

When Hastings died on 17 October 1928, his estate was valued at $265,833, about $3,455,000 in 2016 dollars. He was thus in the same group as the sixty-nine individuals identified by *Canadian Finance* as having a worth of about $250,000. He directed in his will that his wife should have the house, furnishings, and "all my automobiles." He said the trustees should sell his assets and invest the money to pay his wife an income. Upon her death their three children would receive equal shares.

Hastings's assets were largely in the form of government debentures and stocks in Lake of the Woods Milling and in Winnipeg Electric Company, and in Canadian Indemnity, a company owned by the Riley family of Winnipeg. He also owned shares in the Winnipeg Hunt Club, the St. Charles Country Club, the Manitoba Club, the Winnipeg Horse Show Association, and the Lake of the Woods Yacht Club, suggesting a busy social life.

Hastings had been involved in many ventures that helped Winnipeg to grow and develop into an important milling centre. But his estate was comparatively small and his assets were left to his family. He left no money to charity and so the city did not directly benefit from his estate.

Sir James Aikins

James Aikins was born in Ontario in 1851. His father, James Cox Aikins, was
a cabinet minister in two of John A. Macdonald's governments and the lieutenant-governor of Manitoba in the 1880s. James Aikins came to Manitoba in
1879 and founded a law firm that over the years represented many important
clients, including the federal Department of Justice, the Manitoba government, and the Canadian Pacific Railway. Soon after his arrival he also began
loaning money for mortgages in partnership with his brother and his father.
He served on many Royal Commissions and was the Conservative MP for
Brandon from 1911 until 1915. He led the Manitoba Conservative Party in
the disastrous 1915 election when the party was reduced to four seats in the
Legislature. He served on the boards of Wesley College, the University of
Manitoba, and the Canadian Club of Winnipeg. He was a founder and first
president of the present Canadian Bar Association. He also served as honorary
colonel for two Manitoba militia regiments. He was the lieutenant-governor
of Manitoba from 1916 to 1926.

When he died on March 1, 1929, Aikins's estate was valued at $1.7 million.
He had investments in stocks and bonds worth $1.6 million. His money was
held in an investment trust together with the money of other investors as a
managed fund. He did not have a lot of property, although he held $36,000
in mortgages. A yearly income of $7,000 was to be paid to his wife, and when
she passed away in 1931 this income went to his son, Harold Aikins, who was
a partner in the law firm his father founded. He left various amounts of money
to his daughters and to the United Church, the Canadian Bar Association, the
YMCA, the Children's Hospital, and Wesley College, among other beneficiaries. He also left his son, Harold, $100,000 in cash, his library, his shotgun, his
watches and paintings, and some Venetian vases and bowls. Aikins, by leaving
the bulk of his estate to his son, increased the likelihood that his law firm would
survive. The law firm bearing Aikins's name and the names of other partners
continues to serve Winnipeg today.

William Rae Allan

William R. Allan was a son of Hugh Allan, the Montreal shipping magnate
who at one point in the 1800s was Canada's richest man. He was educated
at Rugby School in England, and he went to work for the family shipping
line in 1882. The next year he came to Winnipeg, where he worked in various
businesses, including the Vulcan Iron Works, until he opened his own insurance business. He was a broker and insurance agent along with his partners

for the rest of his life. He had been president of the Union Bank at the time of its merger with the Royal Bank, when he became a member of the Royal Bank's western board.

He was a devoted horse owner and was the president of the Winnipeg Jockey Club. He also belonged to the Manitoba Club and the St. Charles Country Club. He was well liked and described as "friendly and helpful" by a wide range of friends and colleagues.

When he died on March 18, 1926, he had an estate of $49,151, consisting of some shares, the largest holdings being $18,900 in Royal Bank and $17,000 in Lake of the Woods Milling shares. But his liabilities totalled $89,000. After auctioning off all his assets, including the contents of his house on Roslyn Road, and selling his property at Lake of the Woods, there was still a good deal of money owing. Allan, like other members of the city's elite, had undoubtedly been a wealthy man at the beginning of the Great War, but the unfavourable economic conditions in Winnipeg had resulted in losses that left him in debt at the time of his death.

Sanford Evans

Sanford Evans, a former mayor of Winnipeg and a former owner of the *Winnipeg Telegram* newspaper, became a Conservative MLA in 1922 and served until 1936. He also found himself in financial difficulties after the collapse of the boom. His story, of having owned a business during the pre-war boom years from which he was now burdened with debts, was likely a common one among the Winnipeg middle class.

He revealed the state of his finances in a letter to his aunt, explaining why he could not help support his sisters. He said that with the start of the war, his real estate business "completely stopped and with it my income."[8] He was a Conservative and was usually able to get some sort of government work, and had been appointed to the Georgian Bay Canal Commission. He told the government in Ottawa he needed to be paid or he would have to resign. After several weeks of runaround, he "expressed myself pretty strongly"[9] and started home. On the way, he received a cable telling him he would be paid $6,000 for his work on the Canal Commission. In 1917 the Commission was cancelled. At that time, the Millers Association and the Food Controller hired him to work on flour problems. He was employed by the Millers until the fall of 1920. The headquarters of the work was moved to Winnipeg because the Wheat Board, the government agency that was responsible for marketing Canadian wheat at the time, was there. He said he knew all along that when the Wheat Board

William Sanford Evans with wife and daughter, n.d. Archives of Manitoba.

was closed, he would lose his job. The Millers Association decided to move its headquarters to Montreal and wanted him to move there. He decided not to go because it would take years to get established in a new community, and in Montreal, "money matters more than any place else in Canada."[10] Leaving the West would have meant breaking all his ties and giving up any hope of entering public life.

He had gone into partnership with another man who published a daily grain paper and he was getting a salary of $5,000 a year.[11] This was half of what Millers had paid him. He said that Irene, his wife, got a small allowance from the aunt to whom he was writing, but there would be no distribution of earnings from her father's business—a Toronto foundry and manufacturer—until 1923. His wife had sold some jewellery to get a car and fit up the house. He still had debts from 1914 when his business had failed: he had purchased a one-fifth share of the Estevan Coal and Brick Company for $10,000. The company had loans still outstanding and he had been struggling to pay his $7,000 share of the debt. For all these reasons he had not been keeping up with his obligations to his sisters. His aunt had been paying an allowance to his sister Charlotte and had asked him to help. He said he would as soon as possible.[12]

Sanford Evans was a successful politician and businessman but the pre-war and postwar depressions had left him with substantial debts. He did, nevertheless, make important contributions to Manitoba through his political career and his grain industry publications.

Of the millionaires described above, four held half their wealth in the stocks of their own companies. All had shares in local Winnipeg firms like Winnipeg Electric and Great West Life. Several had shares in Canadian Fire Insurance, Northern Trust Company, the Northern Mortgage Company, and Canadian Indemnity. These were all companies that Robert Riley had a significant role in founding, convincing other Winnipeg business leaders to invest. He and his sons continued to be major shareholders and managers for some time. Like Great-West Life, they were intended to create successful companies and pools of investment funds in Winnipeg. These companies and their shareholders thus helped to develop Winnipeg's economy.

Most of the wealth of these men was, then, invested in Winnipeg companies, showing a strong loyalty to their own city. The companies they had stocks in also were often owned by people they knew and had done business with, and this kind of strong connection was an important aspect of the power of the Winnipeg elite.

Some examples of this were the three companies Northern Trust, Northern Mortgage, and Canada Fire Insurance, all founded by Robert Riley, like the others an 1880s arrival. Canadian Indemnity is another Riley company, in which the business elite owned shares, as was Manitoba Cartage, whose president was Hugh Osler. Several business owners held shares in Crescent Creamery, which was owned by Robert A. Rogers, husband of Edith Rogers, Manitoba's first woman MLA, and another member of the small group of business founders and owners in Winnipeg.

However, it seems that the fortunes made during Winnipeg's boom years were only occasionally large enough to create a second generation of business elite members who continued and expanded their family's enterprises. At least two millionaires finished their careers without a great deal of money to leave behind. There were other examples of prominent Winnipeg business people who were bankrupt in the 1920s after having been successful during the boom years.

One such figure was John Machray, the nephew of Anglican archbishop Robert Machray and the lawyer charged with the management of the investment funds of both the Anglican Church and the University of Manitoba. Machray was, on paper, responsible for close to $2 million, but in 1932 Manitobans learned that he had probably been bankrupt since the end of the boom in 1913. He had invested his clients' money heavily in land that, during

Garden party at home of Honourable Robert Rogers, 197 Roslyn Rd. c. 1920. Archives of Manitoba, L.B. Foote fonds, N2233.

the boom, was appreciating in value rapidly. After 1913, the value of many of these properties collapsed. Machray covered up his business problems by using the capital in his accounts to pay his clients' annual interest payments. By 1932, he had used all the funds entrusted to him and close to $2 million was simply gone. This was a disaster for the church and the university, both having to do fundraising in the heart of the Depression to try to replace at least some of the lost money. Machray was convicted of theft and died in prison in 1933.

Another example of financial ruin in the 1920s, with its roots in the collapse of the pre-war boom, were the businesses owned by the brothers William T. Alexander and F.H. Alexander. Before the war they had operated three successful enterprises: the Great West Permanent Loan Company, the Imperial Canadian Trust, and the Canadian National Fire Insurance Company. All these firms were in financial trouble after 1913, and the brothers chose to engage in some questionable practices to try to stay afloat. For example, they arranged huge lines of credit for themselves with the trust company that were never paid back. One of the charges against them was making an illegal loan to their trust company with money from the fire insurance firm—something that was illegal for the proprietors of insurance firms—to add several floors to the Marlborough Hotel, one of their properties. After a lengthy trial, the Alexanders were sentenced to prison terms in January 1929.

Unemployed veterans' march, 1921. Archives of Manitoba, L.B. Foote fonds, N1957.

CHAPTER 4

Unemployment and Unrest

Unemployment was a widespread problem in all the former combatant countries after the Great War. Vast armaments factories closed, throwing people who had been earning good wages out of work. The huge armies went home and the ex-soldiers all began to look for work at the same time. In Winnipeg unemployment provided stark evidence of the city's decline from the economic powerhouse it had been a few short years before. People began losing their jobs in 1913 when the pre-war slump began. There was more work during the Great War, and with so many in the army, workers' wages rose, although wartime inflation ate up much of the additional income. War-related manufacturing stopped after the war, contributing to unemployment. Winnipeg, however, had won only a very small percentage of the massive industrial activity generated by the war. When a Winnipeg factory bid on a project, the high cost of shipping material from the prairies to the seaboard put the Winnipeg company out of the running. Businesses in the city did win contracts to manufacture shell cases and items like uniforms and tents that cost less to ship. Meanwhile, Montreal, Toronto, and other eastern Canadian manufacturing centres generated millions of dollars' worth of activity, filling orders for ships, planes, and all types of weaponry and munitions.

In mid-1920 the postwar depression set in and unemployment rose again. Agricultural prices began to fall and farmers were unable to hire farmhands. As the economy slowed down all over western Canada, Winnipeg, as the centre of the region's distribution, finance, and agricultural processing and marketing, began to see large numbers of unemployed.

The return of troops from Europe intensified all the problems of the early 1920s, including unemployment. Some of the men had married overseas and were bringing wives and children home with them. By the beginning of 1920, 338,000 troops had returned to Canada. Of those who came to Winnipeg, some simply left the train and went home, back to their old pre-war lives and jobs. Many others found there was little work in the city, and unemployment and underemployment would be a problem among the returned men until at least 1925. Some men reacted with anger and frustration, and focused blame on Winnipeggers who had immigrated from the former enemy countries, Germany and Austria.

On Sunday, January 26, 1919, this anger and frustration produced a major riot of returned men in Winnipeg streets. The immediate cause was an outdoor meeting sponsored by the Socialist Party of Canada in Market Square to honour Karl Liebknecht, the German Social Democrat leader and pacifist who had recently been murdered in Berlin. One of the speakers had just begun praising his anti-war work in Germany when a group of several hundred returned soldiers and other young men rushed the stage, many shouting that Liebknecht was a "fritzie" and they were all alike.

The leaders of the meeting sought refuge in restaurants and hotels around the square or on Main Street. The mob pursued them, smashed windows, and helped themselves to money, cigarettes, and cigars. Presumably because he had a German name, Michael Erb's furniture store on the main floor of the Travellers Building at Bannatyne Avenue and King Street was attacked. The plate-glass windows were smashed and furniture was thrown into the street, where some pieces were looted by members of the crowd. Some of the men made their way to the Socialist Party of Canada's offices on Smith Street across from the Marlborough Hotel. The crowd ran up the stairs to the offices and began throwing furniture and pamphlets and books down into the street. They set fire to this material along with a red flag they found in the office.

Groups of men scattered through the city in search of "enemy aliens." They wrecked the Austro Hungarian Club on Selkirk Avenue and damaged other businesses along the street. People encountered on the street sometimes suffered a beating at the hands of the soldiers. Jewish businesses and individuals were also targeted. In St. Boniface, the Edelweiss Brewery, which belonged to Arnold W. Riedle, was attacked, its windows broken and machinery damaged.

Great War veterans demonstrate at City Hall, 4 June 1919. Note the anti-immigrant "Undesirable Alien" banner. Archives of Manitoba, L.B. Foote fonds, N2737.

The police were short-handed at the time, and because the trouble was scattered in many different areas, they were unable to do much to stop the riot. Some people have accused them of standing by and doing nothing, and in some cases this may have been true. The assistant provost marshall at Osborne Barracks, Major Harris, brought fifty troops and a number of wagons to the James Avenue police station to support the police. In the evening a crowd of about 2,500 soldiers and others gathered in the street outside the police station. Chief McPherson went out and said that no arrests had been made and told the men to go home. Harris's men were lined up in front of the station with fixed bayonets, holding the crowd away from the building. The men in the crowd asked that the troops be sent away first and when this was done, they began to disperse. (During a soldiers' riot a few years earlier, in the spring of 1916, the streets around the police station had witnessed pitched battles between police and rioters, and all the windows in the station had been smashed.[1] There was some anti-immigrant violence during that riot, with at least one business owned by a Ukrainian Canadian being wrecked and money stolen from the till.)

Disturbances continued the next day, Monday, January 27, 1919. A large crowd of men crossed the Louise Bridge to Elmwood and gathered at the gate of the Swift Canadian Company slaughterhouse at the foot of the bridge. They demanded that the manager fire all the aliens working there and hire "white labour" to replace them. By "white labour," they meant people of British descent.

Mayor Charles Gray and General Huntly D.B. Ketchen, the commander of regular troops in the city, went to the plant. Gray told the rioters that he wanted to get the alien workers out as much as they did but that they should "go back to the city and show them that you will give them a chance to get rid of the aliens."[2] The men listened respectfully to General Ketchen as he told them much the same thing. Swift manager W.R. Ingram sent a different message when he told them, "I will give any returned man a job here if he can do the work."[3] (Many positions were empty because conditions in the plant were grim. By 1919, in the type of large slaughterhouses found in Winnipeg, the work of cutting up animals was no longer done by tradesman butchers. They had been replaced by assembly lines with each of dozens of specific cuts done over and over by people trained to do that cut and nothing else. This was poorly paid, repetitive work, performed in filthy and dangerous surroundings. There were many injuries.)

The organized soldiers' groups, such as the Great War Veterans Association (GWVA) and the Army and Navy Veterans, and the daily papers were quick to repudiate the violence and destruction of property that took place in the Sunday and Monday riots, at the same time blaming everything on the "Bolshevik" meetings. There can be no doubt that many people in the city found the rioting and the apparent inability of the police to stop it deeply unsettling. There was, however, no great outcry about the unjust and irrational scapegoating of immigrants from eastern Europe. Indeed, in the months ahead an unknown number of such people were fired from their jobs to make places for returned soldiers.

Although this method of finding employment for returned men was problematic, to say the least, authorities wishing to show that they were taking action gave it lip service. An Alien Registration Board was set up to look into the question of firing people. On February 10, 1919, the Registration Board held its first sitting. The members were Sergeant A.E. Moore, a veteran who would be one of the leaders of returned soldiers during the General Strike; Judge R.H. Myers; and a representative of organized Labour, all appointed by the provincial government. The Registration Board's function was in part to "test the loyalty of alien enemies and naturalized citizens born in enemy countries who are suspected of pro-German leanings."[4] At this time the German Empire was well and truly beaten, so the term "pro-German" was no longer a concern.

Mayor Charles Gray speaking to a crowd on 7 June 1919. Archives of Manitoba, N20992.

The Registration Board had an office at 185 Lombard Street and a staff consisting of a secretary, J.H. Mansfield, and at least two clerks. Mansfield was president of an association of vocational student veterans that would call a strike in February 1919 over grievances about what they were being taught. The board set about registering enemy aliens, and during the General Strike they had 27,000 names in their files. In April, Moore and Mansfield met with Mayor Gray, asking him to "have all aliens working for the city replaced by returned soldiers. . . . The Mayor pointed out that the City had already decided on such a policy, but undertook to write to the heads of all City departments."[5]

The Registration Board did not last long and was closed down in August 1919 by Premier Norris, who said it had outlived its usefulness. Its usefulness may have been as a public relations measure to mollify the returned soldiers, and it may have seemed by that time that the danger of another soldiers' riot had passed. Moore, however, warned that "there is every likelihood of a soldier alien rumpus next winter when unemployment will cause unrest."[6] This could be avoided, he said, if the board was allowed to continue and had expanded powers. By the time it closed down, its activities included registering aliens and "supervising" them. However, there was no rumpus during the following winter and the board was not revived.

It is difficult to establish how many workers lost their jobs because of their ethnic origin. What we do know is that, before the Great War, many eastern Europeans were employed by the city, the railroads, and other organizations.

Some had become naturalized Canadians and some who were in Canada as temporary workers were stranded here when war broke out. Subjects of the Austrian and German empires were not allowed to join the Canadian Army in the first years of the war, and several thousand were interned as enemy aliens. Many more were called upon to register as enemy aliens and continued working in Canada during the war, reporting in at regular intervals. Some of these people suffered the injustice of losing their jobs.

Unemployment and underemployment became a chronic problem for Winnipeg, compounded because the general economy of the West was changing. The frantic activity of the pre-war boom—railway building, lumbering, the building of all types of infrastructure—would not resume. As a result, there was much less work for large gangs of men doing general labour, or for tradespeople like carpenters and bricklayers. Winnipeg during the 1920s was slowly developing as an industrial centre and this would generate jobs, but often only for skilled workers. Even in the pre-war boom years, general labourers would most easily have found employment in the spring, summer, and fall, spending the winter in the cities and towns living off their savings. In the early 1920s, more and more of them were unable to find enough work to have savings, and the winter months were times of real distress.

The Federal National Industrial Conference of 1918 and the subsequent Royal Commission on problems of moving from a war footing to peace looked at the problem of unemployment. One of the commission's recommendations was to set up an unemployment insurance system. This was not done in 1918; indeed, it was not finally accomplished until 1940.[7] Until then the unemployed were largely the responsibility of municipal governments and private charities.

The city had organized itself in the past to support unemployed men with relief and work funded with tax dollars. In 1917, as part of a trend away from volunteerism and charity to more professional social work, the city had established the Social Welfare Commission, which was intended to "give assistance in the form of advice, care or relief in cash or in kind, to bona-fide residents of the City of Winnipeg: to undertake such work as may be necessary in order to supply work tests or training for applicants for material relief preparatory to finding suitable employment."[8] The term "bona-fide residents" is significant. Winnipeg and other cities as well complained about having to support unemployed people who came from other communities looking for relief.

The Social Welfare Commission membership in 1921 consisted of six aldermen and the mayor, an executive from Great-West Life, a clergyman, and businessman W.J. Fulton, who also served on the Federated Budget Board, precursor of the United Way, and had served on a Royal Commission concerned with public welfare in the province. In January 1921, for the first time, the commission opened a relief depot in the Rialto Building on Main Street between Bannatyne Avenue and William Avenue. G.B. Clarke, the secretary of the Social Welfare Commission, managed the depot.

As another part of the federal government's efforts to ease the transition of soldiers back into civilian life, in 1918 the Department of Soldiers' Civil Re-establishment was set up to administer pensions and benefits, provide vocational training, and generally help with the problems experienced by demobilized soldiers. This department would be a source of relief support for ex-soldiers. A special fund was created to be administered by the various branches of the privately managed Patriotic Fund across the country. But its activities were limited to the immediate postwar years. The Patriotic Fund had been established in 1914 to create a pool of money that could be used to provide support to the wives and families of men who had gone overseas. It was not a new idea: there were patriotic funds in Britain during the Napoleonic, Crimean, and Boer wars. In Winnipeg, at the beginning of the war, unlike any other branch across the country, the Patriotic Fund had also been used to help unemployed men. In Winnipeg it continued for a few years after the war to support the widows of soldiers who had died and the wives of men who had deserted them. During the winter of 1919–20, between $5 and $6 million was given out through the Patriotic Fund as relief for returned soldiers across the country.[9] The federal government saw this support as temporary, available only until the returned soldiers were integrated back into the labour force. In Winnipeg, this reintegration, for some men, took years.

Also in 1918, the federal government, in partnership with the provinces, opened offices of the Employment Service of Canada in major cities across the country to help the unemployed find jobs.

The philosophy guiding all these agencies was that it was preferable for men to be working for wages than to be on the dole. Traditional attitudes about the nobility of work and the danger of morally ruining people by giving them handouts were much in evidence. If someone wanted to apply for relief, he or she would have first to go to the Employment Service of Canada to certify that there were not in fact any jobs for them at present. The applicant would be investigated to make sure they had no other sources of income. In Winnipeg, once need was established, men might then be sent to the city woodlot at Alexander Avenue and Tecumseh Street, where they would be put to work splitting firewood at fifty cents an hour. If a man could not earn enough this way to feed his family, his earnings could be topped up. By splitting wood, the man on relief proved his willingness to work and was saved from the debilitating and demoralizing effects of being on the dole.[10]

This vetting and processing of relief applicants was used by the Employment Service of Canada at the end of 1920, but with the coming of the New Year it was not long before it broke down under the pressure of huge numbers of men and women applying for aid. By February, the office on Main Street had received 8,223 applications and cheques were simply being handed out with no questions asked.

In February City Council approved additional money for public works so that some men could be employed digging new sewers (thirty-five men were at work in February) and clearing snow from the streets (169 men were organized into thirty-seven three- and four-man teams). There were also wood camps in the bush along the Greater Winnipeg Water District Railroad where firewood was cut for shipment to the city. From January to March 1921 the men in these camps cut 9,500 cords of wood worth $60,000.

While those dispensing relief may have expected the recipients to be humbly grateful, some of the unemployed maintained their dignity and self-respect by arguing that their labour produced the nation's wealth and they should be looked after in times of low employment. The recipients of relief began to organize themselves in January 1921. There were meetings at the Roblin Hotel that were sponsored by the One Big Union, the Socialist Party of Canada, the Ex-Soldiers and Sailors Labour Party, and the Independent Labour Party. There was a large meeting at the Board of Trade auditorium on January 15, during which complaints were voiced about delays in receiving relief cheques due to the paperwork involved. Men receiving help from the Soldiers' Civil Relief Department complained about the same problem. Both agencies were likely overwhelmed by the number of applicants.

Other complaints arose concerning the expectation that women applying for relief should be obliged to take jobs as domestic help. Edith Hancox, an activist who would become the secretary of the Winnipeg Central Council of the Unemployed and run unsuccessfully for City Council, spoke out on January 27 at a meeting of women and girls at the Roblin Hotel. She described as "humiliating" the domestic jobs unemployed women were expected to take. She said that the money for relief was provided by taxpayers, and the women had a right to it without having to take on menial work. She also complained that the seven dollars a week provided to those on relief was not enough to live on. She pointed out that girls were charged higher rent for rooms than men and needed a minimum of $8.50 a week. Indignant letters were written in response to these charges, but Hancox answered that many of the moneyed classes did not know how to treat the girls and women who worked in their houses. Maids were expected to work long hours and sometimes had to put up with the unwanted advances of their male employers.[11]

A recurring question during the interwar years was about which levels of government were responsible for the unemployed. The cities and provinces argued that the federal government should be paying one-third of the costs. Although in the early 1920s the burden was shared by the three levels of government, Mackenzie King later adopted the firm policy that relief was a municipal responsibility. He would maintain this po-

Edith Hancox spoke up for women's rights during Winnipeg's unemployment crisis post First World War. This photograph is from the Winnipeg Tribune, *9 November 1923, when Hancox was nominated for an alderman position.*

sition during the Depression of the 1930s, and Richard B. Bennett took the same position when he became prime minister in 1930. Cities like Winnipeg carried the burden alone for most of the interwar years. King's statement in the House of Commons in 1930 that he would not give five cents of federal money for the unemployed helped cost him the election of that year. Although Labour politicians like A.A. Heaps advocated for it all through the 1920s and 1930s, an unemployment insurance system was finally instituted only in 1940. Bennett had introduced an insurance act, drafted by Heaps, and King did the same when he formed a government in 1935. But a constitutional amendment was necessary, giving the federal government exclusive jurisdiction in this area, before the legislation could become law in 1940.

In 1921, however, federal money was available for the months of January to March, although it was announced that this support would end on April 1. The federal contribution for Winnipeg was $51,000 during those three months. If the federal government stopped paying, the provincial government warned that they would also stop. Mayor Parnell announced that the city, too, would stop providing funds and no new applications would be processed after March 23.

This promised to create an impossible situation. There were regular meetings of the unemployed, including one in Victoria Park at which Hancox spoke.

William Ivens, c. 1921. MLA Winnipeg.
Archives of Manitoba, N70452.

John Queen, c. 1921. MLA Winnipeg.
Archives of Manitoba, N14996.

Representatives of the unemployed, including Edith Hancox, visited Mayor Parnell on March 26 and 29, asking that the relief program be extended for at least another month. They said that there were still 4,500 unemployed in the city. G.B. Clarke of the Social Welfare Commission announced that after April 1, relief in kind—meal tickets, vouchers rather than cash—would be supplied in cases of emergency.

But this was not sufficient for the unemployed, and on April 2, 1921, 600 people attended a meeting in Market Square and paraded through the downtown. The parade was made up of delegations of One Big Union members, returned soldiers, and women and girls who were out of work. Three Labour MLAs—John Queen, William Ivens, and William D. Bayley—and Edith Hancox spoke to the crowd in Market Square, saying that working people must be recognized as wealth producers and that the system had to change. The parade was headed by the Union Jack and the marchers also carried a red flag.

A month later, another parade, the 1921 May Day Parade, was well attended, with at least 3,000 people participating. In response to growing unrest in the country, on May 10 the federal government announced that it would resume payment of relief funds for the summer months. Labour leaders charged that unemployed men were sleeping in boxcars and disabled veterans were being forced to sleep outdoors, that unemployment was on the increase, and that wages were being lowered. Returned men, they said, made up 85 percent of the unemployed, and 50 percent of fathers of children in school were out of work. However, Alderman William Simpson, a Labour member of City Council and chair of the Social Welfare Council, responded that charges being made about unemployment were "wild and unfounded." Simpson said that the men sleeping in boxcars were transients, not local unemployed people, and he and Mayor Parnell said people who needed help were being taken care of.

At the end of May Mayor Parnell announced that the relief office on Main Street would close on May 28, 1921, after which no more aid would be given. He said very few applications were now being received and the Social Welfare Council would handle cases during the coming summer. On June 25, Parnell announced that $190,677 had been spent on relief by the three levels of government, with the City of Winnipeg's share being $66,009 or slightly more than one-third.

In September, a meeting in Winnipeg was attended by representatives of the federal and provincial governments and several Manitoba municipalities. In the report issued after the meeting, several causes were given for the high unemployment being experienced: there was a continued slow-down in the building industry so that men in the building trades and lumbering were out of work: and although rural jobs were often seen as a solution for urban joblessness, many farmers were not hiring. Low agricultural prices were forcing many to leave their land and join the unemployed population. Even farmer soldiers leaving the army had sometimes not gone back to farming, but stayed in cities looking for work. Nevertheless, many politicians maintained that the solution to the unemployment problem was to convince people in the cities to go back to the farm.

In the fall of 1921 there was an additional problem in Winnipeg: large numbers of men who, as happened every year, had come from the East to work on the harvest had decided to wait out the winter in the city in hopes of finding work in the spring. The city delayed starting relief payments in the hope that these additional workers would decide to leave, and about 400 were given train fare to go back east. In November, the city did start to issue meal tickets to the harvesters and provided them with work at the city's wood yard and beds at the Immigration Hall next to the CPR station.[12]

By October 1921 the federal government was promising to once again pay one-third of the costs of relief and the provincial government agreed to do the same. Applications for relief were accepted beginning on 12 December 1921. At about the same time, a quarrel began between Parnell and the mayor of Vancouver over notices that had appeared in the Vancouver papers warning anyone who was not a long-time resident of the city that they could not expect to receive either relief or work during the winter. The mayor of Vancouver, Robert Gale, accused Parnell of sending "indigent" men from Winnipeg to Vancouver, paying their train fare and supplying them with sandwiches to eat on the trip. Parnell fired back, scanning the lists of relief recipients in Winnipeg to discover several residents of Vancouver among the men being supported. Throughout the interwar years, Winnipeg politicians complained that the city was supporting a good number of men who migrated from other communities to collect relief and perhaps find a job.

Plans had been made for some new procedures before the opening of the relief office in December 1921. It had been decided that those applying for relief would not be paid in cash. Work would be compensated with vouchers for food, lodging, and clothing. Immigration Hall number 2 at the CPR station had been set aside as lodging for 250 single men. No application for relief would be accepted unless the person had been out of work for at least two weeks and had registered at the Employment Bureau. For people with rooms or apartments, light, water, and gas would be paid directly to the landlord. Medical care was to be available from doctors who would be on duty in the relief office on Main Street.

Once again the city's wood yard was open for men to earn the support they received. City Council had authorized $53,000 for sewer projects in River Heights on Renfrew and other nearby streets, and crews would once again be employed clearing snow from the streets. There would also be work in the stone quarries at Stony Mountain and a bridge was to be constructed across the Winnipeg River for the Pointe du Bois railroad line. Unemployed men were to be admitted to the Pritchard Baths for free.

The Central Council of Unemployed was not satisfied, and on December 12 there was a meeting in Market Square attended by 300 people. A delegation including Edith Hancox, council secretary, was appointed to talk to Mayor Parnell about problems with the relief system. One of the main issues was the forty-cent per hour rate being paid for sewer work. The group wanted forty-seven cents. Hancox also brought to the mayor's attention complaints received from women applying for relief who had to undergo physical examinations by medical students. She said the students did not always show proper respect for the women.

The year 1921 was probably the worst of the decade in terms of the numbers of people on relief. After that the slowly improving economy produced more jobs until by 1925, unemployment in the city was no longer at crisis levels. Beginning in 1930, conditions would again worsen and remain bad until late in the decade.

North End Farmers' Market, 1931. City of Winnipeg Archives.

PART 2

Politics

City Hall, 1918. Archives of Manitoba, L.B. Foote fonds, N2778.

CHAPTER 5

City Politics and the Trauma of the Strike

On November 28, 1919, Winnipeg voted to elect the mayor and City Council for 1920. The General Strike had been over for five months, but the city was still unsettled, and nowhere was the unsettled state of things more clearly revealed than during that election. Winnipeg historian J. Edgar Rae wrote, "The trauma of the Strike did not dissipate in the summer of 1919. Fear of the OBU [One Big Union] which still gripped the Citizens' Committee (Liberal/Conservative) and Labour's deep sense of injury made it almost inevitable that the struggle would be transferred to the arena of civic politics."[1] Those dynamics would continue to shape Winnipeg civic politics for the first half of the next decade.

In November 1919 there were seven wards in the city represented by fourteen aldermen, half of whom came up for election each year for a two-year term. There were therefore seven seats to be voted on in 1919. Any man or woman could vote as long as they were twenty-one years old, a British subject by birth or naturalization, and owner of property with an assessed value of no less than $100 or a tenant or leaseholder of property assessed for at least $200.[2] Boarders or lodgers were not eligible to vote, a rule that disenfranchised large numbers of people. Property owners could vote for aldermen and school board trustees in any wards in which they owned property. Everyone could vote only once for the mayor. If bylaws involving the creation of a debt were to be put to a vote at election time, only property owners, usually referred to as "ratepayers," could vote. In 1919 there were 31,367 property owners in the city and 23,695 eligible tenants for a total of 55,063 voters resident in Winnipeg.

Non-resident property owners numbered 6,734, all of whom were eligible to vote. The Liberal/Conservative campaigners encouraged the non-resident property owners to travel to Winnipeg to cast their ballots.[3] The number of potential voters was, therefore, 61,797 and the population of the city in 1921 was 179,097, including those below the age of twenty-one. So only approximately one-third of the population could vote.

Labour members of City Council supported instituting universal suffrage, but they did not have the votes during the 1920s to pass a motion in favour of the change. In the mid-1930s they were able to pass a motion to give everyone over the age of twenty-one the vote. However, when the matter reached the Manitoba Legislature's Law Amendments Committee, it was dropped and not added to the City of Winnipeg Act. Universal suffrage was finally established in Winnipeg in 1942.[4]

Candidates for mayor and aldermen had to be qualified electors and able to read and write. To run for mayor there was an additional qualification: ownership of property assessed for at least $2,000. This was eliminated during 1920. A similar stipulation that candidates for aldermen must own property worth at least $500 had been removed in 1918. A motion introduced by Labour Alderman Abraham Heaps to raise the annual indemnity paid to aldermen to $1,200 was passed around this time. Raising the amount paid to aldermen and eliminating the property qualifications for mayor and aldermen were important reforms that made it possible for a broader cross section of the city's population to run for office.

The 1919 City Election

In the months leading up to the November 28, 1919, vote, two political camps formed. The Board of Trade organized the Citizens League, just one of many such political groups of Liberal/Conservative candidates and aldermen that have, over the years and under many names, put forward non-Labour candidates in Winnipeg. During the 1920s the Better Civic Government Association (1923) and the Civic Progress Association (1929) were similar groups. Groups like this continued to function in the years after the 1920s.

The Citizens League's goal in 1919 was to provide support during the campaign to ensure that the victory won by the Citizens' Committee of 1000 during the strike would not be threatened by a Labour victory in the civic election. The extent of the preparations they made indicate it was clear that the

League was not at all sure of winning. The League's first organizing meeting took place at the Board of Trade building on August 20 and a nominating committee was established to find candidates for the executive and a fifty-person executive committee. The elections took place September 22 at the Board of Trade. The president was Dr. Jasper Halpenny, a prominent surgeon who had sat on many medical association and Board of Trade committees. One of the vice-presidents was Alvin K. Godfrey, previously a member of the executive of the Committee of 1000. He was an American who founded Monarch Lumber and became a citizen in 1913. Two more doctors, Dr. W.F. Taylor and Dr. N.K. McIvor, were also vice-presidents. The secretary was a lawyer, F. Sparling, who would later run for mayor, and the treasurer was J.D. Waugh. Many of the people involved with the Citizens League had been active with the Committee of 1000 during the strike. The League endorsed aldermanic and school board candidates in all seven wards, as well as the candidacy of Charles Gray for re-election as mayor.

Robert A.C. Manning gave the main speech at the September 22 organizational meeting. Manning was a lawyer and a long-time organizer for the Conservative Party who had been a prominent member of the Committee of 1000. He was born and educated in Winnipeg, and was a well-known hockey player as a young man and the president of the first Manitoba Hockey League. His father was a coal dealer and Manning inherited the business. He was called to the bar in 1901. He was a fiercely loyal Conservative and had worked for the party during the Roblin regime. He was a Winnipeg City alderman, ran unsuccessfully for mayor, and served as the reeve of Fort Garry Municipality from 1912 to 1914. Manning was well liked by his friends but, in the words of his obituary, "he was an old fashioned, uncompromising party man. As such he made many political enemies."[5] He died in a car accident in 1929.

In 1919 Manning laid out the basic themes on which the Citizens League would campaign. The first was that many Labour candidates were dangerous radicals. Manning said, "There was a definite plan of the reds to seize control all over the country . . . the objects that lay behind the strike must be stamped out and to assist in this representative citizens must be elected to the council."[6] He was using the language of the "red scare" that gripped Canada and the United States for a time after the Russian Revolution of 1917. Fear that the Left would start a revolution, as had happened in Russia and some European cities, was used in both countries to justify a wide range of actions directed at Labour and Social Democratic activists. It is difficult to say to what extent the fears were genuinely felt and how far they were just used as an excuse to cynically attack political opponents. In the case of experienced political men like Manning, it was probably the latter motivation that predominated.

By "representative," Manning meant "not Labour," and that was the second theme: that Labour politicians would ignore the rest of the population and represent the wishes of only working-class people. Only the Liberal/Conservative politicians backed by the League could be counted on to represent the whole population.

A third theme put forward by the League was that there was a difference between the radical left groups and "sane" Labour—the adherents of traditional trade unions, usually international unions affiliated with larger American organizations. Early in the 1919 campaign, on November 20, the *Free Press* carried an unsigned editorial headed "Extreme Types Are Winnipeg's Chief Foes," arguing that "Labour radicalism is rampant though challenged by sound labour unionism." As proof of this split in the Labour movement, it quoted a resolution passed at the Dominion Labour Congress in September 1919. The Congress denounced the OBU, saying it was "founded on force" and "gambled its whole future on the success of sympathetic and national strikes."

It was true that there was a split in the Labour camp, and Liberal/Conservative politicians happily used it in their campaigning, especially in the early 1920s. There were many points of view among the supporters of Labour, ranging from Marxists to the Independent Labour Party (ILP) supporters who believed in gradual reform through the existing system. The ILP leaders were mostly British and their influences came from the British Labour movement led by people like Kier Hardie. The Social Gospel had an influence as well with its focus on the evils caused by unregulated business. In the Labour union movement, the most important division was between union leaders like Robert B. Russell of the One Big Union, who were working to establish industrial unions or "general unions," as they were called in Britain, on one side, and the older craft and trade unions on the other. The membership of the general or industrial union included workers from all areas, from highly trained tradesmen to general labourers. These unions often believed in being involved in politics and in working toward establishing a social democratic state. The more conservative leaders of the older craft unions followed the lead of Samuel Gompers, one of the founders and for many years the president of the American Federation of Labor. He believed unions should concentrate on matters like collective bargaining and labour legislation and steer clear of left-wing politics.

After the General Strike the OBU began a recruiting drive in Winnipeg and attracted many new members. For many, the OBU served as a fraternal organization and maintained the camaraderie they had enjoyed during the strike. The older trade unions, however, maintained control of the Winnipeg Trades and Labour Council (WTLC) and its assets and, helped by their organizers, managed also to retain the status of being the unions with whom companies signed contracts. The OBU acquired members but, with a few exceptions such as the Street Railway staff, did not represent them with the employers. The struggle went on for a time but the recession that began in 1920 and lasted until 1925 caused workers to be less militant for fear of losing their jobs. Union membership in all unions declined from the high numbers achieved at the end of the war, but the international unions could be said to have won the contest with the OBU.[7]

The Citizens League began at their first meeting to plan for changes to how the mayor and aldermen were elected in the city. They passed a resolution recommending that not just property owners but also their spouses should be allowed to vote on money bylaws in civic elections. This suggestion was sent to City Council and it was included in the next set of amendments of the City Charter, an example of the simple but effective relationship the League enjoyed with Council.

Labour held a convention in October to prepare for the election and select a candidate for mayor. There were 400 delegates present. Representatives from the Dominion Labour Party, the largest Labour party at the time, and the ex-Soldiers and Sailors Labour Party as well as various unions chose Seymour Farmer as the Labour candidate for mayor.[8]

Seymour Farmer was chosen as Labour candidate for mayor in 1919 and was elected mayor of Winnipeg in 1923. This photo is from 1941 when he was an MLA. Archives of Manitoba, N26779.

Farmer had been involved in Winnipeg and Manitoba politics for fifteen years. Born in Cardiff, Wales, he came to Canada in 1900 and worked as an accountant for the International Elevator Company. He was married and had four children. He had been the secretary of the Direct Legislation League, the vice-president of the Dominion

Labour Party, and he had been one of the organizers of and was the general
secretary of the Independent Labour Party. He was also a member of the
Manitoba Legislature and in the provincial election of 1920 he had received
the second-largest number of votes of any of the Labour candidates. He would
continue to serve on City Council and as an MLA for many years, winning
his last election as a CCF MLA in 1945. Farmer and his fellow MLA Fred
Dixon were good friends and in the 1920s lived close to each other in the Lord
Roberts neighbourhood.

Nominations for council and the school board had to be in the hands of
the city clerk, Charles J. Brown, by November 19. There were Labour and
Citizens League candidates in all seven wards and a full slate of candidates
from both groups for the school board election. Brown reported that it was
the busiest nomination day he had experienced in his eleven years on the job.
Many of the nomination papers had long lists of signatures, proof that large
numbers of people were eager to play some role. As in past elections the may-
or, Charles Gray, was nominated by his two friends Alex Jamieson and R.A.
Harvey. Seymour Farmer collected a number of names including that of his
friend and fellow Labour politician Fred Dixon. They often nominated one
another and worked on each other's campaigns.[9]

City Clerk Brown wrote to all the returning officers warning that, given the
atmosphere in the city, "there may possibly be some disorder on this election
day." Each polling station had a special constable, usually the school janitor,
who had the power to arrest. Thirteen of the busier polling stations had a
regular uniformed police constable on duty. In the event there was no disorder
but a larger voter turnout than was usual.

The renomination of Charles Gray for mayor guaranteed some stormy
election meetings. Gray was very unpopular with many people because of
actions he took during the strike, such as deploying the special constables who
were hired to replace the striking police force. Probably he was most hated for
his decision to read the riot act and call in the Mounted Police to clear Main
Street on Saturday, June 21, 1919. On that day the Mounties charged through
the crowd on Main Street, firing their pistols and causing the deaths of two
men. Gray was a lightning rod for the outrage of Labour voters.

Charles Gray was not a typical member of the city's elite and did not seem
to participate in the social life of the wealthier families. Born in London,
England, he was an electrical engineer. He had served on the Board of Control
for a year before being elected mayor for 1919. At several election meetings
Gray was greeted by raucous crowds. At Aberdeen School on November 18,

*Charles Gray, c. 1920. He was re-
elected mayor in the 1919 City Council
election. Archives of Manitoba.*

1919, he was invited and attended in spite of John Queen's prediction that he would "never come to a Ward 5 meeting."[10] Gray was greeted with polite applause when he rose to speak but he was soon being heckled by a section of the audience that showed its hostility "in what at times amounted to a regular fury."[11] Gray stood his ground and finished his remarks.

Seymour Farmer also spoke at the meeting. He said that City Council had never "done one thing to alleviate the lot of working people." Farmer maintained that civic employees should be free to organize in any way they saw fit. Gray responded that promises made at election time were often either fraudulent or naive, and that Labour candidates had no idea of the difficulties in the way of fulfilling their promises. At one point Gray shouted at the crowd, "The trouble with you people is not that you are sore at me. You would be sore at anyone who held the position I held." A voice said, "You'll never hold it again." And Gray answered, "Yes I will and I'll get a majority right here in this ward."[12]

Gray attended a meeting at St. John's High School where he was again heckled and at times could not make himself heard. At another meeting at Kelvin School in the south end on the evening of November 20, Gray spoke again, this time to a sympathetic audience. At that meeting a man asked a question from the floor about the ads the Citizens League had placed in the papers. He said he had been a member of Alderman John Sullivan's committee but had resigned because he objected to the ads. The city was deeply divided between two warring camps and feelings were running high.

It may be that Farmer wanted to avoid any repetition of the rowdy meeting at Aberdeen School, but he did not attend two subsequent meetings where Gray spoke. On the evening of Sunday, November 23, he addressed a stand-ing-room-only crowd at the Columbia Theatre. Farmer said that the vote, which would take place on Friday of that week, was about the same issue facing people the world over: "whether the people of Winnipeg are content to be dominated by an old system which keeps them in slavery and maintains itself by fraud or whether they will turn to progressive people in the community and march onward with truth."[13]

Farmer's platform described the world he was inviting people to march toward: it would have universal suffrage, a city-operated dairy to ensure an adequate supply of fresh milk in the city, and all homes worth less than $3,000 exempt from city taxes. At the same time it was proposed that vacant land should be taxed to force speculators to develop their land holdings. The municipal dairy idea was on the ballot on election day and was narrowly defeated, 5,006 to 4,800.

On election day a record number of people came out to vote. Many were surprised at the strength of the Labour vote—a measure of the anger and disappointment Labour supporters were feeling. Seymour Farmer held his own against Mayor Gray at the beginning of the counting, winning majorities in the three North End wards. But when the results from the wards south of Notre Dame Avenue were in, Gray was the clear winner with an overall tally of 15,670 votes to Farmer's 12,514.

By the end of the day, Labour had elected two new members—aldermen John Blumberg in Ward 6 and Herbert Jones in Ward 7—producing an evenly divided council, with seven Labour and seven Citizens League aldermen. Although they did not have a majority, this was the best result Labour had ever had, and marked a turning point in Winnipeg politics. Labour aldermen and -women would keep their platform before the voters at election time and throughout the year, and behave like a city administration in waiting.

The tie in the number of seats meant that the mayor would play a central role during 1920, frequently casting his vote to break a tie. When the numbers were not tied, the mayor's main function seemed to be to "keep the others from fighting," as Mayor Ralph Webb would later say. In spite of the increased Labour support, the city was still geographically divided between north and south, Alderman Ernest Robinson in Ward 4 being the only Labour member south of the CPR yards.

Once the election was over, both sides of the divided Council began to put forward suggestions to change the way in which it was elected. The Labour aldermen favoured universal suffrage. At the second Council meeting in 1920, aldermen Heaps and Queen moved that Council "go on record as favoring the adoption of adult suffrage in municipal elections." They asked that the Legislative Committee of Council prepare an amendment for the City Charter, giving the right to vote to "all persons male or female, British Subjects by birth or naturalization, 21 years old, resident in the city for 6 months before going on the voters' list."

Counting the votes for the Winnipeg proportional representation election, 1920. Archives of Manitoba.

The Citizens League councillors wanted to push through changes they had started to plan before the election, and they had no interest in broadening the vote or abandoning the property qualification. The Council vote on Heaps's and Queen's motion was tied. Mayor Gray cast the deciding vote, defeating the motion[14] and establishing a pattern that would continue throughout 1920 for votes on all questions.

On 7 January 1920, *Canadian Finance*, a local business paper, carried an article supporting a different way of changing the voting method. The piece criticized Winnipeg's existing seven-ward division. Each ward elected two aldermen although the populations they represented varied greatly. Ward 3, a large ward in the centre of the city, stretching from St. James Street to Balmoral Street with a northern border at Notre Dame Avenue and a southern border at the Assiniboine River, had the largest population at 43,705. The next largest was Ward 5 between Selkirk Avenue and Logan Avenue with 34,301. The other wards ranged from 11,000 to 25,000. The number of voters also varied greatly, ranging from 3,600 to 15,000.

Table 1. Old Ward System.

Ward	Voters	Population
1	12,035	25,942
2	4,694	18,131
3	15,520	43,705
4	7,575	24,372
5	5,533	34,301
6	9,323	25,373
7	3,694	11,554
TOTAL	58,374	183,378

Source: City of Winnipeg Municipal Manual (1920), 108, 191.

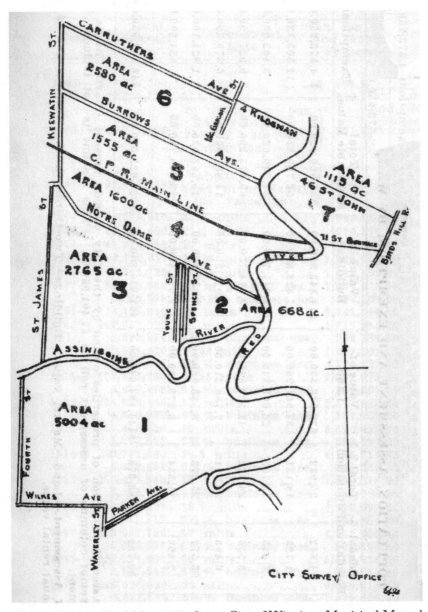

City of Winnipeg Ward Map, 1907. Source: City of Winnipeg Municipal Manual *(1920), 192.*

The new governance model put forward by *Canadian Finance* and the Citizens League proposed that the number of wards should be reduced from seven to three. The western boundary of the three wards would be Kenaston Boulevard, and St. James and Keewatin streets. The new Ward 1 would extend south to Wilkes Avenue, and the northern boundary was moved from the Assiniboine River to the centre line of Portage Avenue. It thus would take in residential areas in the west end, Armstrong's Point, and the Hudson's Bay Reserve area south of downtown. The ward extended east to the Red River. Ward 2 encompassed the old wards 2, 3, and 4, and ran from the centre line of Portage to the CPR tracks and east to the Red River. Ward 3, made up of the old wards 5, 6, and 7, was north of the CPR and included Elmwood. The six wards, numbers 2 to 7, where significant Labour support existed, were thus reduced in number to two.

Under the new system each of the three wards would elect six aldermen, three each year for two-year terms. The populations and the number of voters in each ward would be much closer than before—Ward 1 had 20,466 eligible voters, Ward 2 had 21,070, and Ward 3 had 18,728. The percentage of the population who could vote in each ward was 35 percent in Ward 1, 31 percent in Ward 2, and 26 percent in Ward 3. The total populations, including non-voters, were Ward 1: 58,206; Ward 2: 67,032; and Ward 3 in the North End: 71,709. These numbers still covered a wide range but they were closer than under the old system. So aldermen from Wards 2 and 3 were representing more people than those from Ward 1 but they were elected by roughly the same number of voters.

Table 2. New Ward System.

Ward	Voters	Population	Percent
Ward 1	29,216	58,206	35
Ward 2	31,235	67,032	31
Ward 3	26,155	71,709	26

Source: City of Winnipeg Municipal Manual (1921), 117, 199.

The method of voting also changed to the single transferable vote. This method presented the voter with the usual ballot with all the candidates' names, but instead of just marking one name, the voter placed a number beside each name, from 1 to the total number of candidates, with number 1 being the voter's first choice. A number of votes required to be elected, or quota, was established once the total number of votes cast in the ward was known. Any candidates who succeeded in achieving the quota were declared elected. Then, if three people had still not been elected, the number 2 choices were counted and transferred to the totals of the remaining candidates until three collected enough votes to be elected.

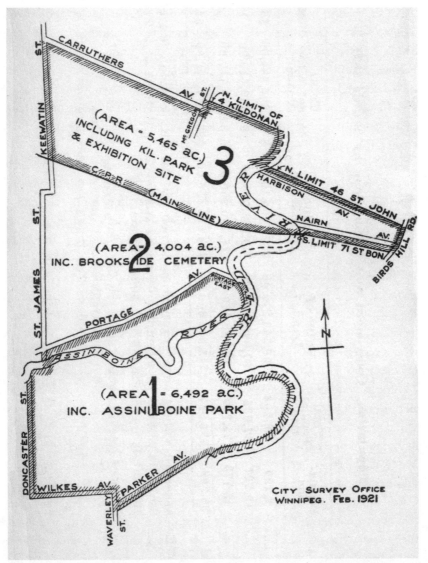

Wards 1, 2, and 3. Source: City of Winnipeg Municipal Manual *(1921), 200.*

It was argued that this method of voting would give a more accurate picture of what voters wanted. It was also pointed out by the supporters of the plan that the reduction of the number of wards from seven to three would reduce duplicate voting—ratepayers voting in any wards in which they owned property—by about 50 percent.

The Labour group on Council opposed these changes. At a special meeting of Council on February 12, presentations about the proposed changes were invited. The galleries in the council chamber were crowded and noisy. The Citizens League plan was presented by R.A.C. Manning. He was continually interrupted by heckling from the gallery and Mayor Gray called for quiet. When Seymour Farmer spoke on the proposals, calling them undemocratic and a step backward, he was cheered and applauded by people in the gallery. Mayor Gray then asked the police to remove the people in the gallery and those standing on the floor of the council chamber. The Labour aldermen also left the meeting at that point to protest the mayor's action.

At the regular Council meeting the following Monday, the Labour councillors attempted to discuss the legality of the mayor's action, but this motion was defeated with the mayor's casting the deciding vote. Once again the galleries were crowded and the mayor threatened to have them cleared when the crowd became noisy. The people in the gallery then settled down and regular business proceeded.

The changes were finally approved by Council on March 15. Aldermen Fisher and Sparling moved that, "with a view to more equal representation," the changes should be proposed as an amendment to the City Charter, and it passed with a vote of eight to six. The plan was then sent to the Legislature with a request to amend the City Charter. When the changes reached the Law Amendments Committee for consideration, there was a crowd of about 100 in the committee room. Labour had twelve speakers registered to speak, all of whom advocated universal suffrage. Jesse Kirk, who would be elected as Winnipeg's first woman councillor in 1921, said that she valued human rights more than property rights and equality of rights more than special privilege. Mrs. Roe, speaking for the Women's Labour League, said the property qualification for voting was a relic of the past and it was time to start building the new Canada that was promised during the war. Labour lawyer T.J. Murray argued that everyone contributed to taxes whether directly or indirectly and should therefore have a vote. The supporters of the changes merely restated what was being proposed and defended the idea that the spouses of property owners should be allowed to vote. John W. Dafoe, who had supported the changes in the *Free Press*, said that the Labour members had shown themselves to be obstructionists and not reformers. He argued that universal suffrage was too big a change to be made without further study. Dafoe said the new system could well work in Labour's favour because they could be sure of electing all the aldermen in Ward 3 and if they could take enough seats in Ward 2, a mixed ward, they might well gain the majority on Council. To achieve this, he said, they would have to modify their policies and present a more moderate program to attract a wider cross-section of voters.

Although no city election in the remainder of the decade would be as lively as the 1919 contest, and Labour would not do as well in succeeding elections, Labour aldermen were now established as a disciplined group on City Council.

❖

The problems produced by the General Strike were still very much on the minds of Winnipeggers in 1920. In August 1920 Labour aldermen A.A. Heaps and Herbert Jones made a motion that Council ask for the release of the strike leaders from prison.[15] Heaps argued that some of the prisoners were members of Council and of the Legislature, proving they had the confidence of the people. Alderman John Sullivan spoke against the motion, saying that it would appear to condone what the men had done. He said with some feeling that many men had been shot for less. Sullivan said that it would set a bad example for the many foreigners in the city: "I am a British Subject by choice. I took an oath and I think that I would be breaking that oath by voting to let traitors out of jail."[16] Labour Alderman Ed Robinson replied, "This is the request of elected representatives of the people declaring that the ends of justice have been served and that these men should be set free. They are not criminals, they are no more guilty than we are. . . . For Alderman Sullivan to talk of traitors—all I can say is that I am surprised."

Frank Fowler spoke next. He said, "I regret very much that this resolution has been brought to Council. It is not for Council to decide this matter. Our duty is not to interpret the desires of the citizens of Winnipeg in a matter of this kind. I am not going to vote for a resolution purporting to express the desire of the citizens of Winnipeg for the release of these men." He said there was nothing in Heaps's motion to indicate that he thought they had done wrong, but they had been convicted of a crime. Fowler then waffled and said he would, he thought, vote for a motion that petitioned for the release of some, adding that the city solicitor had given his opinion that the motion was out of order. Fowler, who was acting mayor, cast the tie-breaking vote, defeating the motion six votes to five.

The city elections for the 1921 and 1922 mayor and Council saw Edward Parnell run for mayor as the Citizens' League candidate. Seymour Farmer was the Labour candidate for 1921, and in 1922 Parnell was unopposed. The elections did not excite the same kind of emotion that the city witnessed in 1919. The strong, angry feelings about the strike were beginning to fade. At an election meeting in Elmwood for Independent Labour Party Alderman J.L. Wiginton, the *Tribune* reported that "strike events were dragged in considerable detail before the meeting by a few persons wanting particular information but the majority of the 100 electors present indicated they were tired of talking and hearing about the strike."[17]

Abraham A. Heaps was one of the jailed 1919 strike leaders. He served on Winnipeg City Council from 1919 to 1925, as well as in the House of Commons from 1925 to 1940. Along with his involvement in housing issues, he was instrumental in drafting unemployment insurance legislation as well as old age pension in Canada. Archives of Manitoba, Jewish Historical Society Collection, 575.

The animosities aroused by the strike were nevertheless still in evidence during the campaign, and the trials of the strike leaders early in the year had served to keep them alive. By the fall of 1920 there were also divisions within the Labour movement, with the American Federation of Labor-affiliated craft and trade unions that dominated the Trades and Labour Council on one side, and the supporters of the One Big Union on the other.

On November 3, 1920, the Dominion Labour Party had nominated a slate of candidates for Council with Seymour Farmer as their choice for mayor. But the party then split over the nomination of William Hoop for alderman. When Hoop was nominated, many of his fellow party members resigned from the Dominion Labour Party because they did not want to be on the same slate with him. Fred Dixon went so far as to say he would not support Hoop for dogcatcher. Seymour Farmer briefly withdrew from the race for the mayor's office, but then was convinced to reconsider.

Bill Hoop was a long-time Labour leader and a member of the Dominion Labour Party. He worked for the Winnipeg Trades and Labour Council in the early 1920s during their struggle with the OBU. During a debate earlier in 1920 between two speakers for the international unions and two representatives of the OBU, Hoop had charged that the OBU was responsible for the failure of the General Strike because of its radical ideas. Many Labour supporters were outraged by this assertion. During 1921 the people who had left the Dominion Labour Party established the Independent Labour Party, which continued to run candidates for many years until it became part of the Co-operative Commonwealth Federation (CCF).[18] William Hoop ran unsuccessfully for City Council in Ward 2. In 1927 he ran again as an independent and was again defeated.

In 1921, Edward Parnell could be said to have been the last Winnipeg mayor in the 1920s who came from the city's business elite. A successful businessman, he was also president of the Board of Trade during his first term as mayor. This close connection between the Board of Trade and the mayor's office had been common in the past. He had also been a member of the executive of the Citizens' Committee of 1000 during the 1919 strike. Parnell had been president of the Canadian Manufacturers Association before being elected mayor and had been on the founding board of the Winnipeg Foundation. He was born in England and came to London, Ontario, as a boy. He owned a successful bakery there and served on the London City Council for eleven years. He came to Winnipeg and in 1911 went into partnership with Winnipeg baker John T. Speirs. Their partnership was in response to the arrival of Canada Bread, a company started by George Weston. Weston was buying up bakeries in Winnipeg, including a large share of Speirs's and Parnell's bakeries. They were allowed to continue in business as long as they did not directly compete with Weston products. Their plant on Elgin Avenue was worth over $500,000, and Speirs and Parnell operated sixty delivery wagons and produced 100,000 loaves a day. [19]

Parnell attempted to set a conciliatory tone during his campaign, even though it was clearly too soon after the General Strike to do so. He said that if Farmer were elected he intended to do everything in his power to assist him, and that "if the citizens declare themselves in my favor as I expect they will, then I will expect and will welcome Mr. Farmer to get behind me in the supreme interest and effort to make our city everything it should be."[20]

Parnell said he was not against labour unions and his bakery was unionized, but he was not a supporter of radical leftists who wanted to overthrow everything. This position differed from the Citizens League rhetoric of the 1919 election that called for the eradication of the objects behind the strike. Business-oriented politicians would now make similar distinctions between "radical" and non-radical labour groups for the rest of the 1920s.

J.W. Morrison, running for Council as an independent, commented that the Citizens League would make it impossible for the Council to operate in the conciliatory way that Parnell favoured. He said the League candidates were not disposed to bridge the gulf between factions and would not "attempt to carry into effect the principles of cooperation and united community advocated by Edward Parnell."[21] This turned out to be true.

Parnell made the construction of Memorial Boulevard in the area north of the Legislative Building one of his main proposals, and said it would be "an act of criminal neglect if we allowed the opportunity that now offers to be lost." He was principally referring to the Hudson's Bay Company's plan to proceed with a new store on Portage Avenue if the boulevard was built.

To address the housing crisis, he promised to work to create a new, comprehensive housing scheme. He felt the Winnipeg Housing Commission should aim to build 600 to 700 houses. During the two years before the 1920 election, Council had spent a good deal of time and energy on the housing crisis and Parnell had participated in the issue as a member of the Board of Trade executive.

❖

Housing was one of the most challenging postwar problems facing Winnipeg. It was one of the major struggles of the early 1920s between Labour and Liberal/Conservative aldermen, the two groups having diametrically opposed views on what to do about the problem. The ILP members of Council wanted the city to build public housing and then rent units out. The Liberal/Conservative aldermen did not want the city to be in the rental business in competition with private landlords. They favoured a loan program to help people to build new homes. The Board of Trade became involved, establishing a fund to pay off defaulted loans and a second private loan fund created with capital provided by local businessmen.

The shortage of good-quality housing, especially affordable housing for working families, was not a new problem in Winnipeg. In the 1913 report of the Winnipeg City Planning Commission there is a description of living conditions in a sample of 2,222 specific houses in the city. The commission made recommendations about such matters as overcrowding, the lack of natural light and air in cottages that were built too close to one another on small lots, the quality of construction in many homes, and the need to revise the building by-law. The recommendations provided a foundation for work done in the 1920s.

Cities across Canada and in all the combatant nations faced housing problems as the war ended and hundreds of thousands of men returned home. In the crowded North End of Winnipeg conditions were especially bad, with several families often sharing the same single-family house. As the troops came home, the crowding was about to get worse.

At the same time owning land and rental property and investing and speculating in building lots were activities participated in by many Winnipeggers from the earliest days of the city. A lot of people still owned houses and lots they had been holding and paying taxes on and they saw the end of the war and the return of the troops as a golden opportunity to finally cash in on their investments. They, along with real estate agents, were inclined to argue that the problem was not a housing shortage, but rather a buyer or renter shortage.

In Winnipeg private construction of new housing had declined during the war years.[22] In 1913 and 1914 a total of 3,392 houses and 149 apartment blocks had been built, but between 1915 and 1917 the numbers declined to 135 new houses and 9 blocks. Meanwhile, the population of the city had increased by 43,000 or about 25 percent, from 136,035 in 1911 to 179,087 in 1921. The return of demobilized soldiers in 1919 brought several thousand additional people looking for housing.

A National Industrial Conference was convened by the federal government in 1918 to discuss ways to ease the country from war into peace. In their report the commissioners said "a cause for unrest which we met in practically every place we visited was the scarcity of houses and the poor quality of some of those that did exist."[23]

The Federal Government passed an Order-in-Council on December 3, 1918, authorizing a $25 million appropriation to be made available to provincial governments under the War Measures Act to be loaned to municipalities for the construction of new housing.

Winnipeg Council action on housing had begun in March of 1918 when Alderman Cockburn and Commissioner Arthur Puttee moved that a housing survey be done of "at least a portion of the city." E.W.J. Hague, the assistant chief health inspector, presented the results of the survey to the City Council Health Committee on December 31. This study found that in some areas, especially in the North End, overcrowding was producing, in Hague's words, "slumdom" conditions. A total of 1,031 families were found to be living in space meant to accommodate 361. Rents, like all the other components of the cost of living, had risen during the war. In 1918 alone the increases averaged 20 percent. The majority on the Health Committee voted to table of the report in Council, ensuring that it would be considered further.

On January 17, 1919, the federal government formally announced the housing program. Manitoba's share was to be $1.5 million.[24] The federal program stipulated that the loans would be repayable over twenty to thirty years and were to range between $2,000 and $4,500, depending upon the type of house and building materials used. The loan could not exceed 85 percent of the value of the house and lot, so borrowers had to be able to raise the remaining 15 percent elsewhere. In addition, the people receiving the loans were not to have an income greater than $3,000 a year. The houses were to have all modern conveniences—sewer and water—and they were to be occupied by the person taking out the loan.

A City Council special committee on housing was appointed, consisting of three labour aldermen, A.A. Heaps, Ernest Robinson, and W.B. Simpson, and two Liberal/Conservative members, R.H. Hamlin and H. Gray. Almost immediately, on January 23, 1919, A.A. Heaps proposed that Winnipeg should take $1 million of the federal money and build 300 houses on the old Exhibition Grounds.

Heaps, who was born and grew up in Britain, was familiar with the public housing that British County Councils had been building since the 1890s. With the end of the Great War Britain passed a Housing Act that envisaged the construction of large housing estates financed with public money. In mid-1920 London County Council announced a plan to spend $150 million over the next two years to put up 19,000 cottages.

In Winnipeg, however, those in the real estate business were opposed to the city government building and renting housing. Two days after Heaps made his first proposal those present at a real estate meeting said the thousands of troops returning to the city could be accommodated in the available vacant properties or privately constructed houses.

Many aldermen agreed and wanted to limit the City's role to simply lending mortgage money. There were some non–Labour Party members of council, like Alderman Fisher, who were open to building public housing. George Fisher had originally come to Winnipeg from Scotland to be manager of the Scottish Co-operative Wholesale Society, and was familiar with the British public housing schemes.

On February 14, 1919, a public meeting was convened by the Housing Committee to discuss the issue, with A.A. Heaps in the chair. The minutes provide a glimpse of the wide range of views in the city.[25] Board of Trade

Jesse Kirk, 1921. City of Winnipeg Archives, City Clerk's Department.

representatives like N.T. McMillan, a real estate developer, and former mayor Thomas Deacon were opposed to the City building houses.

Several others at the meeting disagreed and spoke in favour of reserving all the money to provide housing for soldiers and their families. Jesse Kirk, a future Labour alderwoman, said there was no doubt about the scarcity of small comfortable modern houses for rent to veterans. Margaret McWilliams, a Liberal and another future member of City Council said the local Council of Women gave top priority to providing houses for returned men and for the families of those who had not returned. She was opposed "to the bringing up the children of these men in overcrowded conditions."

J. Winning, president of the Winnipeg Trades and Labour Council, was also at the February 14 meeting. He said that workers were not earning enough to be able to build their own homes and that the City should build homes for them to rent.

Heaps thanked the attendees for their ideas and adjourned the meeting. He must now have seen clearly how difficult it was going to be to come up with a plan that everyone would support. At the end of March 1919 A.A. Heaps moved that the committee apply for $1 million to build 400 houses, work to start as soon as the weather permitted and enough labour could be found. But the opposition of other committee members continued to delay any application for funds from the provincial government. Instead, council voted to wait and see what regulations the Province formulated for lending the federal money.

In mid-April 1919, with no action having been taken, a *Tribune* editorial accused the City Council of not showing "the activity that reasonably might have been looked for."[26] Manitoba Finance Minister Edward Brown said that he wondered what the Council was doing. Edward Parnell, president of the Board of Trade, said the Board was eager to work with the city to get houses built and Council approved the idea of cooperating with the Board. A.A. Heaps had still not given up on public housing, proposing 1,000 houses using a "town planning" method, laying out streets according to well-defined plans.[27]

In mid-May 1919 the General Strike intervened and Council passed a motion to lay over further work on the housing question until the strike was settled. There can be no doubt that the housing situation was one of the factors contributing to the strike.

Once the strike ended, Council moved to appoint a new housing committee that would consist of aldermen and citizens. A.A. Heaps was unavailable, having been arrested with other strike leaders on June 18. The *Winnipeg Tribune* and the Board of Trade exerted pressure on Council to make a start. When Council members did not show up at a housing meeting the mayor called another for a few days hence. The *Tribune* commented, "If enough of the @1200 a year aldermen show up Council may adopt a scheme so that a few houses may be constructed before the weather is too cold."[28]

Then on July 9 came the meeting at which the issue exploded. W.B. Simpson moved acceptance of the Council Housing Committee's original report. Then Liberal/Conservative aldermen Gray and Hamlin made a motion that everything in the report after the first paragraph be deleted and new wording substituted. The new wording omitted any mention of the City building and limited the scheme to simply advancing mortgage loans to citizens, the money to be used to build suitable housing.

These tactics outraged Gray and Hamlin's colleagues on the Housing Committee, who saw that they had been superseded without consultation or explanation and resigned. Alderman George Fisher "accused City Council of playing with the proposed housing scheme and branded council's latest attempt to solve the housing shortage problem as a joke." Fisher announced that he would not attend any meetings of the new committee selected to manage the plan.[29]

A three-hour debate followed and all the various reports and options were discussed all over again. A.F. Pulford and Frank Fowler then moved that the city Committee meet with the Housing Committee of the Board of Trade to explore options for housing. This was defeated. Then, in what seemed like an attempt to throw the Labor members a bone, Liberal/Conservative Aldermen Alexander McLennan and Robert Hamlin moved that the city purchase land and erect twelve houses that citizens could apply for. This was declared out of order and the Pulford and Fowler motion was passed. During this scene some Liberal/Conservative Aldermen voted with Labor—housing was an issue that could cause councilors to break ranks.

Finally, on August 5, 1919, Council began to act on the amended Special Committee on Housing Report of July 15. The City would make loans for

85 percent of the value of the house to individuals wanting to build houses for their own use. The individual borrowers would have to find the other 15 percent themselves. The functions of the proposed Housing Commission were to ensure such things as: the building lot met their standards in terms of its size, location, price, and being connected to the city sewer and water; that the value of house and lot was such that the applicant had at least 15 percent of the necessary cash to put in; cost of the materials being purchased was legitimate; and the house was built under supervision of the commission.[30]

On August 18 the Board of Trade housing committee set up a fund intended to protect the City from losses due to defaults. It would amount to 10 percent of the total loans and would be deposited with the City of Winnipeg Sinking Fund Trustees to invest and manage.

Heaps, now out of prison on bail, and the other Labor members made a last attempt to amend the plan by having the loans cover 90 percent of the cost and the borrower fund 5 percent. Their motions were defeated.

In November 1919 the Commission borrowed an additional $50,000 from the Province and $40,000 was loaned out immediately to twelve borrowers. This amounted to average loans of $3,000. As 1920 began the Commission seemed to have settled into a regular routine of approving loans but the numbers of houses resulting were very small.

Table 3. Total Construction of Buildings in Winnipeg, 1920 to 1923.

Year	Commission Loan Houses	Total Loans	Total Buildings Erected in Winnipeg	Total Cost of All Construction (millions)
1920	153	$517,000	2,501	$8.3
1921	206	$856,000	3,201	$5.5
1922	219	$855,000	3,473	$6.8
1923	134	$477,000	2,716	$4.4
Total	712	$2.7 million	11,891	$25.0

Source: City of Winnipeg Municipal Manual.

The Housing Commission continued to loan money for three years until the end of 1923. They made 712 loans for 712 houses, the loans totaling $2.7 million. By the end of 1924, fourteen of the loans had been paid off and others were in various stages of being repaid. After 1923 it was decided that there was no longer a need for the Commission loans "in view of the improved housing situation and the fact that private funds had become available at reasonable rates of interest to meet all possible requirements."[31] The Commission continued to exist but now its function was solely to manage the outstanding loans and their repayment. The personnel of the Commission did not change a great deal and in 1930 W.E. Milner and W. H. Carter were still serving as representatives of the Board of Trade. By that year, $1.5 million—more than half of the total amount loaned—had been repaid.

In their annual report for 1923, the last year new loans were made, the Board of Trade expressed great pride in the accomplishments of the Commission of which they were part: "The work of the Commission has built a town in the heart of Winnipeg of an assessed value greater than any other town in Manitoba." The assessed value of the houses constructed was $2 million and the city would collect $60,000 in taxes every year from the owners. Revenue for City Hydro would be $17,500 and the homeowners would use water worth $6,500 (see Table 3).

❖

During the civic election in November 1920, both Farmer, the Labour candidate for mayor, and his opponent Edward Parnell made a new housing scheme one of the main planks of their platforms. Farmer said Labour wanted municipally owned housing, a model earlier championed by A.A. Heaps. It would be self-supporting, using rents to cover expenses and loan payments. The *Tribune* reported that another Labour candidate in the 1920 election had charged that Heaps's housing program had been wrecked by "private interests" because it was a Labour idea.[32] Parnell wanted to continue with the Housing Commission as it existed with Board of Trade representation. He began to advance his proposal to build Memorial Boulevard, and he also encouraged people to vote, commenting that election meetings had been poorly attended and there seemed to be a general apathy in the city. This was in contrast with the huge crowds and noisy debate in the meetings of a year before.

The 1920 election was the first in which the new three-ward division of the city was in place and the first time spouses of ratepayers were able to vote. In practice, this meant many women voted for the first time. The first woman council member, Jesse Kirk, won a seat. It was also the first time the new transferrable vote system was used. There was enormous confusion among voters, and in some polls as many as 25 percent of ballots were rejected.

On December 5 Parnell was elected but with the relatively small majority of 920 votes. He won a majority in Ward 1 and Farmer won majorities in Wards 2 and 3, proving that there was substantial Labour support in Ward 2.

House moving at Ellice Avenue and Sherbrook Street, 1922. Archives of Manitoba, McAdam fonds, 167.

This support did not translate into Council seats for Labour. The new Council would have six Labour aldermen and eleven Liberal/Conservatives. Ward 1 elected three Citizens' Committee aldermen; Ward 2 returned two Citizens' and one Labour candidate; Ward 3, one Citizens' and two Labour. This was a big change from the 1919 election when the two sides were tied.

On December 15 the *Canadian Finance* newspaper lamented that out of 90,000 possible voters, only 30,000 bothered to vote in the municipal election. The paper opined that Labour would have elected more except that One Big Union and American Federation of Labor supporters would not select candidates from the opposing Labour group on their ballot as second choice. To show that the city was not as polarized as people said, the paper pointed out that Mrs. Kirk, Labour, and Daniel McLean, Citizens' Committee, were both elected partly by supporters of their opponents, naming them as second choice.

Running in his second election in the fall of 1921, Parnell was re-elected by acclamation. He encouraged people once again not to be apathetic about voting in the aldermanic elections. "No matter how much confidence you may have in your mayor, he is more or less controlled by the Council, as it has the voting power," he said.[33] The 1921 election resulted in six Labour alderman and twelve Liberal/Conservatives to serve for the 1922 year. Parnell was ill and in February he took a six-month leave in Victoria to build up his health. He did not improve and died in June. Frank O. Fowler, who had been acting for Parnell, was the only candidate nominated in the by-election to succeed him.

Frank Fowler was a Liberal and a tough, experienced politician. He had come to the West in 1881 from Huron County, Ontario, and homesteaded for ten years near Brandon. He became a grain buyer and served as the reeve of Oakland Municipality. He sat in the Legislature as a Liberal from 1896 to 1903 and he was a Winnipeg alderman from 1908 to 1922. He moved to Winnipeg in 1902 to work as the secretary-treasurer of the Northwest Grain Dealers Association. He was also the manager of the Winnipeg Grain and Produce Clearing Association, which provided services to the Grain Exchange. He was a dedicated poker player and took part in weekly Saturday-night games at the Fort Garry Hotel. He was typical of the Ontario-born business leaders who had led the Committee of 1000 and managed to control City Council throughout the 1920s.

Fowler had been one of the authors of what Labour called the "slave pact," the Council measure that produced much irritation among Labour supporters during the decade. Passed during the General Strike on June 9, 1919, over the objections of Labour aldermen, it established that prospective employees of the City would henceforth have to swear an oath stating, "I agree that if I am hired I will not join or remain a member of any union or association that is directly or indirectly affiliated with any organization that can give orders to the union. I will not take part in a sympathetic strike and I can be fired for breaching this agreement."[34] The Liberal/Conservative aldermen believed that City workers, whose unions had participated in collective bargaining and signed contracts with the City in early 1919, had been guilty of a betrayal when they walked out in sympathy with the General Strike. The Council wanted to make sure this never happened again.

Not all non-Labour leaders were in agreement. A group representing the Canadian Problems Club went to see the mayor and Council to plead with them to abandon the pledge they were asking civic employees to sign. Council was not interested in modifying its position, Alderman Fowler responding to the group with a succinct "no chance."[35] The measure was a red flag to Labour aldermen for a decade and they repeatedly attempted to get rid of it, but efforts to change it were always voted down by the Liberal/Conservative majority on Council.

It was finally rescinded in September 1930, when a group of union members asked for a Board of Conciliation to consider the matter. Council agreed to follow the ruling of the board and the oath was replaced by a simple statement signed by the worker and a representative of the union he or she chose to belong to, promising not to participate in any sympathetic strike. The change was made with the support of both Labour and Liberal/Conservative aldermen.

In the November 1922 civic election there were once again two candidates for mayor. Farmer was running for the third time, and opposing him was John K. Sparling, a lawyer who had been born in Montreal and came to Winnipeg in the 1880s. At the time of the Yukon gold rush, he went to Dawson City where he lived for a number of years. It is not recorded whether he found any gold but he was the chair of the library board. He had been a Winnipeg alderman since 1917, and was chair of the police commission and had served on the boards of the General Hospital and Wesley College. He was a prominent supporter of the Boy Scouts. He had also been heavily involved with the Citizens' Committee of 1000. After his defeat in the election for mayor, he left politics. He died in 1941.

In the 1922 election the renewal of the Winnipeg Electric Company's franchise to operate the street railway system became the major election issue. The street railway operated under an agreement signed with the City in 1893 and embodied in Bylaw 543, passed in that year. The agreement stipulated that the City had the option to buy the streetcar company in thirty-five years, which would be in 1927, if it so chose and an agreement could be reached. If the City did not purchase the system, the franchise would continue with a

Winnipeg's Osborne Bridge, c. 1925, featuring Winnipeg Electric Company's street railway cars. The issue of the city buying the streetcar franchise was hotly contested in the 1922 election. Archives of Manitoba, N9831.

review every five years. Winnipeg Electric paid the City a share of the profits every year and a tax for each car in service. Over the years there had been various agreements arrived at to dispose of irritants between the City and the company.

A special committee of Council had been formed to handle the matter of the franchise. The position of the company, as put forward by Vice-President and General Manager Andrew McClimont in April, was that they wanted a ten-year renewal of the franchise. McLimont said this plan would allow the company to sell ten-year bonds to raise the money necessary to carry out all the repairs and upgrades they had undertaken to complete in various agreements with the city.

Winnipeg Electric did enjoy support from some Winnipeggers, including some aldermen, partly because it was one of the few local companies that was profitable and paid dividends. The company tried to expand its support by promoting Customer Ownership campaigns that offered stock to the general public and relatives of their employees. In 1927, when a lot of people were trying their luck on the stock market, a campaign sold 5,000 Winnipeg Electric shares to Winnipeggers in three hours.

During the Great War the company came close to bankruptcy because of the advent of jitney taxis on the streets. Jitneys, often owner-operated Model T Fords, were a phenomenon common to most North American cities at the time. They swarmed the busiest streetcar routes at rush hour, draining off the company's fare income. Jitneys were hugely popular with commuters, who got to ride in comfort for the same cost as a streetcar ticket and did not have to stand waiting in the cold for an overcrowded streetcar. In 1918, because of the intervention of the Board of Trade, City Council passed legislation removing the competition by making jitneys illegal.

Winnipeg Electric not only operated the streetcar service, it owned two hydroelectric dams and a coal-fired power plant in Winnipeg, and sold electricity to private and commercial customers. It also owned two coal gas plants that piped gas for cooking and lighting into customers' homes.

In July 1922 Council's special committee recommended acceptance of McLimont's ten-year plan. Labour members on Council, who wanted a publicly owned street railway, were strongly opposed to this recommendation and instead supported beginning negotiations to purchase the street railway. No agreement could be reached and the special committee recommended that the issue should be put to the voters in the November 25 municipal elections. The question of who should be allowed to vote on the franchise renewal then arose. At the Council meeting on November 20, the Citizens' Committee members used their majority to pass a bylaw stipulating that the franchise would be renewed for ten years, subject to the results of a referendum, and a motion establishing that only ratepayers would be able to vote on the bylaw followed.

On the same day Sparling published a newspaper ad laying out his position on the franchise:

- Tax and financial conditions made municipal ownership impossible, even in 1926, a year in which the postwar depression seemed to be over.
- Toronto had a publicly owned street railway and they were "spending millions experimenting with municipal ownership."
- Winnipeg could afford to wait ten years and learn from Toronto.
- There were vital problems with the Winnipeg Electric Company that needed to be addressed now and could not wait until 1926.
- The agreement had been negotiated and a referendum decided upon.
- Farmer wanted municipal ownership run by a radical Labour council.

Winnipeg Electric's Float in the city's fiftieth anniversary parade. City of Winnipeg Archives, no. H-14.

Then Sparling used the Liberal/Conservative majority to postpone a referendum on the issue until a later date, and so it was not actually on the ballot in the November 25, 1922, election.

On November 22 the Independent Labour Party (ILP) candidates for mayor and alderman held a well-attended special meeting over this issue with Fred Dixon in the chair. The speakers said that the majority on Council was depriving 50,000 Winnipeg citizens of the right to vote by putting this question to ratepayers only and at some later date, after the civic election. The issue of who should be able to vote on the franchise came up repeatedly at other campaign meetings. The ILP argued that public ownership of street railways was the best way to ensure they were operated as a service and not just for the profit of shareholders.

Farmer and the ILP ran as the champions of City-owned transit. The idea had strong public support. Farmer countered Sparling's assertion by passing out information about the successful publicly owned streetcar services in Toronto and Minneapolis.

On November 23, two days before the 1922 election, Dafoe pointed out the dangers inherent in Sparling's actions. In his *Free Press* editorial he said that it was very unfortunate that "the majority on City Council under the leadership of Alderman Sparling deliberately threw the issue into municipal politics." Dafoe, one of the most experienced politicians in the city, had argued for some months that the franchise renewal should be voted on in a referendum open to all voters so that it could be decided apart from other issues. The result of Sparling's actions, wrote Dafoe, was that the "mayoralty contest has become itself a referendum on the extension of the franchise" rather than the question of who was best qualified to run the city. Those who did not favour the extension of the franchise were given no other option than voting for Farmer to demonstrate that opposition.

Alderman Sparling attempted to repair the situation by reminding voters that he had been the chair of City Hydro's board and asserting that he was not against public ownership. He tried to reassure the voters that the issue of the franchise would be voted on all in good time. But the damage had been done. He also ran a campaign that, as usual, painted Farmer and the other Labour candidates as dangerous radicals who would spend money and be guided by "new ideas." He was a formidable and well-connected opponent who could be expected to win, but his blatant use of the majority of Liberal/Conservative aldermen, a tactic that normally worked, clearly alienated many Winnipeg voters, who did exactly as Dafoe had predicted and elected Seymour Farmer, Winnipeg's first socialist mayor. In his third run for the office, he defeated Sparling with impressive majorities of 3,910 overall, and of 2,873 and 4,377 in Wards 2 and 3, respectively.

On election night in 1922, Farmer and his supporters had waited at the ILP rooms on Sargent Avenue for the results to come in. When it was clear that he had won, they paraded to City Hall. Another larger parade arrived from the North End with "banners flying," according to the *Tribune*. Farmer then went to the *Tribune* office on the corner of Smith Street and Graham Avenue and spoke to the crowd. He thanked the *Tribune* for its balanced coverage of the election and for supporting his position on the street railway franchise. He said the election result was proof that the citizens agreed with him.

Woodsworth spoke as well and interpreted Farmer's election as proof that the city had changed in the years since the General Strike. He said voters were no longer impressed by the Citizens' Committee's attempts to scare them with stories of what would happen if socialists gained power: "The old bogeys no longer work. The ingredients are poured in the glass as before but the result is not the same. When you cry 'Wolf, wolf' too often it no longer produces the same scare."[36]

Seymour Farmer, like Fred Dixon, had been deeply affected by the war and conscription and the events of the General Strike. They were supporters of the Dominion Labour Party and then the Independent Labour Party. They had also both been influenced by the writings of Henry George, a nineteenth-century writer who was in favour of public ownership of utilities. George was suspicious of government, believed in free trade, and opposed militarism. His central idea was the single tax. He believed that if unimproved land, held by speculators, was taxed, it would provide for the municipality's needs as well as encourage the owners to develop their property. When a large amount of land was left undeveloped, held out of use, rents were forced up and the municipality was starved for tax revenue.

A number of Winnipeggers were "single taxers." Farmer and Dixon shared these views with Louis St. George Stubbs, a lawyer who would become a judge; Daniel W. Buchanan, the owner of a tree nursery; and a bookshop owner, Dr. Robert Mobius. They met in Mobius's bookshop to discuss political theories.

❖

One of the major projects of Farmer's time as mayor was the construction of the Hydro steam plant on Ellen Street. It was an innovative project for its time and represents the sort of facility the city might have seen more of if Farmer had been able to work with a Labour majority on Council. The Ellen Street steam generator, called a "standby plant," was built as the result of a tornado that struck the Portage la Prairie and Winnipeg area on June 23, 1922, six months before Farmer was elected. Three people were killed, including an eight-year-old Winnipeg boy who touched a live power line that had been brought down by the wind. In Portage la Prairie the damage was extensive, while in Winnipeg a few buildings had their roofs torn off and there was debris scattered in the streets. The roof of the Lydia Court Apartments was destroyed and the tenants of the building were forced to retreat to the basement. The roof of the King Edward Hospital in Riverview was damaged and the roof of a verandah on the hospital was torn off. A Seventh Day Adventist convention had just begun in East Kildonan. Attendees had erected fifty tents, almost all of which were destroyed. The Thistle Curling Club rink was also badly damaged.

The most important result of the storm, however, was that because transmission towers were blown down between the city and the dams on the Winnipeg River, the city was without power. Both Winnipeg Electric Company customers and those who bought power from Winnipeg Hydro, including rural Manitoba customers, were affected. City Hydro was out until 5:30 p.m. and was not completely restored until the following day because of damage to power poles lining the city streets. Dozens of poles belonging to both companies had to be replaced and tangles of wire cleared from the streets by emergency crews.

The Winnipeg Electric Company used its standby plant on Martha Street to keep the streetcars running and restore power to some users almost immediately, although they, too, were hampered by the destruction of transmission lines in the city. The company made sure to place newspaper ads informing anyone who had not noticed that their steam-powered standby plant allowed them to restore power much more quickly than their rivals at City Hydro.

Out of this natural disaster the Winnipeg Hydro standby plant on Amy Street emerged. The decision to build the plant was taken in December 1922. In February 1923 a special committee of City Council identified a strip of land close to the river near the high-pressure pumping station as the best location for the new standby plant. After discovering that the riverbank was too unstable to build on, the committee recommended Victoria Park and that another piece of land be found nearby to provide the area with a park. The new park, which still exists at the foot of Selkirk Avenue on the bank of the Red River, was purchased and named Norquay Park.

It is sometimes said that the choice of Victoria Park, an important rallying point during the General Strike, was intended as an insult to Labour, but the fact that Labour Alderman Abraham Heaps was involved in the decision and did not protest on those grounds seems to bring the idea into question. Heaps introduced the Bylaw 10689, which provided for the purchase of the northern portion of the park by City Hydro. The money from this sale was used to purchase land needed for Norquay Park.

Acquisition of equipment for the plant, which eventually cost $750,000, got underway in February 1923 when three steam-driven turbo generators were ordered from a Glasgow firm. A contract for the boilers was let in May to a Toronto firm. Construction of the steam plant building was begun immediately and installation of the new equipment was scheduled for early 1924.

The Amy Street boiler room accommodated two electric and three steam boilers that generated the steam to drive the turbines. The electric boilers could raise water temperature from cold to steam in five minutes and they were powered by electricity from the dam at Pointe du Bois—an efficient way to utilize the dam's off-peak surplus power. Three super-efficient furnaces burning pulverized coal mixed with air and blasted into the furnaces through nozzles heated the coal-fired boilers.

As a standby for the production of electricity, the plant would remain idle most of the time. The general manager of City Hydro, John G. Glassco, therefore argued that a central heating plant connected by underground pipes to the buildings of downtown customers would make efficient use of the boilers when they were not needed for generation of electricity. This type of plant was well suited to the Winnipeg climate and was already in use at the Agricultural College in Fort Garry and to heat the Legislative Building and Law Courts. In 1928 the Winnipeg Heating Company would open a central heating system in River Heights with a steam plant on the corner of Rockwood Street and Dorchester Avenue and a network of underground pipes to deliver steam to individual houses. Winnipeg Electric had a similar but much smaller heating plant in the basement of the Street Railway chambers on Notre Dame Avenue and Albert Street, but it supplied steam only to some of the buildings in the same block.

Glassco estimated the city could earn $75,000 a year to help defray the fixed costs of the plant. He also planned to connect the steam to the city's high-pressure pumping station next door and said that would halve the cost of operation for that facility. In the normal manner of Winnipeg officials, he

Amy Street Plant, October 1985. University of Manitoba Archives, Kip Park fonds.

realized his opinion alone would not win the needed approval and he commissioned a report from S.J. Neiler, a Chicago central heating expert. Neiler recommended that the City go ahead, verifying that the soil was suitable for laying underground mains. Arguments in favour of the heating system were that it would eliminate smoke from many chimneys and the widespread litter of ashes in downtown alleys, as well as reduce the number of wagons delivering coal to individual buildings.

The summer of 1924 saw downtown streets torn up to lay the pipes, encased in concrete, for the central heating system. Traffic was disrupted and the cartage companies were asked to keep their horse-drawn vehicles off Main Street to avoid congestion and accidents.

On November 12, 1924, a banquet was held in the generator room of the plant to celebrate its completion. Mayor Farmer, for whom the plant was "a very high and creditable achievement for the people of Winnipeg," rose to toast "our new public utility." He said it was "a bright spot in the somewhat gloomy view which some people took of local conditions."[37]

The standby plant and central heating service were a success. In 1925 advertisements placed by Winnipeg Hydro before the civic election stressed the savings customers had already realized through using the central heating utility. One nine-storey office building reported that they had hoped to lower costs from the $9,000 expenditure they had made operating their own heating plant to about $7,000. Their experience had been better: a reduction to $6,000, a saving of 36 percent. Other customers had experienced reductions of between 20 percent and 30 percent in their heating costs. The reduction in the amount of ashes in the city lanes and in the number of chimneys in the downtown were also cited as positive results. Even Liberal/Conservative aldermen Sullivan and Alexander Leonard pointed out, perhaps grudgingly, that combining the two functions, standby plant and central heating, was actually saving the city $75,000 a year through greater efficiency.

City Hydro was, contrary to the arguments of its opponents—those opposed to public ownership, friends of the Winnipeg Electric Company and the Taxpayers Association—a successful enterprise and overall during the 1920s produced surpluses and kept rates low.

In 1926 City Council hired Price Waterhouse for an outside audit of the utility. The auditors found that the utility was in good shape financially, although surpluses were less than they had been before 1920. The most important issue that the auditors commented on was that City Hydro was recording too little depreciation in its accounting, resulting in apparent overexpenditures or smaller surpluses. The decline in surpluses was also attributable to the costs of expanding the Pointe du Bois dam and building a second transmission line to the city, the auditors said. Rates had been been reduced from 3.5 cents per kilowatt to 2.5 cents and this had also affected the bottom line, although it was a nice benefit for the customers.

While the production of cheap electric power was intended to foster the growth of industry in the city, growth was slow in the early 1920s. Both Glassco and Winnipeg Electric therefore initiated programs to increase the number of customers using electricity. In 1920 City Hydro opened a showroom at 55 Princess Street where all the latest appliances could be viewed by Winnipeg householders. Special rates were created for cooking and water heating and Hydro set up a repair department. In 1924 Hydro instituted a range program, and 1,652 electric stoves and 1,500 electric water heaters were installed in Winnipeg homes in just three months. The program was extended to apartment blocks where 1,741 new stoves were installed. The ranges remained the property of the City and at first no rental was charged for them. In July 1926 this program was discontinued because it was losing money. The program required all the locations to be rewired so that the higher voltage needed by the stoves and water heaters could be delivered. This work was done by Winnipeg Hydro.

❖

Farmer was nominated for a second term as mayor in November 1923. In October, in preparation for the upcoming civic election, a Better Civic Government Association was founded with the sole purpose of opposing Mayor Farmer's re-election. The association began working to ensure that the voters realized that Farmer had damaged the city by making socialistic statements that made investors nervous about investing in Winnipeg.[38] Robert Jacob, a lawyer who had been born in England and came to Manitoba at the age of thirteen, opposed Farmer. He was a Liberal who sat on the Winnipeg School Board from 1913 to 1923 and he sat as one of the ten Winnipeg MLAs from 1922 until 1927. He was briefly the attorney general in Tobias Norris's last government.

The *Free Press* said that Jacob and Farmer were very close on many of their policies. Jacob expressed his support for the energetic development of City Hydro during the campaign; Farmer's victory in 1922 had taught the Liberal/Conservative candidates to make their support for publicly owned Winnipeg Hydro very clear. But he also said, at a Gyro Club lunch at the Royal Alexandra

Hotel, that he was running because there was widespread demand for a candidate who would "oppose class government in the city." He disapproved of the mayor's being openly a representative of the Independent Labor Party. He said there was a "distinct cleft" in the Council between Labour and non-Labour aldermen and that there was "strife and turmoil where dignity and cooperative effort should obtain."[39] This was perfectly true, but both factions were equally at fault and neither appeared to want the situation to change. Jacob also repeated the usual theory about the harm Labour councillors and the Labour mayor were doing to Winnipeg. At an election meeting he said that financial men had informed him that "just as long as Winnipeg is represented by a Mayor who claims to be the standard bearer of the ILP—a party with a membership which includes extreme radicals and socialists—just so long will there be no money for investment in Winnipeg."[40]

Farmer spoke at the same meeting and continued his strategy of running against the Winnipeg Electric Company. He made its relations with the City his central topic. He listed the outstanding problems the City was having with the company: during his first term some tax arrears had been collected but the company still owed the City $610,000 in taxes and $414,000 for paving done along the streetcar lines. With regard to an issue that had dragged on for over a decade, money was also owed the City for burst water mains damaged by a phenomenon called "electrolysis." Because the streetcar tracks were not properly bonded with copper to create a complete circuit from the company's generating station to the cars and back, electric current jumped from the tracks into the ground. In some places the city's cast-iron water pipes, excellent conductors of electricity, sustained damage from the current travelling along them. The company had been ordered to pay the City for this damage but so far it had not done so.

Farmer warned that now that the company had completed the Great Falls hydro dam, it was aggressively marketing power, and Council would have to withstand this campaign in order to protect Winnipeg Hydro's market. He suggested that Robert Jacob was not really a supporter of City Hydro and was sympathetic to the Street Railway Company. He again handed out a pamphlet that showed that publicly owned streetcar systems in other cities, such as Toronto and Detroit, were very successful. He also denied that Winnipeg was in a depression because it had a Labour mayor. The economic situation was due to a multitude of factors that were, he said, beyond the scope of municipal government to solve.

John Dafoe noted in an editorial before the election that "in the opinion of many impartial observers, Mayor Farmer has, during the past year, acted as the representative of all the citizens and has not been influenced by the spirit of faction . . . in his capacity as mayor it can hardly be said that he has not acted fairly and impartially." Nevertheless, Dafoe argued, he might not automatically be given a second year in office because Farmer had been formally nominated by the Independent Labour Party and had stated he had been true to the party's policies. For this reason the election would be fought as a contest between two definite groups and re-election for Farmer could not be automatic.[41]

On the night of the election, the *Tribune* claimed to offer the best election coverage. The paper had hung a screen on the wall of Holy Trinity Parish Hall across the street from the newspaper's building at Smith Street and Graham Avenue and used a large magic lantern projector to show the crowd the re-sults as they came in. When there was nothing to report, the screen projected movies and cartoons, and the Princess Patricia's regimental band played to entertain the crowd.

When it was clear that he had won, Farmer was carried through the streets on the shoulders of his supporters. At the *Tribune* office he stood on the small balcony over the front doors and delivered his victory speech to the crowd. Later, in front of the *Free Press* building on Carlton Street, Farmer said his election was a vindication of the actions of the ILP members of Council and showed that it took "more than a well oiled machine and a big campaign chest to check the advance of democracy."[42] Farmer enjoyed strong support throughout the city and won the largest majority to date in a mayoral election: 20,189 votes to Jacob's 15,546. He increased his vote over 1922 in all three wards, winning Wards 2 and 3 and improving his total in Ward 1. He clearly had the support of many non-Labour voters.

The *Winnipeg Tribune*, in an editorial the day after Farmer's victory, said it was clear that Winnipeggers would not be duped into voting on false issues of class antagonism: "Mayor Farmer had been a prudent, painstaking and efficient chief magistrate; why punish him? Why ride him down in remorseless indif-ference to the public service he had rendered?"[43] Dafoe also praised Farmer after his victory but then qualified his statement by adding that "the vote that he received . . . is not to be taken as any indication of public approval of the program of the Independent Labour Party. It was due rather to particular issues that were raised during the campaign." He suggested that Farmer's victory was due to his strategy of criticizing the Street Railway Company. He wrote, "It is quite evident from the result that even the suspicion that a candidate is not a whole hearted supporter of the City's hydro electric enterprise places him under a serious handicap and the suggestion ... that a candidate may be too friendly to the Winnipeg Electric Railway Company is also one that may be used with damaging effect."[44]

Nevertheless, the election again resulted in a City Council with a Liberal/Conservative majority.

Main Street in 1925, showing CN Railway Station (Union Station), Archives of Manitoba, McAdam fonds, 435.

CHAPTER 6

Towards a New Consensus

On November 14, 1924, the city clerk received nominations for the civic elections and the second half of the 1920s at City Hall began. In many ways it would mark a new approach, but the basic situation remained the same. There were only two candidates for mayor: the incumbent Seymour Farmer and Colonel Ralph Webb, the manager of the Marlborough Hotel and the candidate of the Liberal/Conservative group on Council. Webb was not well known in Winnipeg, having lived in the city only since the previous year.

During the first week of the campaign Winnipeg got to know Webb's point of view. He pledged support for Winnipeg Hydro and the public ownership of the utility. In fact, he stated that City Hydro would be one of the tools he would use to revive the local economy. What was needed, he said, was to attract industry to the city by letting people know about Winnipeg's low power rates. He tried to make contact with a broad spectrum of Winnipeggers, speaking to working-class men in Weston, to a Ukrainian audience on Selkirk Avenue, and to businessmen at a meeting in the McIntyre Block. His message was that Winnipeg was in a slump and everyone had to work together to get the city moving again. At one of his meetings, the *Free Press* reported, "The candidate on rising said it was time to stop grousing and get together under a good common sense leader to pull things out of the rut.... You want a man big enough to look after the best interests of the City. It's time for a change."[1]

Webb tried to make the question of who was best equipped to pull Winnipeg out of the four-year recession the central issue of the campaign.

Webb claimed he did not believe in "isms," only in the rule of the majority. He exhorted people to get out and vote. He was generally received enthusiastically by audiences. Having been in the city only for a year, he was able to dissociate himself, to some extent, from the General Strike. He attempted to rise above the lingering bad feelings with a new positive message about eliminating the divisions that were hindering the city's growth. He said, "There should be no division between those in the north end and those in the south end of Winnipeg . . . we should be one united body working toward the one goal."[2]

Farmer defended his record on fighting for public ownership of utilities and encouraging the construction of the central steam heating facility. He claimed that Webb was opposed to public ownership and labour unions, charges that Webb denied. Farmer argued that there was little that city government could do to alter the economic situation. At a meeting on November 19 at Isaac Brock School, he addressed the often-repeated charge that a Labour mayor had discouraged investment by saying he had always encouraged and supported any business ventures wanting to start up in the city. He admitted that Colonel Webb had worked hard to bring conventions to the city, but that he would be able to do no more as mayor except "turn the city hall into an annex for advertising the hotel business." Taking an approach that was probably opposed to the instincts of many Winnipeggers, he criticized Webb for being a "booster." He argued that boosterism could be overdone and the city was still suffering from the results of pre-war boosterism. Referring to the failed real estate schemes of the boom years, he said, "Look at the miles of sidewalks you have running by vacant lots. You have to build gradually."[3]

In a newspaper piece he asked if the city's future would once again be placed in the hands of a booster and if civic planning was to be based on "hot air." He reminded his readers that "Winnipeg was to be the Chicago of the North; land values were boosted, land speculators were boosted into retirement in California and municipal debt was boosted by many millions."[4] Farmer's arguments for slow, steady growth were probably realistic for a city like Winnipeg, where a reasonable approach might be to slowly and carefully lay the foundations for future development. But this did not sound very compelling to Winnipeggers looking for a revival of the good old days when people came to the city to get rich.

Webb disagreed with Farmer, stating that the mayor did indeed have a role to play in economic development and should take the lead in any area that would help develop the city. He said that if the city had a few boosters in City Hall, it would make a big difference to the length of the bread lines, and insisted that what the city needed was "sound business boosting." He seemed to offer a way out of the recession and he seemed to be an energetic man who could bring change. As an example of his methods, Webb claimed credit for the decision by the Province to gravel the Lord Selkirk Highway from St. Norbert to Emerson, an improvement that would bring more American tourists to the city. He said Mayor Farmer had agreed to contribute some civic funding for the project only after Webb had asked him to. (Farmer denied that Webb had influenced this decision.) Webb claimed that the road project would provide jobs and promised to promote the completion of the Hudson's Bay Railway as another means to create jobs.[5]

Ralph H. Webb, c. 1941. Mayor of Winnipeg from 1925 to 1927 and 1930 to 1934, and MLA from 1932 to 1941. Archives of Manitoba.

City Hydro and relations with the Winnipeg Electric Company were, as usual, important issues. Farmer returned to the perennial question of the franchise and warned voters that the following year, 1925, was when some final decision would have to be made about whether the City should renew the company's franchise or purchase the street railway. Both men said that on the issue of the franchise, they would put the question to all the electors and abide by what the people wanted. The ILP speakers asked where the money was coming from to pay for Webb's newspaper advertising, and accused him of being a friend of Winnipeg Electric.

At a later meeting Farmer warned that Webb would take the city back to the days of special privileges and concessions to private interests. Webb consistently claimed that he was not connected to any particular group or interest in the city. He said he was asked to run only after several others had refused, a claim he habitually would make at election time and one that may well have been true. In addition to appeals for unity in the city, he brought out the old Liberal/Conservative claims that Farmer sought only to represent Labour voters.

During the election campaign a delegation of 600 unemployed men marched to the Marlborough Hotel to ask Webb what he would do for them. He told the men he could not do much until he was elected but they were welcome at his committee rooms where they could sit and keep warm. He wondered why Mayor Farmer had not employed some of them to work at the polls for the election. In general, during his years as mayor, Webb would say he was more interested in job creation than in keeping people on the dole.

In this, his first election campaign, Webb was able to marshal support from many army officers, including Lieutenant General Richard Turner, one of the Canadian Corps' most senior commanders, testifying to his organizational skills and effectiveness as a commanding officer during the war. These testimonials were published in the papers as letters to the editor. Webb's campaign manager, General R.L. Patterson, no doubt solicited them.

On election day, November 28, Webb won with a 4,700-vote majority, a new record. The total turnout was greater by 5,000 votes than the previous year. Webb won majorities in Wards 1 and 2 and reduced Farmer's majority in Ward 3. Webb made his victory speech in front of the *Tribune* building and then broadcast a message on CKY Radio. He paid tribute to the fairness of Mayor Farmer's campaign, and said that he now stood with a closed door behind him and before him was another open door: "Behind this closed door let us shut and imprison for life the antagonisms, enmities and quarrels of the past. Let us all as citizens of Winnipeg close up our ranks, bridge all our cleavages and see if we cannot by cooperation and mutual effort make of this city what is best for all of us."

Farmer commented, "It is quite evident that the people of Winnipeg are weary of the long drawn-out period of depression and have decided to make a change and voted for Mayor Webb accordingly."[6]

❖

Who was this newly elected Ralph Webb? He was born at sea, on a ship carrying his parents from India home to England, in 1887. He came to Canada in 1902 and, after working on a whaling boat, as part of a railroad surveying crew, and as a foreman in a cement plant, he spent a few years in the lumber business, finally taking control of the Gold Medal Furniture Company in Toronto. He volunteered for the army in 1914 and went overseas.

Webb had a distinguished war record. He fought as a lieutenant at the Second Battle of Ypres, Canada's first major battle of the war. He won the Military Cross for his bravery while leading convoys carrying wounded men from the battlefield. He was quickly promoted and by 1916 he was the commanding officer of the 47th (British Columbia) Battalion. He received the Distinguished Service Order and the Croix de Guerre, and was mentioned in dispatches six times. Historian John H. Thompson described how, at Oppy Wood in March 1918, Webb's fighting career ended: "Struck by a shell fragment high on the hip, his left leg was almost torn from his body. Covered with his own blood, Webb sawed off the shreds of his now useless member with his trench knife and tied off the pumping fermoral artery with a shoelace. 'Boys,' he told a startled group of his soldiers as he proffered them the severed leg, 'I won't be needing this again.'"[7] Webb had a wooden leg that made a creaking sound when he walked and it was said that every time he took a step, he collected another vote.

After his injury Webb was given a job managing a rest club for Canadian officers recovering from wounds. This experience enabled him to go to work in the hotel business when he returned to Canada, managing the Windsor Hotel, the CPR's flagship Montreal hotel. In 1923 he came to Winnipeg to manage the newly expanded Marlborough Hotel. He moved from the hotel

The Marlborough Hotel, c. 1925, which was managed by Ralph Webb before he became Winnipeg's mayor in 1925. Archives of Manitoba.

business to promoting tourism. When the Second World War broke out, he again volunteered and became the head of catering for the Canadian Army, introducing an efficient system of messing and providing, he claimed, better quality food than he had eaten during the Great War.

Ralph Webb saw the role of the mayor as that of a salesman, and he worked hard to sell Winnipeg to investors and tourists. One of his first acts as mayor was to put up a large electric sign on City Hall, which blazed forth "Welcome to Winnipeg." For many people he lifted the sense of gloom that had hung about since the strike and attempted to set out on a new course. He was successful as a politician, winning election as mayor seven times in the decade from 1924 to 1934 and sitting as a provincial Conservative MLA from 1932 to 1941.

As 1925 began Webb's victory helped to create a sense in the city that the long postwar recession was over and things were improving. There were several large New Year's dances. At the Board of Trade building over 3,000 people celebrated. There was a Scottish theme with pipers, and the proceeds from the event were going toward building a Scottish hall in the city. At the Fort Garry, 700 people danced in the rotunda, the Palm Court, and the various ballrooms to the music of two dance orchestras. The Royal Alexandra hosted 600 people and the Marlborough had 500. Railroad employees celebrated in the rotundas of the two big train stations. Souvenirs or party favours were given out at all these events. There was also a large dance at the Alhambra Dance Hall on Fort Street to the music of Eddie Elliot's Blue Medley Orchestra; it was a costume dance and there were prizes for the best costumes.[8] The *Free Press* began to blow its whistle at 11:55 p.m., and at midnight whistles and bells all over the city began to ring in the New Year. The Carillon at St. Luke's Church and many other church bells rang out. It was a livelier New Year's Eve than the city had seen for a while.

The editor of *Canadian Finance* wrote an optimistic editorial in the January 7, 1925, issue. He quoted from a report issued by the National City Bank that said that Canada was sixteenth in the world in terms of its total assets and second in the world in total growth in wealth in the period from 1877 to 1922. The population was increasing.

That spring, the Industrial Development Board was established to foster industrial growth in the province and city. It was not a new idea. The Board of Trade had had committees in the past whose role was to encourage local industry, and their building at Main Street and Water Avenue was the setting for displays of local products. The new Industrial Development Board was a

John Bracken, 1925. He was premier of Manitoba from 1922 to 1943. Archives of Manitoba, L.B. Foote fonds, P7392/5.

new attempt to encourage industry. It was supported by the Province, City Council, and the Board of Trade. The chair was Premier Bracken, and the vice-chair was William H. Carter, representing the Board of Trade. City Council was represented by Mayor Webb and three aldermen. The Trades and Labour Council had members, as did the CPR, CNR, the Bankers Association, the Bond Dealers Association, Winnipeg Electric, and Winnipeg Hydro.

The Development Board's first task was to make an industrial survey of "resources, the markets, existing industries, transportation and power, raw material and labour, and related data on all phases of information which might help investors and promoters."[9] This was updated each year. One large development during the year was the incorporation of a sugar beet processing plant. The Development Board had purchased processing equipment and located it at the Agricultural College so it could be tested and the students could become familiar with it. Also, a new packing plant was built in St. Boniface by Harris Abbatoir Company. The year 1925 was also when the Memorial Boulevard project finally began, and there was intense activity acquiring land and beginning the construction of the new streets and the Hudson's Bay Store.

The Development Board lobbied different levels of government and encouraged development. Their yearly reports showed a growing industrial sector in the years between 1925 and 1929. In 1927 the largest types of business in terms of number of plants were eighty-three shops involved in various aspects of the printing industry, fifty-one businesses making bakery products, and forty-one clothing and hat manufacturers. The largest employers were the printing industry, which employed 2,451 people, and clothing manufacturers, which had 1,714 employees.

There had been growth in manufacturing during the Great War, although Winnipeg's share of war-related contracts was much smaller than Montreal's or Toronto's because the city's great distance from the seaboard added heavy shipping costs to Winnipeg products. In February 1921 *Canadian Finance* reported on the growth in manufacturing in the city during the war. In 1910 there had been 177 establishments with $26 million in capital invested, and the total value of goods produced amounted to $32 million. By 1918, 745 establishments with a total investment of $84 million turned out products worth $118 million.[10]

As the 1920s wore on there was an ever-increasing emphasis on building the city's manufacturing capacity. The Industrial Development Board reported that between 1924 and 1928, manufacturing output grew from $102.2 million to $159.2 million. Between 1925 and 1927 the number of establishments grew from 785 to 789, total salaries increased from $6.2 million to $7.1 million, and wages paid rose from $20 million to $21.8 million. The number of people employed grew from 20,000 to 23,000. The net value of the products they produced grew from $52.4 million to $62.5 million.[11]

Ralph Webb was confident that Winnipeg could develop its tourism industry by encouraging Americans to visit. During his first term, in May 1925, Mayor Webb was part of a trip sponsored by the *Winnipeg Tribune* to show that it was possible to drive from Minneapolis to Winnipeg in twelve hours. A convoy of eight cars left Winnipeg City Hall at 4:00 a.m. on Friday, May 15, intending to arrive at Minneapolis City Hall at 4:00 in the afternoon. Mayor Webb was in the lead car, a large Studebaker touring car driven by Roy Parkhill, who was representing the Young Men's Section of the Board of Trade. The mayor had made it clear to everyone that the trip was not a race. An effort had been made to clear the road of traffic so they would have a better chance of making the trip in the time allotted.

The cars of 1925, even the big Studebaker, were not as well built as those of today and there were plenty of mishaps on the road. The Studebaker, in spite of needing the repair of a flat tire and a broken fuel line, arrived in front of the Minneapolis City Hall at 4:30 p.m. Two more cars arrived soon after, and the rest of the convoy, having suffered various mishaps, such as catching fire and rolling into a ditch, came later. The streets outside City Hall were lined with cars and everyone blew their horns to welcome the Canadians. A celebratory banquet was given in the Nicolett Hotel. Webb explained that he wanted to make the northern part of the Jefferson Highway the busiest part.

The Jefferson Highway was more a route than a highway, consisting as it did of a series of local roads cobbled together. It began in Winnipeg and ended in New Orleans. Webb promoted the route and developed good relations with the Jefferson Highway Association as part of his strategy to encourage American tourists. It is still possible to follow the route most of the way from north to sourth, and there is still a Jefferson Highway Association, which marks the way with the same distinctive signs with a blue letter J that marked the route in the 1920s.[12] (There were and are other named highways but they have now been largely superseded by the much faster interstate numbered route system.) All along the way cities used the Jefferson Highway as a means to attract tourism and "boost" their communities, and Mayor Webb was convinced that promoting the highway could contribute to the revival of Winnipeg's economy. He seemed to be right—it was later calculated that during 1925 alone, American tourists had spent $3 million in Winnipeg.

Of the U.S. tourists who came to Winnipeg in 1925, two-thirds came by car and one-third by train. Among other reasons, the Americans came to Canada to buy British goods, which were not available or much more expensive at home. There was also a visit of 7,000 American Legion members attending a convention during the summer.[13] A national conference of Canadian veterans' groups met in Winnipeg in November to negotiate the formation of a single Royal Canadian Legion that would unite all veterans, ending their division into a number of different associations. Mayor Ralph Webb was the chair of the Winnipeg Unity Committee. Webb also organized a Tourism and Convention Bureau to capture as much of the lucrative convention business as possible.

On November 12, 1925, the Independent Labour Party nominated Fred Tipping to run against Mayor Webb in the election for the 1926 mayor and Council. Tipping had immigrated from England, arriving in Winnipeg in 1905. He worked as a Baptist clergyman when he first arrived and later became the supervisor of manual education at Lord Roberts School. He had been active in the Labour movement, helping to found the Social Democratic Party of Canada in 1911 and the Democratic Labour Party in 1918. He was

more moderate in his views than Labour leaders like Robert B. Russell and
other founders of the One Big Union. In 1917 he was elected president of the
Trades and Labour Council. In the fall of 1918 he was appointed to a Royal
Commission set up to reach a settlement in a dispute between the Metal Trades
Council and their employers. The commission's report was considered to be
more favourable to the employers than the workers, who became discouraged
and began to return to work. Tipping signed this report, and some, including
Russell, accused him of being a traitor. Tipping then resigned from the pres-
idency of the Trades and Labour Council.

It appears that Tipping's reputation was restored by 1925 because among
those nominating him for mayor were John Queen, Seymour Farmer, Marcus
Hyman, and William Ivens, all prominent Labour politicians. Among those
who signed Webb's nomination papers were Edith Rogers, Liberal MLA;
Robert W. Paterson, owner of Winnipeg Paint and Glass and a Conservative;
Alex Macdonald, owner of a large grocery wholesale; Horace Chevrier, a
pioneer merchant in Winnipeg and owner of the Blue Store on Main Street;
Elisha F. Hutchings, the owner of Great West Saddlery; and Robert J. Gourley,
who had worked for the Union Bank and was a successful businessman. J.L.
McBride, the business manager of the International Brotherhood of Electrical
Workers, also signed, and he was forced to resign from his post as secretary of
the Winnipeg Trades and Labour Council because of his support for Webb.
A representative of the more conservative craft unions, he had opposed the
Independent Labour Party in the early 1920s. He declared himself to be a
Conservative and ran unsuccessfully for City Council in 1926.

Minnie Campbell, the widow of former Attorney General Colin Campbell
and an active Conservative Party supporter, spoke at the nomination meeting:
"When there is no vision the people perish. That's the reason we were dead and
almost buried for two or three years." Now, she said, Webb had restored people's
confidence. The *Free Press* said that Webb had to win so that the recovery he
had started could continue.[14]

During the campaign, the question of whether the City should purchase
the Street Railway at the end of the company's franchise agreement in 1927
arose once again. Andrew McLimont, general manager of Winnipeg Electric,
had said that the company was worth $13 million. John Blumberg, another ILP
candidate, said that the Street Railway should be properly evaluated before
any negotiations began. The attitude of the Liberal/Conservative majority on
Council was that there would be no negotiations because Council had already
voted to accept the Winnipeg Electric Company's proposal that the franchise

be extended for ten years. They had only to wait for the deadline to expire and the extension would become reality. There was also the issue of the zoning of hydroelectric sales by the City Hydro utility and Winnipeg Electric. A proposal had been made that City Hydro should serve the city and Winnipeg Electric would provide electricity to the rest of the province. Labour was suspicious of the proposal; Webb said nothing would be agreed to until Council was sure it would benefit Winnipeg.

Webb emphasized his accomplishments: the all-weather gravel road to Emerson, constructed due to his "sticktoitivness"; the Winnipeg Convention and Tourist Bureau, which he created and managed and which had brought $3 million to the city in 1925; and moving the long-standing issue of the Memorial Boulevard along so that the project was now underway, with the long-awaited beginning of construction on the Hudson's Bay store. He also claimed that he had attracted industry to the city. "Let Webb finish his work. He deserves a second term," said his ads.

Labour candidates chose to accuse Webb of not being sufficiently digni-fied. He responded that the city could not "afford dignity right now. What Winnipeg wants is the backbone to produce something." At another meeting he said, "I have not been looking for robes and gold chains. Winnipeg needs salesmanship of its opportunities to the world."[15]

Webb and his supporters argued that Winnipeg had to become a man-ufacturing centre to offset the losses of wholesale and distribution business due to the construction of the Panama Canal and the growth of other western cities such as Vancouver, Calgary, and Saskatoon. Winnipeg's cheap hydro rates were, as always, touted as the way industry would be enticed to locate in the city. Webb suggested this was how the unemployment problem would be solved. He pointed to the founding of the Industrial Development Board during 1925 as an important step in building up the city's manufacturing sector.

The *Tribune* had supported Farmer during his time as mayor but they were lukewarm about Ralph Webb. In an editorial on November 24, 1925, the ed-itor wrote that it was customary to give a mayor a second term unless he had mishandled things. But, he said, "Mayor Webb is not an ideal Mayor by any means; he has shown no particular aptitude for handling the city council or attending to the routine business of the city, and he has said and done things that had even his friends on edge wondering what was going to happen next."[16] He had done nothing to create better feeling between Labour and non-La-bour elements, "which after all is one of the main problems facing Winnipeg." Webb occasionally said ill-considered things in public that outraged Labour

members. During the 1926 civic election campaign, for example, he said he
would like to dump certain Labour aldermen in the river. Labour politicians
charged him with uttering threats and only dropped the charges after Webb
apologized. But, said the *Tribune* editorial, he had worked hard and played a
part in getting two or three issues launched that had been hanging fire. This
conditional endorsement from what was a conservative paper is revealing.
Clearly, Webb had not had unquestioned success in his first term. The voters,
however, proved ready to give him their solid support.

On November 27 Webb was elected with another record majority—over
10,000 more votes than Fred Tipping. Webb won Wards 1 and 2 with large
majorities and he came within 100 votes of winning a majority in Ward 3, the
North End heartland of Labour support.

Webb continued his tourism policy, beginning the year 1926 by travelling
to New Orleans with the famous Pines to Palm Tour. The idea for this excur-
sion originated with Wesley McCurdy, the business manager of the *Winnipeg
Tribune*. McCurdy had worked for both the *Free Press* and the *Tribune*, ran
his own advertising agency for a time, and eventually became the publisher
of the *Tribune* and in 1942 a vice-president of the Southam newspaper chain.
Designed to publicize Winnipeg as a tourist destination, the Pine to Palm Tour
caravan of twenty-eight cars carrying seventy-nine people left Winnipeg in
the morning on January 23, a day when the local temperature was a relatively
pleasant −10°C. Led by an "administration car" carrying McCurdy and other
Winnipeg *Tribune* representatives, the caravan included Mayor Webb and
provincial and federal government representatives, as well as cars sent along by
other Manitoba communities such as Brandon, Portage la Prairie, Gretna, and
Neepawa. There were cars for the Young Men's Section of the Board of Trade,
the Rotary Club, the Manitoba Motor League, and, of course, representatives
of the Winnipeg press. A local garage sent a travelling repair van to take care
of breakdowns on the road. The travellers carried many small bags of No. 1
Northern Red Spring wheat, Manitoba's most important export, to give away
to Americans, and the cars were decorated with banners to let people know
they were from Manitoba.

They arrived in New Orleans on February 4 and were given a warm welcome. They left for home just three days later, missing Mardi Gras by ten days.
No doubt the *Tribune* was not interested in paying for the delegates to enjoy
themselves too much. While in the Big Easy, Ralph Webb was offered the job
of Tourism Chief by the mayor.

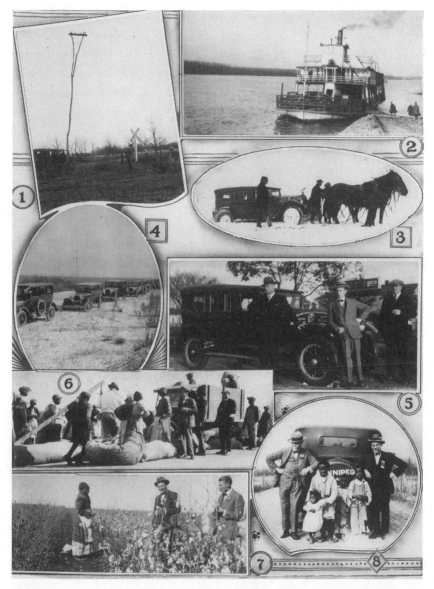

A collection of photographs from the Pine to Palm Tour. Archives of Manitoba, Events, 174.

The cars returned north by a different route along the Mississippi Scenic Highway, following the river for 3,058 kilometres. They returned to Winnipeg on Ash Wednesday, February 17, and were welcomed home with a banquet at the Royal Alexandra Hotel, preceded by a massive parade through the streets. The organizing committee encouraged merchants to decorate their windows and fly every flag available. They called on the general public to welcome the group: "The Winnipeg Pine to Palm tourists have made history and crowned Winnipeg and Manitoba with fame and glory. So let Winnipeg rise to the occasion and extend to our heroes of the trail a welcome home of a warmth, magnitude and enthusiasm never before experienced in Winnipeg."[17]

The *Tribune* commented enthusiastically on the significance of the trip, saying the tour had "placed Winnipeg and Manitoba definitively and finally on the tourist map. . . . Winnipeg is now known in the far south not in an indefinite hazy sort of way, but a real city with a fixed location—strong, virile and enterprising. . . . a city of real quality furnished the adventurous spirits who made up the party."[18] It may have been one of the few occasions when a large number of Americans could tell you where Winnipeg was.

❖

Nominations for the 1926 civic election were received on November 13. Mayor Webb, running for a third term, once again faced Fred Tipping in the contest.

During the year Council had dealt with a number of issues related to the City's dealings with the Winnipeg Electric Company. The question of whether the City should purchase the Street Railway at the end of its franchise period in 1927 was no longer an issue at the time of the 1926 election. On February 11, 1927, the renewed franchise period for Winnipeg Electric's control of the streetcar service began. The first franchise had lasted thirty-five years; the renewal was for five years. In future the City would have the option to purchase after each five-year period.

During the election campaign Tipping and other Labour candidates criticized Council decisions that seemed to favour the Winnipeg Electric Company. In one area there had actually been cooperation between City Hydro and the company: in the fall of 1926 there was a Better Lighting campaign designed to encourage commercial customers to provide more lighting outside their premises. The campaign was run jointly by Winnipeg Hydro and Winnipeg Electric, and it was the first time the rivals had cooperated on a project.

Other outstanding issues were resolved. In the case of the $43,083 the company owed the City to repair damage to water pipes due to electrolysis, Council voted to accept the company's offer of $38,000. The balance of the costs would be absorbed by the waterworks budget. This was done over the objections of the Labour members and John S. McDiarmid, a Liberal. (McDiarmid served on Council only in 1925 and part of 1926 until he was elected as a Liberal MP. He voted with Labour on more than one occasion during his short time on Council. Between 1953 and 1960, at the end of his career, he became a lieutenant-governor.)

In July, Council debated whether or not to purchase power from Winnipeg Electric. The purchase was becoming essential since consumption in the city was growing and would soon outstrip the generating capacity of the dam at Pointe du Bois. The alternative would be to build a second City Hydro dam at Slave Falls, downstream from Pointe du Bois, a site on which the City had an option. The Labour members and McDiarmid voted to delay the agreement to purchase power until a study had been done on the feasibility of developing Slave Falls.

In the end both the power purchase and the development of Slave Falls as a hydro dam site occurred. The agreement to purchase power had been approved by Council in the summer of 1926. During the 1926 civic election Webb defended the agreement, saying Winnipeg needed the extra power now, and Slave Falls, which he confirmed would be built, would take several years to complete. He reminded voters that John Glassco, the manager of Winnipeg Hydro, had recommended the purchase agreement. Webb said it was a good business proposition, since the City would buy power and resell it at a profit. Tipping criticized the deal and his campaign advertised the relative costs and benefits of purchasing as opposed to producing power.

Tipping and the ILP also wanted the Housing Commission to once again become active in providing mortgages. Alderman Simpson pointed out that overcrowding continued. Many of the large homes in the Hudson's Bay Reserve area between Broadway and Assiniboine avenues had been turned into tenements. One house had seventeen families living in it and fifteen gas ranges operating under its roof. Tipping charged that the Housing Commission had ceased making new loans because the city was cutting into the mortgage business of loan companies. The Housing Commission remained in existence but it concentrated solely on managing the outstanding loans, claiming the housing crisis had been solved and new loans were not required.

Tipping also published a list of all the Council and committee meetings Webb had missed; Webb's defence was that in each case he was absent on city business and that he was more effective meeting with people who could potentially benefit the city than chairing council meetings where he did not even have a vote unless there was a tie. (Every Winnipeg mayor before Webb and for a good many years after shared the frustration that came from the relative powerlessness of the office to affect what Council did. The current Executive Policy Committee system is intended to give the mayor more control over Council priorities and decisions.)

None of these three areas of attack—Slave Falls, housing, or absence from Council meetings—seemed to do much damage to Mayor Webb's campaign. However, in the 1926 campaign some new voices were heard. One of Webb's supporters, Rankin Leslie, ran for Council that year. In a speech on November 25 he suggested hiring a city manager as a way to make the city administration more efficient. Like many people, Leslie felt that expecting the aldermen to manage complex developments like the construction of Memorial Boulevard caused delays and prevented careful planning. Leslie said that having Mayor Webb run the Tourism Bureau made his workload too heavy and the city needed a dedicated manager in that position. He also supported the idea that was popular among the business community that City Hydro should be administered by a commission and not City Council. Neither the city manager nor the Hydro Commission became a reality at the time, although a tourism manager was hired.

Leslie had worked in the insurance business, living in China for three years. In 1916 he had become the Manitoba manager for London Life. He was active in the On to the Bay Association, which promoted the completion of the Hudson's Bay Railroad. He was one of the directors of the new Northern Paint Company, which Robert Paterson started in 1926. Paterson was a friend and political ally of Webb's. Leslie also became a director of the Finch Shoe Company, of which Webb and Paterson were also directors. Leslie's political positions were slightly different from the usual Liberal/Conservative candidates and represented a slight blurring of the lines between the two factions on Council. He said in a speech on November 23 that he did not care if the Council had a Labour majority. He wanted decisions to be made on their merit, not on the basis of old animosities: "I represent some of the younger generation who are absolutely fed up with the bear garden performance at City Hall. We want to see some new blood in the city Council that will make for harmony and decency."[19] Leslie lost his election, coming fifth in Ward 1 with a vote of 1,581 out of 12,698 ballots cast. He was, along with Liberals John McDiarmid and later Ralph Maybank, representative of a new more moderate non-Labour view in city politics but his vote suggests he did not have many sympathizers.

John Bracken and Ralph Webb with King Prajadhipok and Queen Rambai Barni,
31 August 1931. Archives of Manitoba, L.B. Foote fonds, P7392/5.

On election day, November 26, 1926, Ralph Webb was once again victori-
ous, though with a reduced majority. His vote dropped from 23,627 in 1925 to
19,925 in 1926. Tipping's vote was virtually the same, 12,703 compared with
12,686 the year before. The decline in Webb's vote may have been due almost
entirely to lower voter turnout, suggesting that he had failed to motivate some
of his supporters to once again support him. Ralph Webb served his third term
as mayor in 1927 but did not run again in the 1927 civic election.

At his going-away banquet in the Fort Garry Hotel at the end of his first
three years, Mayor Webb looked back on how, as a newcomer in 1923, he had
not been impressed by the atmosphere of the city, remarking that "its people
seemed to have forgotten that they were not living in the 1890s. Millions of
dollars were being sent away from the city because businessmen were not
taking the trouble to develop trade." He commented that much still needed
to be done and Winnipeg was still in need of all-weather roads.[20] In making a
toast to the city, Bracken said he agreed with Webb but noted that all-weather roads were built at a great price and the citizens might not like having to
raise a million dollars a year to pay the principal and interest on the debt. The

remark brings into focus the difference between the two politicians. Webb was a promoter who saw the need to invest in things that would bring a return; and Bracken was focused on keeping the debt low, paying the bills, and making a few carefully negotiated deals to benefit the province. His careful pay-as-you-go approach appealed to Manitobans and kept him in power for two decades but it meant that Manitoba still had pretty bad roads in the 1950s.

General Robert Paterson, who had originally nominated Webb in 1924, recalled at the tribute dinner that troops returning to Winnipeg after the war had found it a "pretty dreary place," but had put their shoulders to the wheel for the city's re-establishment and a "new move" had begun. Webb became associated with this idea that the city could be resurrected from its depressed condition and once again set on the road to greatness.[21]

With Webb no longer running for mayor, for the next civic election, November 1927, Colonel Daniel McLean was the candidate of the Liberal/Conservative group and John Queen ran for the Independent Labour Party.

McLean was one of the Ontario-born businessmen who made up a large percentage of the city councils in the 1920s. He was not a wealthy man and he did not socialize with the city's elite or belong to their clubs. He was a Conservative, a Mason, and a member of St. Giles United Church. He was born in Halton County and worked in the milling industry in Ontario and then in Morden after coming to Manitoba in 1892. He moved to Winnipeg and was the manager of the Winnipeg Machinery and Supply Company before setting up his own real estate and insurance brokerage. He and his family lived in the North End on Redwood Avenue, and he was an alderman representing the area, with some breaks, from 1906 to 1942, when he retired. He also served on the Board of Control in 1913–14 and was an MLA in 1914–15. During the First World War he took the first troops from Winnipeg to Valcartier in 1914. He later recruited and took the 101st Battalion to France, where he led them from 1916 to 1918. After coming home he served on the staff of Military District 10 in Winnipeg until March 1919. He was elected mayor in 1928 and 1929.

McLean's opponent in November 1927, John Queen, was a successful Labour politician. He was born in Scotland and came to Winnipeg in 1906. He served as an alderman from 1916 to 1919, and as mayor of Winnipeg seven times between 1935 and 1942. He was also an MLA from 1920 to 1936 and leader of the Independent Labour Party from 1930 to 1935. He was involved in leading the Winnipeg General Strike and was one of the people charged with sedition. He was sentenced to a year in jail and was in prison when he first won a seat in the Legislature.

As the 1927 civic election campaign began, there was exciting news from the North. New York financier Harry Whitney had announced he would invest in developing the large copper and nickel deposit at Flin Flon. The Whitney interests intended to build a 3,000-ton smelter at Flin Flon at a cost of about $10 million. They had been testing a new smelting technique that would allow the ore to be processed in Flin Flon rather than being shipped to a smelter in British Columbia. The new smelter would be powered by electricity rather than coal, and a hydro power plant was being built at Island Falls on the Churchill River northwest of Flin Flon in Saskatchewan. The Flin Flon mine and town, which did not yet exist, would soon be connected to The Pas by rail.

In December 1927 The Pas was packed with people and there was not "a house, shack or store to rent."[22] The excitement was because Hudson Bay Mining and Smelting, the Whitney firm, had announced that altogether it would invest $55 million in Flin Flon. People looking for jobs and prospectors wanting to stake claims were flooding in. The other area mines—Sherrit Gordon, Mandy, Gordon Murray, and the Bingo mine—were all getting a second look. Winnipeg expected to benefit from the activity in the North. The mine was in large part an accomplishment for Premier Bracken but it probably helped solidify support for McLean by indicating that business could produce jobs and growth.[23]

At the same time there was an announcement that the Marlborough Hotel had gone into receivership. Ralph Webb was not involved with the hotel by this time but he had originally come to Winnipeg to work for the owners, W.T. Alexander and F.H. Alexander, who would soon be charged with fraud. Their companies, the Great West Permanent Loan and Imperial Canadian Trust, also went into receivership. One of the charges against them was making an illegal loan with money from a third company, the Canadian National Fire Insurance Company, to greatly expand the Marlborough Hotel before Webb had come to Winnipeg to manage it. After a lengthy trial the Alexanders were sentenced to prison terms in January 1929. This scandal may have contributed to Webb's decision not to run again for mayor, though there was no suggestion he had been aware of the Alexander brothers' dishonesty.

The civic auditorium was a major issue during the election campaign because the question of creating a debt to build it was on the ballot in the 1927 election. The bylaw was rejected by the ratepayers. McLean and Queen agreed on the other big issue of the day: the need to build the dam at Slave Falls. The new hydro plant would be approved in a referendum the following year.

On election day, November 25, 1927, Dan McLean won with 23,366 votes, giving him a comfortable majority of 6,874 over Queen, who received 16,240 votes. McLean increased his vote over Webb's of the previous year and Queen received 3,500 more votes than Tipping had gotten the year before. This was a heartwarming result for an old politician like McLean. The voter turnout was the largest ever recorded. Alderman Alfred H. Pulford, another veteran Winnipeg politician, had originally been nominated in the race for mayor but a "group of citizens" visited him and asked him not to run. He agreed, thus avoiding a split in the Liberal/Conservative vote.

The following year, in the election of November 23, 1928, Mayor Dan McLean was elected by acclamation. The big issue was the bylaw to build a new City Hydro dam at Slave Falls, nine kilometres downstream from Pointe du Bois. It was not contentious; all candidates on both the left and right were in favour. No one dared to campaign against the construction of the publicly owned dam, although there were still those who felt it would be better to purchase power from Winnipeg Electric. Dan McLean placed the following ad in the papers: "Citizens! There is opposition to Slave Falls and we need a 2/5 majority. Get out and vote. Ladies vote and bring your friends. This is my final appeal to you for action in this all-important matter."[24] On election day, November 23, the Slave Falls bylaw passed with a two-fifths majority with solid support in all three wards. Construction began in the summer of 1929.

E.D. Honeyman, a Liberal lawyer who was running for the first time in 1928, would be an alderman for ten years. Like Leslie in 1927, Honeyman campaigned saying he wanted more unity of action and thought on Council. He said he wanted an end to the partisan scrapping in the council chamber. Once elected he did break ranks and vote with the Labour members on occasion.

With the economy improving, the need for more hydroelectric power was clear. Winnipeg was already buying extra power from Winnipeg Electric and had approved the new dam at Slave Falls to supply her growing electricity consumption, but one last power site remained undeveloped on the Winnipeg River: Seven Sisters. This was potentially the best of all hydro sites. Passing over seven rapids, the river fell eighteen metres, the biggest drop on the river. By consolidating the rapids into one waterfall, the dam was provided with a flow of water capable of driving turbines that would produce more power than any of the other Winnipeg River dams. Construction began in 1929 and the first half of the power plant with three turbines was completed in 1931. The plant was not completed until 1952, when the sixth turbine was installed.

The 1929 visit of members of the Manitoba Legislature Assembly and officers of Winnipeg Electric Company to Seven Sisters Dam. Archives of Manitoba, Events, 53.

The provincial government had applied for a lease of the site, but there was controversy over whether the dam should be built by the Province or the Winnipeg Electric Company. Premier Bracken kept his options open, refusing to withdraw the Province's application. He called in J.T. Hogg, an Ontario Hydro engineer, to write a report with recommendations about the best option for the government. In March 1928 Hogg delivered his report, stating that it would not be economically feasible for Manitoba to build the dam.[25] It would be preferable to allow Winnipeg Electric to do the work on the condition that they guarantee a supply of electricity to the province for thirty years at a certain price. The agreement should also stipulate that after thirty years the province would have the option of assuming ownership of the facility.

Bracken did not let Winnipeg Electric know that this was what was contained in the report, but negotiated with Andrew McLimont and the Winnipeg Electric lawyer, Edward Anderson, for the best possible price for the thirty-year contract. Bracken was able to secure a price lower than the best price that had been achieved in Canada up to that time—13.80 per hp for a 30,000 hp contract.

The report had come to Bracken the day after the Legislature rose in 1928, so it could not be discussed or debated. There was a huge uproar when he announced his decision to contract with Winnipeg Electric, and he was attacked by the opposition parties. In the fall of 1928 there was a by-election in Lansdowne constituency that gave the opposition parties an opportunity to use the Seven Sisters agreement as an election issue.

During the campaign Colonel Fawcett Taylor, the Conservative leader, charged that Bracken's party had received a donation of $50,000 from Winnipeg Electric in return for the decision to let them build the dam. He got this figure from a Conservative Party supporter who alleged the information came from his brother-in-law James Coyne, who was on the Winnipeg Electric board. Coyne denied telling him anything and subsequently it was discovered that the informant had made up the $50,000 figure. Bracken denied these charges and campaigned solely on the hydro deal, carefully laying out its merits at meeting after meeting. The Bracken candidate, Donald McKenzie, won by a majority of 200 votes. Taylor kept calling for a Royal Commission and finally Bracken set one up. In the end the commission did not find any wrongdoing. Winnipeg Electric refused to have its books audited, but it was established that they had made donations of $3,000 to the Progressives, $3,500 to the Conservatives, and $500 to the Liberals.

At the same time it came to light that William Major, Bracken's attorney general, and William Clubb, the minister of public works, had purchased Winnipeg Electric stock because they were privy to the upcoming deal. Major had actually told Conservative member John T. Haig about the deal before it was made public, and Haig offered to get him some stock. Several others bought stock at the time, including the Speaker of the House and even John Queen, who invested seventy-five dollars. In the end everyone who bought stock claimed to have lost money.

Although Clubb and Major were obliged to resign from Cabinet, there was no long-term damage, and after the Legislature rose for the 1929 sitting, Bracken reappointed them. So the effects of a scandal like this were not very serious at this time.

The last civic election of the 1920s took place on November 22, 1929. For the first time since the introduction of preferential voting, there were three candidates for mayor. Marcus Hyman was running for the ILP, Dan McLean was running for a third term as mayor, and Ralph Webb had been asked to run by the Civic Progress Association, the 1929 version of the citizens' groups that always backed the Liberal/Conservative campaigns. They had also asked Dan McLean to step down and run instead for alderman in Ward 3. He rather testily announced he was running for mayor and didn't care what the Civic Progress Association thought.

McLean ran on his record. Speaking on CKY Radio, he took credit for finally getting the Slave Falls project underway. He pointed out that several other issues, including building an auditorium and the Exhibition, looked as though they would soon be resolved, although they actually were not. He mentioned the new Town Planning Committee, which had begun the work of zoning the city for various uses.

Webb, as usual, said that he had been asked to run only after the Civic Progress Association had asked a number of other possible candidates and been refused. He avoided mentioning McLean's candidacy. He once again talked about the importance of building the tourist industry, the fourth-largest industry in Canada. His business experience and positive attitude were cited as important qualities. One ad said that once he was mayor again, "this city will once more take a big step towards its great destiny."[26]

Marcus Hyman had a more exotic background than most Winnipeg politicians. He was a lawyer who had studied at Oxford as a Rhodes Scholar. He had worked as a tutor for the children of an Indian maharajah. In 1934, as an MLA, he introduced the first group anti-defamation legislation to be passed into law. The Act made it illegal to libel a group, including Jewish citizens. As a campaigner he was witty and sharp-tongued. He attacked Webb's record, charging that he had not really accomplished much. He answered John Dafoe's often-repeated objection that the ILP had injected party politics into Winnipeg Council, commenting that he was "surprised that a man of Mr. Dafoe's immense learning and knowledge of affairs was apparently unaware of how the party system had permeated municipal administrations in Great Britain." The heavy sarcasm and the reference to how things were done in Britain may have lost him votes.[27]

Hyman attacked Webb, saying the newspaper ads of the Civic Progress Association called for new blood at City Hall but Ralph Webb was not new. He was just "our old stager," meaning someone who has been through many battles and given faithful service. For his part, Webb pretended to forget Hyman's name whenever he mentioned him in a speech. He called Hyman a "knocker" and said, "I don't mind what Mr. Hyman says. I'd be glad to compare my record with his any day, even if he is a Rhodes Scholar. We want a City that will go ahead 100%. We don't want to be led by a knocker."[28]

Webb called for a positive attitude on the part of Council and an energetic approach to attracting new business to the city. He said that "the most important thing facing us is to find work for those who need work." The stock market crash had just happened and its consequences were beginning to be felt. He was not surprised that support for the Communist Party was on the rise. The recipe for communism, he said, was "no grub, no fuel, no place to sleep and lack of sympathetic contacts," and that if he and his audience were in the same place they might be Communist supporters as well.[29] He accused McLean of not really doing anything during his two years in office. Referring to a habit of Mayor McLean's, Webb said if he was elected he would not sit in the mayor's gilded office every morning, reading the papers from other cities. Instead, he would be out trying to get the city mentioned in the papers so people in other cities would be reading about Winnipeg.

The *Free Press* supported Webb, and after the vote Dafoe said that his election was a "personal tribute to Colonel Webb. The people believe that he will give leadership for an active and progressive administration." Dafoe called for "as much cooperation as possible between the two sections of council. Team play all around is what the City requires just now." Even so, he could not resist pointing out that ILP vote had declined from the 44 percent won by John Queen two years before to the 33 percent garnered by Hyman the day before: "Mr. Hyman's campaign did not secure for him the confidence of Winnipeg voters."[30] Dafoe added that the election of Civic Progress Association candidates Herbert Andrews, Ralph Maybank, and A.J. Roberts showed that the people believed the "City should be making greater progress and that the City Council should deal more promptly and effectively with the City's business and should do more to help on the development and advancement of Winnipeg."[31] The aldermen named were younger, and Maybank, at least, was a Liberal, the law partner of local Liberals Albert B. Hudson and Herbert Symington. Roberts was a druggist and Andrews was another lawyer, the nephew of Alfred J. Andrews, a former mayor and one of the prosecutors in the General Strike trials. Herbert Andrews was a decorated veteran of the Great War and a well-known hockey player. Andrews, Maybank, and Roberts, being new to Council were, Dafoe hoped, more likely to compromise and work with both Labour and Liberal/Conservative colleagues to accomplish things. As it happened these younger men did have an impact, but it was limited. Andrews died in a car accident in 1935; Maybank was elected to the Legislature, and between 1936 and 1954 he was a federal MP for South Winnipeg.

One of the bylaws to be voted on in 1929 was to create a debt to build a new swimming pool to replace the Cornish Avenue baths that had been condemned. *Winnipeg Tribune* journalist Vernon Thomas wrote a column supporting the new baths. He said that the Cornish pool had seen 65,318 visitors in the year before it was closed, and pointed out that fully 25 percent of the population had no other place to bathe because they were living in rooms with no hot-water bathing facilities. Between 3,000 and 3,500 large houses were subdivided in the area and occupied by many families, making bathing difficult. Thomas said public baths were therefore a very important municipal service.[32] On election day the baths bylaw was passed and the Sherbrook Pool was built as a result. A bylaw to expand the Central Heating Plant to serve more customers also passed.

In the 1929 election Ralph Webb was elected with 22,622 votes. Marcus Hyman received 13,821 votes and Dan McLean received 7,273. Webb would be elected three more times and would be mayor of Winnipeg until the end of 1933.

The City Council of the 1920s saw a good deal of partisanship but there were moments when Labour and Liberal/Conservative aldermen united in support of specific issues. Toward the end of the decade, there were signs of a more cooperative attitude. Of most interest was the emergence of the Independent Labour Party as a strong and united group on Council. Later in the 1930s John Queen was elected mayor seven times and Labour had several majorities on Council.

PART 3

Class and Culture

View of Fort Garry Hotel from Union Station, 1914. Library and Archives Canada, Topley Series, Mikan 3304579.

CHAPTER 7

The Elite in an Unhappy City

In the 1920s, economic and political conditions in Winnipeg had changed and the position of the city's political and business classes no longer seemed as unassailable as it had been. Sir Douglas Cameron's wife, Margaret, had reportedly once said, "Rich people don't come to Winnipeg. People come to Winnipeg to get rich." It is perhaps telling that in the 1920s, she and her sons moved to Vancouver, the West's new boom town.

The lesson of the General Strike for upper-class families was that their previous largely unquestioned control of the city would now be questioned. While they, as represented by the Citizens' Committee of 1000, had contributed to the failure of the strike, there were few signs that people took much satisfaction from the victory. Many spoke of a pall hanging over the city. The old, confident boosterism of the boom years seemed to have evaporated.

Pioneer Winnipeg store owner Horace Chevrier spoke in 1922 about the "period of depression and gloom" the city was going through. On January 1, 1920, John Dafoe, in his New Year *Free Press* editorial, referred to Winnipeg as an "unhappy city" with large numbers of people "cultivating grudges and looking for revenge." At a meeting where Ralph Webb was nominated for a second term in 1925, Minnie Campbell gave a speech in which she remembered that "we were dead and almost buried for two or three years," referring to the immediate postwar, post-strike period.[1] (Campbell, the widow of Premier Roblin's attorney general Colin Campbell, was one of the last active

Delegates representing the provincial chapter of Imperial Order Daughters of the Empire, Fort Garry, 20 April 1921, with Minnie Campbell (first row, fourth from left), the widow of Attorney General Colin Campbell. She belonged to Winnipeg's elite and participated in its many organizations. Archives of Manitoba, P2506A-5.

Conservatives from the Roblin era. She was an important leader in the IODE and a prominent member of Westminster Church but through the long years of Liberal and Progressive governments in office from 1915 to the 1950s, she was no longer as influential as she once had been.)

In November 1924, at the opening of City Hydro's Amy Street power plant, former mayor Thomas R. Deacon spoke, representing manufacturers. Deacon was the owner of Manitoba Bridge and one of the managers against whom the General Strike had been called. He said that since manufacturers in western Canada were considered to be highwaymen or criminals, he was surprised he had been asked to attend, a comment that revealed the state of mind of the city's business leaders. At a meeting during the strike, someone in the audience called out that businessman Augustus Nanton's house should be burned down. The comment had to be taken seriously. Nanton, his sons, and his servants took turns patrolling the grounds of his house on Roslyn Road, armed with a pistol. His wife and daughters went to stay elsewhere for the duration of the strike. A barn on a farm owned by Nanton in Rosser Municipality was burned during the strike and a number of horses were killed. This incident was likely overblown because of the emotional atmosphere at the time, but it nevertheless must have made a deep impression on the Nantons and people like them who felt they had done a great deal for the city.[2]

One result of the city's traditional leaders' new sense of insecurity was the increased attention paid to putting some distance between the elite and everyone else. A manifestation of this was the Winnipeg Blue Book of 1926–27. Many large eastern cities such as New York and Philadelphia had social registers, published regularly, listing socially prominent families and other information such as club memberships. Many smaller cities published a social register of "historically and socially important families," as the Connecticut Social Register of 1900–01 said, or "An Authoritative Register of Elite Torontonian Families," as the Toronto Blue Book of 1928 claimed. In Canada in the 1920s, Montreal, Toronto, and Vancouver all had a Blue Book with slight variations in their titles.

There was also a Winnipeg Society Blue Book and Club List for 1926–27. The book contained a directory of thirty-six pages of entries for families, and forty-four pages that listed the members of forty-six of the city's clubs. About 600 families had entries, and the club membership listings contained many hundreds more people not listed in the directory section.

The editor of the Winnipeg Blue Book was Arthur Tunnell of Toronto. He was involved in the publication of many reference books, and from 1932 until his death in 1969 he was the editor of the *Canadian Who's Who*. For part of that time his partner was the poet and prose writer Charles G.D. Roberts. For the *Who's Who* Tunnell decided who would be included by sending questionnaires out to prospective entries. There is no indication in the Winnipeg Blue Book how the entries were chosen, but it is possible that Tunnell made that decision based on research in newspapers and other sources. It may also have been that, like other such publications, whoever wanted to pay a subscription fee would be included.

The names of families are listed alphabetically, with the husband's name coming first and the wife's maiden name included in smaller type. The address is given and the location and name of the family's summer residence, if there was one. The names of any children, including those who had married, come next. Then the entry gives the club memberships of the man and his wife, represented by numbers. The Manitoba Club, for example, was number 14 in the club list, and that number would appear under the names of its members in the directory.

What use would be made of such a directory? It could be a useful reference for hostesses wanting to send out invitations. It also established which families were the most important, who was securely a member of the city's upper class and who was not. Addresses, summer homes, club memberships, the maiden name of a man's wife were all listed as markers of status and success. It was, in short, a tool for setting out the boundaries of the city's upper class and demonstrating its exclusive nature.

Clubs

The club membership lists recorded a larger group of people who were important enough and wealthy enough to belong to exclusive organizations. Membership in at least some clubs was restricted, granted after nomination and votes of the membership, and payment of often large fees or the purchase of shares. It was, therefore, a reliable measure of status.

In addition, the clubs and, to some degree, the summer resorts where people had cottages, constituted safe zones where these families could socialize with people of their own kind without being intruded upon by people from outside their circle. To take one club listed in the Blue Book as an example, the St. Charles Country Club history describes it as "both a place of refuge and a showpiece, a sanctuary for some and a place of pride and passion for others." In his preface to the history, Alan Sweatman describes the discussion over whether to increase the membership in the 1960s in order to bring in more revenue. One of those who resisted increasing the size of the membership above the 550 of that time cited the benefit that "I know most of the present (members) or I know who they are."[3]

The Gyro Club was one of the newer types of service clubs, like Kiwanis and the Rotary Club, that grew quickly in the 1920s. The club's historian explained: "A large proportion of our members were ex-service types from World War One, restless, active and seeking some outlet for excess energy in a world which was just beginning its recovery and at times seemed rather flat." He described the process of admitting new members: "All applications for membership were submitted to and secretly voted upon by the membership at large and a single black ball sufficed to exclude an applicant. It soon became evident that personal prejudice and petty spite was being exercised against certain applicants. Several members resigned in protest when candidates whom they had proposed or seconded were rejected. The black ball count was reduced to one in five."[4] The writer does not say who the potential blackballed members were, but there was clearly a desire to be able to limit membership.

It may be that the Blue Book was useful to the women of the city's upper-middle-class families who played a major role in establishing and maintaining the borders of "society," and that their activities helped to strengthen society as an entity with an unassailable right to control the city. While their husbands may have taken the lead in the area of business and making money, it was the women who organized a social life appropriate for a leading family. Expensive and exclusive parties and dances were given, using the city's large railroad hotels as showplaces for their clothing and jewellery and their ability to spend money on the best food and the best dance bands. The managers and some staff of these hotels would have been able to offer useful advice on the correct way to do things, having risen through the ranks and worked in company hotels in the more sophisticated eastern cities such as the Windsor in Montreal and the Chateau Laurier in Ottawa. Also, many members of Winnipeg's upper-middle class travelled, an opportunity to observe how things should be done as they crossed the Atlantic in modern liners and stayed in good hotels abroad. The cars that upper-middle-class people drove; the neighbourhoods they lived in, steadily farther removed from the city centre; and the schools their children went to were all means of creating distance between themselves and the general population.

Neighbourhoods

The process of creating exclusive neighbourhoods had begun early in Winnipeg as wealthy people moved from the Point Douglas area to the so-called Hudson's Bay Reserve between Broadway and Assiniboine avenues, an area marketed as exclusive. In the decade before the Great War, people who could afford to moved from the Broadway area to Fort Rouge, Roslyn Road being the most expensive and desirable street for people wanting their homes to add to their status. Well-to-do people in Winnipeg were tending to move further west during the 1920s.

The western limit of their migration was the area next to Assiniboine Park, where the town of Tuxedo was finally starting to see some construction. Before the Great War, real estate developer Frederick Heubach had purchased a large tract of land and issued a prospectus for a garden suburb that was to incorporate expensive homes with a landscaped setting by the Assiniboine River. In 1901 David Finkelstein had gone to work for Heubach's real estate firm as a clerk and eventually became a partner. Heubach passed away in 1914, never having seen the development begin. His son Claude and David Finkelstein carried on with Tuxedo after the war. There were several other smaller landowners in Tuxedo, including some British investors. Finkelstein was Tuxedo's mayor for forty-six years and Tuxedo's Council consisted of other landowners. By keeping

Olmstead plan for the Tuxedo suburb, c. 1910, including proposed site of the University of Manitoba, which never materialized at the location. Library and Archives Canada, Mikan no. 183858.

control of the municipal council, they were able to ensure that only the kind of large luxury residences they wanted would be built in Tuxedo. They blocked the construction of cheaper, smaller houses and of businesses in the south end of the municipality, where the Canada Cement Plant and inexpensive housing for the plant's workers were located. Generally, over the years, representatives of these residents were never able to win a seat on Council.

David Finkelstein was the main promoter of Tuxedo. He was born in Poland to Jewish parents and came to Winnipeg as a boy. He appears not to have been an active member of the city's Jewish community or to have been close to his Winnipeg relatives.[5] Until the 1950s Tuxedo remained an area with an unwritten caveat that property would not be sold to Jews, and Finkelstein supported this.

During the 1920s, people began moving to the area that is now called Old Tuxedo between the Assiniboine River and Corydon Avenue, and by 1930 about twenty large homes had been built. The first houses were built on Park

Boulevard facing the Assiniboine Park. A number of people involved in the grain business had houses built on Park Boulevard, and Lamont and Handsart streets. There were also lawyers, a dentist, a surgeon, people who worked for the government and for Eaton's, two owners of piano businesses, and a broker. The number of houses built in the 1920s was small, but the movement from the city was significant enough to establish Heubach's projected suburb as a reality. Tuxedo would continue to struggle until the 1940s and 1950s, when Finkelstein's perseverance began to pay off and a significant number of luxury homes were built in the town.

Roslyn Road, a street that in the years before the Great War had become home to some of Winnipeg's wealthiest people, began to change during the 1920s. Of fifty houses, 40 percent did remain with the same owner throughout the decade. About half of the remainder changed hands once and half more than once, and seven houses actually sat vacant for a year or more. In four cases the original owner died. Three houses on Roslyn seem to have taken in boarders or created suites. Robert L. Richardson, the owner of the *Winnipeg Tribune*, died early in the decade and his wife let parts of their house to two renters. Most people who sold their houses moved to another part of the city, but three moved into apartments, four moved to another house on Roslyn, and another three, all widows, moved into either the Royal Alexandra or Fort Garry hotels when their husbands died.

The trends that would eventually destroy Roslyn Road—subdividing the houses and building apartment buildings—began in the 1920s with the demolition of one house for the construction of the Blackstone Apartments in 1927 or 1928. The building at 139 Roslyn became the Fort Rouge Preparatory School, owned by E.E. Johnson. In 1925, City Council received a petition from homeowners on Roslyn west of Osborne Street, asking for assurances that no apartments would be built in their area. Council confirmed that this would not happen. Sir Charles Tupper objected to this petition. He owned property in the area, although he did not live there. He may not have wanted any limits put on what development could take place on Roslyn. It would not be until the 1960s, when the city changed the zoning to allow multi-storey buildings, that most of the large houses were demolished and replaced by high-rise apartments.[6]

In the days of the Winnipeg boom before the Great War, Roslyn Road had been home to business owners like Augustus Nanton, David Dingwall of Dingwall Jewellers, John Galt of G. and J. Galt Grocery Wholesalers, and

Douglas C. Cameron, owner of Rat Portage Lumber. But in the 1920s the street was no longer the exclusive preserve of the city's elite. The residents were still well off, but they tended to be managers of other people's businesses. There were also five medical doctors and a number of lawyers living on the street.

Further west, in Crescentwood, Dromore Avenue was an example of a more exclusive street, safe from apartment blocks and finishing schools. Like Roslyn, Dromore was inhabited by managers rather than owners. Dromore also saw about 42 percent of its twenty-five houses stay in the hands of the same owner while the rest changed hands either once or twice. But the new owners were the same sort of people as the sellers—managers or lawyers—and none of the houses took in boarders or were divided into suites.

Herbert M. Tucker was an example of Dromore residents. He lived at 201 Dromore. He came to Winnipeg from Ontario in 1906 to work in the new Eaton's store, rose through the ranks at Eaton's, and by 1925 was one of the company vice-presidents and a board member. There were other people on Dromore in management positions at Great-West Life, Canadian Pacific, various banks and trust companies, and grain companies. Albert B. Hudson, the lawyer who had been an attorney general in the Liberal Norris government and who eventually became a Supreme Court Justice, lived at 208 Dromore

Views in Crescentwood, c. 1900–1925, Albertype Company. Library and Archives Canada, Albertype Company fonds, Mikan no. 3334801.

until 1927, when he moved to an apartment in the Fort Garry Court. The house was bought by Sanford Evans, a former mayor of Winnipeg. Unlike those on Roslyn Road, the houses on Dromore survived and continued to be single-family homes.

Schools

Many affluent families in Winnipeg sent their youngsters to Ontario or Quebec to be educated in private schools like Bishop Strachan School, Trinity College School, Upper Canada College, or Bishop's in Lennoxville, Quebec, while in Winnipeg there were the Tuckwell School for boys and the Rupertsland College for girls.

Across North America at this time, the uses of private schools helped create an exclusive and protected environment for the children of the elite. In a time when the old elites were feeling eased out by newly rich people, restricted access to desirable schools was one way to preserve social status.[7] In Winnipeg, sending children away to school in the east or enrolling them in private schools in Winnipeg was, in the decade before the Great War and during the 1920s, a way to ensure that they met other young people from their own social class. They would not only learn the subjects in the curriculum but would become comfortable in and familiar with an upper-middle-class social environment.

Some young women from wealthy families went abroad for post-secondary study. Mary Machray, daughter of lawyer John Machray, graduated from University of Manitoba and went to Paris to study at the Sorbonne. Elizabeth Dafoe, the daughter of *Free Press* editor John Dafoe, went to New York to study librarianship and experience a carefully chaperoned winter in the great city.

Sanford Evans, a former mayor of Winnipeg, had daughters attending Bishop Strachan School in Toronto in 1918. He was told Bishop Strachan would have to raise everyone's fees by fifty dollars because of the inflation in costs due to the war. Boarders were charged from $450 to $650 per year, depending on their age. That is roughly equivalent to a range of $5,400 to $7,800 in 2016 dollars. The basic curriculum was English, Latin, French, German, mathematics, singing, sewing, and drill. Additional fees were charged for subjects such as Italian, Greek, Spanish, bookkeeping, shorthand, dressmaking, embroidery, piano, violin, harmony, counterpoint, and the history of music.[8]

By encouraging and training their daughters and sons and creating social events where their children could meet each other, the Winnipeg elite also ensured the future of their social group. Young women of this group had debutante seasons during which they were presented at an array of social functions

The social page from the 20 May 1922 Winnipeg Tribune *shows Marjorie Glassco (first from right), daughter of John Glassco, manager of City Hydro. She was one of the socialites of the city's elite and her photo was often featured in the* Tribune's *society pages. Here, along with Martha Anderson and Geraldine Wood, she's promoting Humane week, which was to feature an animal parade in Winnipeg.*

as eligible partners for marriage. In December of 1925 there was a coming-out party at the Royal Alexandra Hotel for Marjorie Glassco, the eldest daughter of John Glassco, the manager of City Hydro. The guests included Sir Stewart and Lady Tupper, Mr. and Mrs. Robert Rogers, and many other prominent lawyers and businessmen. This party at the Royal Alexandra would likely be just one of a number of events during Marjorie's debutante year, a year of great expense for her father. At the end of it her parents hoped that their daughter would have attracted a proposal or two. Marjorie had gone to the Compton House School in Montreal, and in 1923 she won a Girl Guides Silver Medal for saving someone from drowning. She was socially active in the 1920s, attending dances and working with the Junior League. But it appears that she chose not to marry. In 1937 she was still listed as Miss Glassco. Rose Halter, the daughter of Maurice and Rhoda Halter, had her coming-out dance in November 1924. She had graduated from the University of Manitoba in the spring of the same year. For the next couple of years her name appeared in the lists of guests at dances at the Royal Alexandra Hotel, and in August 1928 she was married and became Mrs. Schreiber.

Travel

Some people sent their daughters on sea voyages so they could see other countries and perhaps meet potential husbands on board the liners. The first-class sections of the ships were like floating private clubs, sealed off from the lower orders, in which any young people one met would be from a "good" background or at least rich. If we are to believe numerous interwar Hollywood movies set on ocean liners, first class was also a favourite haunt of confidence men and card sharps.

A best-selling book of the 1920s was *Planning a Trip Abroad* by New York journalist and popular historian Edward Hungerford.[9] The book was clearly intended for people who could afford to travel but had perhaps not done much of it. In the 1920s Americans sailed for Europe in large numbers because the value of their dollar was sky-high compared with the currencies of many struggling European countries. A five-week trip could be made for $500 American if one travelled second class on the railways and took a less expensive ship. When choosing a steamer, Hungerford said, the decision depended upon the traveller's tastes and pocketbook. There were a lot of new liners because many ships had been sunk during the war and they were now being replaced with "new tonnage which is of an excellence not known before."[10] Large, slow steamers were the most comfortable because they vibrated less. In an inside cabin on the lowest deck, the passenger would feel the least roll, and in an outside cabin on the top deck, the most. The lowest rates were charged between September 1 and March 1. The winter westbound rates, 10 percent lower than regular rates, were charged between November 1 and June 30. In these periods the ships were not full and service was better than in the busy summer season. The most luxurious ships sailed from New York to Cherbourg and Southampton. The second-tier ships, nearly equal in comfort and speed, sailed to Liverpool, Plymouth, and Boulogne. One could also travel in a "cabin" ship that charged 50 percent less than liners and was just as comfortable, if somewhat slower. Instead of first, second, and third class, cabin boats had only cabin class and steerage.

Hungerford offered advice on what to pack for the voyage. He suggested not taking a steamer trunk because they cost a lot to transport. English ships allowed 150 pounds of free baggage; French ships, 66 pounds; and German lines, foreshadowing the stinginess of modern airlines, did not allow any. He also gave suggested amounts to tip the various stewards—dining room, cabin, smoking room, bath, and deck. It was important to see the bath steward early so that he would assign you a good time for having your bath. He would come to your door each day to let you know your bath was ready.

One example of such a trip was taken by Winnipegger Betty A.W. McLimont, the daughter of the general manager of Winnipeg Electric. She had taken a long voyage between February and May 1922, when she sailed, properly chaperoned, with some friends to Cuba, through the Panama Canal, and on to Valparaiso in Chile, Buenos Aires, Portugal, Spain, Paris, London, and home. She later travelled to the Orient by ship. She and her parents spent the winter abroad in 1924, coming home in April, and in 1925 she went to New York with her family in the fall.

Dances

Dances, lunches, bridge parties, and other entertainments might take place in private homes or in a hotel. Unlike house parties, public dance halls were seen as places where girls might be exposed to unwanted advances. The general rule was that young women should not go to public dance halls unless accompanied by a slightly older married couple as a way to ensure the girls were not preyed upon. In January 1925 there was a dance at the home of Robert T. and Minnie Evans at 10 Ruskin Row. Mr. Evans owned the British America Elevator Company. The party was given in honour of his sixteen-year-old daughter and her friends, who were "not outs"—that is, girls who had not yet come out as debutantes. The Evans house was one of the biggest in Winnipeg and there was plenty of room for the party. In the ballroom, Frank Wright's Orchestra played the "latest music" for fourteen dances.

Exclusive dances could also be held in Winnipeg's Fort Garry and Royal Alexandra hotels. In early 1924 a group called the New Dancing Club put on a "deb party" at the Royal Alexandra in the Tapestry Room, one of the smaller rooms in the ballroom area of the hotel. A "club" dance was one for which tickets would have been bought and was thus a private event. In attendance were a number of young women who were in their debutante year. Margaret Mathers, the daughter of Chief Justice Mathers, was there. Her older brother Frank and his wife were with her. Also at the dance were a number of young

10 Ruskin Row, c. 1900–1925. Library Archives Canada, Albertype Company fonds, Mikan no. 3334730. In 1925 Robert T. Evans owned this home, which was one of the biggest in Winnipeg, and threw a lavish party in honour of his sixteen-year-old daughter. The party included an orchestra.

men, potential grooms and dancing partners, including John Rogers, who was with his older sister Margaret Konantz. They were the children of Edith Rogers, Manitoba's first female MLA. The New Dancing Club seems to have attracted younger people, but their dance of February 9, 1924, was hosted by Kathleen Osler and Edith Kirby, both middle-aged ladies who would act as chaperones and make sure the evening went well.

There were other club or association dances that would control admission by the sale of tickets. These dancing associations would come and go, and in one season, from October to April, might sponsor five or six dances in the Royal Alexandra or the Fort Garry. In 1923 there was a series of Assembly Dances at the Fort Garry Hotel, the final one taking place on February 10. Among many other guests were Mrs. Hugh Sutherland, by this time an elderly woman; Lady Tupper, then middle-aged; and other women from the same social group, such as Jean Riley, Muriel Galt, and Louise Phillips. Their husbands were businessmen and lawyers.

Fort Garry Hotel ballroom, 1926, one of the venues where Winnipeg's elite attended dances. Library and Archives Canada, Mikan no. 3348979.

In 1927 the 200 Dancing Club offered five dances during the winter, all held in the Gold Suite at the Royal Alexandra. At the February 12 dance there were many young men and women present along with older people such as Louise Phillips and Lady Tupper, and younger married people such as Alice Galt now Mrs. Weiss, one of the daughters of George Galt who had been a debutante about fifteen years before.

The senior members of the city's upper class continued to be patrons for a list of annual balls or large formal dances that had been going on, in some cases, for decades. The Rose Ball, for example, was organized each year by the Fort Garry Chapter of the Imperial Order Daughters of the Empire (IODE), and in the 1920s it was usually held at the Fort Garry Hotel. Because of the importance of the IODE, this ball attracted community leaders such as the mayor, premier, and lieutenant-governor; General Huntly Ketchen, commanding officer of Military District 10; and former premier and magistrate Sir Hugh John Macdonald.

Beginning in 1906, the Old Timers' Association had held an annual ball. In the 1920s Richard D. Waugh, former mayor and first head of the Manitoba

Liquor Control Board, was the chair of the club. He was a genuine old-timer, having come to Winnipeg from Scotland when he was a small boy. Waugh's wife, Harriet, was a member of the Logan family that traced its roots in the city back to Red River Settlement times. The Waughs might have been present at any of the society balls held in the big railroad hotels, but the Old Timers' Ball was interesting in that attendance was not restricted by factors like wealth or social position. All that was required was long residence in Winnipeg. It was also probably the only such social event that also included some Metis attendees. Fred Genthon, an award-winning fiddler, was one of the Metis musicians who came to play Red River jigs each year at the ball. The ball was important, too, because it gave Winnipeggers a ready-made history and pedigree, a connection to a past that stretched back long before the arrival of the first immigrants from Ontario. Of course, this pedigree paled in comparison with the several-thousand-year history of the area's Indigenous people.

On April 18, 1925, the Royal Alexandra was the scene of another annual dance: the annual Military Ball put on by General Ketchen and his officers from the headquarters of Military District 10 at Fort Osborne Barracks. There was a huge crowd of attendees, including a good many militia officers who joined the professional soldiers on this occasion. The band of the Princess Patricia's—the regiment was stationed in Winnipeg during the 1920s—provided music during the reception, and then the Canary Cottage Orchestra played "the latest tunes" for the eighteen dances following dinner. Military balls like this one and others sponsored by the militia regiments had been a feature of the city's social life for many years and were quasi-official occasions at which army officers, politicians, and public servants joined the city's business and legal elite to dance.

During the war the fighting in Europe overshadowed the formerly carefree social life of the city. Balls and dinners had to have a serious purpose, such as fundraising for the Red Cross, the Patriotic Fund, or for some specific battalion so that the men could enjoy comforts like cigarettes, magazines, or new socks. A week before the Military Ball of 1925, a dance was held at the Minto Armouries to celebrate the anniversary of the Canadian victory at Vimy Ridge in 1917. With so many returned soldiers in the city, there were many social events sponsored by the various Winnipeg battalions and veterans' groups.

With the end of the war and the coming of the 1920s, good causes continued to be funded by social events. In April 1920, for example, a ball was held to raise funds for the Polish Relief Committee. Winnipeggers had supported relief work in Poland throughout the war. The ball was in honour of Polish

The front page of 30 December 1923 Winnipeg Tribune *featuring the news of the wedding of Josephine Anderson and Lloyd Pulford. In attendance are Betty Limont and other daughters of Winnipeg elite.*

Consul Buckowiecki-Olszewski, and the patrons were the mayor, the premier, Charles F. and Mary Czerwinski, and Minnie Campbell. (Charles Czerwinski was a local manufacturer and businessman, born in Ontario of Polish parents.) All these entertainments created a small exclusive world in which the upper middle class could socialize among themselves.

A Policeman's Ball was held on February 16, 1929. It was not an event that was in any way restricted and around 2,000 people crowded into the Royal Alexandra to dance to one of several bands or participate in a whist drive in the lobby. The patronesses were leading members of the upper class, such as Muriel Richardson, Louise Phillips, Lady Macdonald, Edith Rogers, and Alice Bracken, the premier's wife. But the committee also included Lydia Farmer, the wife of the successful Independent Labour Party politician and former mayor.

Winter

As a city with a long winter, Winnipeg had always supported a lot of winter sports. The 1920s continued this tradition with some modernization. Snowshoe "tramps" took place on the frozen rivers. A favourite route was to walk along the frozen Red River to Lockport, have lunch, and walk back, aiming to be home before midnight.

A favourite place for winter activities was a tea room called the Cabbage Patch, on North Drive in Fort Garry. In 1929 the group that would become the Wildwood Club purchased the site and built a clubhouse. The Cabbage Patch had been a meeting place for people who participated in winter sports like snowshoeing and skiing. On January 17, 1925, for example, the first sports day of the year took place at the Cabbage Patch and the riverbank was "thronged with spectators." The *Tribune* newspaper story refers to "the jump," a wooden ski jump built on the high bank and ending on the frozen surface of the Red River. The social page includes a picture of a group of young women in ski clothes, standing on the jump. They all look very happy and they are dressed in sweaters and ski pants with tightly wrapped legs. The buttressing under-garments of their mothers' time were now much simpler or gone altogether, freeing them to ski, skate, and snowshoe more comfortably.

For many years the Winnipeg Skating Club had been active in the city. In 1924 the club built a two-storey, red-brick and stucco building at 51 Smith Street. The clubhouse had an indoor ice sheet measuring fifty-two by twenty-two metres on the main floor, and administrative offices and a lounge upstairs. Each year a skating carnival was put on by the Skating Club at the Amphitheatre Rink, the largest indoor rink in the city at the time. The Amphitheatre Rink, or "Amp," was located west of the site of the present Great-West Life building and was originally built as a venue for the city's annual horse show. It had always had an ice surface in the winter. The carnival included various figure-skating performances by adults and children, and the members practised at their own rink at 51 Smith Street. In 1921 the theme of the winter carnival was "Alice in Wonderland," and the story was acted out on the ice. The Skating Club attracted women from the city's elite: Aurelia Rogers, wife of the former cabinet minister, and Muriel Galt, the widow of one of the partners in the large Galt grocery wholesale company, were on the organizing committee; Galt participated in the carnival itself. There was a large informal dance at the club after the carnival, to which many of the members wore their costumes. On February 4, 1922, the *Tribune* carried a special section on a winter carnival to be held between February 5 and 11. It was a much bigger event than the usual Skating Club events that had taken place in the past. It was, however, not repeated on the same scale. Instead, there was a carnival the next year in St. Boniface and the Skating Club continued its usual annual event.

On December 11, 1929, the papers carried a big spread about the new Winter Club on Smith Street and Assiniboine Avenue. The Winter Club was built on the property that had been occupied since 1924 by the Winnipeg Skating Club and it was the successor to the earlier organization. The new club was advertised as one of the finest in Canada. It was at once a symbol of the economic recovery that had taken place in the years since 1925 and of the continuing health and exclusivity of the Winnipeg elite. The message the new building conveyed was that while there had been rough times during the postwar depression, now Winnipeg was in a new period of posterity.

The contract for the new building had been let in June 1929, and construction carried on through the summer and fall. The Winter Club now had an ice surface of more or less the same size as the old skating club, but it had added badminton courts and two squash racquet courts. In the basement was an eighteen-by-nine-metre pool with a three-metre deep end and three diving boards at one, two, and three metres. The pool area was lit by a skylight. There were new locker rooms and there was a restaurant and a lounge for young people. Bowling alleys were added later.

The outside of the building was brick and stucco with half timbering. Window shutters and the columns on either side of the entrance were painted green. There was an area in the basement with nets and a putting green so members could practise their golf swing and take lessons from the St. Charles Country Club pro during the long winter months. There were instructors for badminton, figure skating, and swimming, all experienced men who had formerly worked at places such as the Chateau Lake Louise and Banff Springs Hotel.

Membership was limited to 650, and there were three classes of members: active members who participated in the available sports; non-active who used the club but did not play sports; and military members, who included the officers of the permanent forces stationed in Winnipeg. Badminton seems to have been a favourite sport of the military at the time and there was a five-team league that included teams from the Minto and McGregor armouries. The membership consisted of people who often also had memberships at the St. Charles Country Club or other local golf clubs. There was a mixture of the older Winnipeg families and business people who had come to Winnipeg since the war. The Winter Club allowed these people to remain active during the winter. Members were described as people who were interested in fostering healthy recreation and amateur sports for themselves and their families.

The opening celebrations in December 1929 included a dance at which James and Muriel Richardson—he was the honorary president of the club—acted as hosts. During the dance Mademoiselle Charlotte of the Montreal Skating Club and Oleh Peterson, the skating pro at the Winter Club, gave a figure-skating demonstration.

The Winter Club was also another exclusive area where the city's upper middle class could socialize without the intrusion of outsiders. The club building was closed to the outside and the interior spaces could not be seen. Although it was near the centre of the city, surrounded by residential streets, no one but members could actually participate in or know about its services. Its size and the quality of the facilities demonstrated that the members were successful and in control and ready to meet the future with confidence. However, the collapse of the stock market just weeks before the official opening would cast an increasingly dark shadow over the club and its members. Winnipeg would soon be entering yet another long period of difficulty and testing.

Main Street, 1929. University of Manitoba Archives.

CHAPTER 8

A Diminished Roar

The 1920s are commonly seen as a "roaring" time when Victorian morals were replaced by much more relaxed and permissive attitudes. People usually think of jazz, speakeasies, short skirts, and fortunes made on the stock market. Did any of this apply to Winnipeg, a city very far from the centres of fashion? The answer is, yes, in some ways. For one thing, Canada did not really "roar" in the 1920s. As we have seen, the first half of the decade was a time of recession, and, unlike the United States, Canada and cities like Winnipeg suffered much more from the after-effects of the Great War. But Winnipeg was very much in touch with the outside world through movies, newspapers, and the new medium of radio. Many ideas and mores changed during the decade. An interesting example and evidence of the changes that were taking place was the "advice column" of the *Winnipeg Tribune*.

Problems of the Heart

In Winnipeg in the 1920s young women and men were often confused about the changes in dress and behaviour and just how they should behave. One place they turned for advice was the newspaper "agony" or advice column. By the 1920s almost all homes in Canada received a daily paper, and papers had a vast readership. One of the popular features were the articles by advice columnists Dorothy Dix and Beatrice Fairfax, who were syndicated in hundreds of daily papers in the United States and Canada and were presumably read by tens of thousands of women and men. In Winnipeg, the *Tribune* carried Betty Vincent and her daily column "Problems of the Heart" during the 1920s. She had been published before in the *Tribune* between 1914 and 1916 with a weekly column: "Advice to Lovers."

When introducing her to its readers as a new member of the *Tribune* staff in May 1921, the paper said that Vincent would answer questions about love, etiquette, and home problems. Betty Vincent, readers were told, received letters from thousands on "problems of the heart and knotty questions. She puts her experience at the service of *Tribune* readers." Vincent was an American journalist and published a column called "Courtship and Marriage" in the *New York Evening World*. This column was carried by other papers across the United States. The *Tribune* appears to have been the only paper that published "Problems of the Heart" in Canada.

"Problems of the Heart" was a letters column. Vincent received letters from men and women living in communities across the prairies, although the majority were Winnipeggers. Based on some of her comments, she must have lived in Winnipeg for at least part of the time. In 1926 she was asked if she was a Manitoban and she answered, yes, that although she owned land on Vancouver Island, she was here in Winnipeg "problemating."

Before the 1920s the usual school-leaving age had been fourteen, the point at which many young people passed into the adult world and were expected to find a job and contribute to the family income. Once young people were working, issues like marriage and boyfriends or girlfriends came up. In the 1920s this slowly began to change as jobs were hard to find and more young people stayed in school, hoping to find better jobs with higher wages by getting more education and perhaps even finishing high school. In Winnipeg the school division followed a nationwide trend and established a junior high school. After a successful trial at Earl Grey School, junior high or intermediate schools were started in the Lord Selkirk and Lord Roberts areas in 1920.[1] New curriculum was developed to challenge the intermediate students, who could become bored if the material used in grades one to six was simply taught again. Staying in school probably meant that young men and women were thrown together more in social situations than if they had gone to work.

Younger girls and women, aged fourteen to their early twenties, seem to have been Betty Vincent's particular area of concern, and her columns were overwhelmingly devoted to females in this age group. By far the majority of letters published asked about relations with the opposite sex. Her answers to a list of questions sent by a fifteen-year-old were typical of the common sense and conservative advice she gave. She told the young person that fifteen is the age at which one begins to be grown up. She said not to let boys put their arm around her and not to go for car rides with older boys. She counselled the girl not to try to get a boy away from another girl, reasoning that he had some rights, too, and should be allowed to choose whom he wants to be with.

A twenty-year-old wrote that she had been asked to marry by someone five years older. Vincent told her she must not keep him dangling but give him an answer. But she said to think carefully before turning him down: "a good home and a good husband are the best things a woman can have in this world."[2]

However, as a professional woman herself, she frequently advised young women to get a profession like teaching or journalism so they could earn their own living. Asked about a choice between teaching and being a hairdresser, she emphasized that teaching was a profession in which the person could do much good. She was, then, counselling women to be independent and to do something useful with their lives.

Vincent had very little time for adulterers. Her correspondents sometimes wrote that they were involved with someone who was married and with whom they were very much in love. In one case she advised the young woman to give the married man a "good clip in the face, which is what he deserves."[3] In another she warns a young letter writer not to run away with a married man because "men frequently tire of a relationship that is not sanctioned by society."[4] In answer to another writer, whose married friend was having an affair with a married man and wanted to know what she should say, Vincent told her to leave her friend to her fate: "She deserves the punishment she will get and you'll get no thanks for interfering."[5]

In matters of dress and appearance, on the other hand, Vincent was fairly liberal. She was positive about the new fashions and the young people trying them out. Sophisticated youth, she wrote, "are modern, they are daring, but somehow they are nice, with their smart shingled hair, slim gowns and their spirit of fun and fair play."[6] In November 1926 she wrote to one of her correspondents who had asked about cutting her hair: "I say cut it. I believe in being up to date and if the fashion says 'shingled heads' you will always find me with a shingled head."[7]

But Vincent's advice about relationships was conservative, and this may have been motivated simply by a desire to protect young women from some pretty dire consequences. In 1920s Canada a marriage breakup or the pregnancy of a single woman were arguably much more destructive and difficult events than they are now. Women who became pregnant while they were unmarried

Detail of the 20 November 1926 Winnipeg Tribune *featuring Betty Vincent's "Problems of the Heart" column along with hat fashion tips and other articles directed at female readers. University of Manitoba Archives,* Winnipeg Tribune *fonds.*

could face harsh treatment from their families and society. If they asked for help from a religious charity or from the relatively new secular Children's Aid Society, they might well have their children taken from them and put up for adoption.[8] Vincent never discussed actual sexual intercourse, but its risks in an era when birth control was not widely practised underlay much of the advice she gave.

In August 1921, two girls aged sixteen asked if it was correct behaviour to go to River Park with boys. A new dance pavilion had opened at the park in the spring of that year. Vincent said they were too young to go to public dance halls with boys unless they were accompanied by an older married couple.

Another young woman said that her parents had told her to stop "hanging around" at the front gate when her boyfriend brought her home at night. She asked if it was all right to ask him to come and sit on the porch with her. Vincent said, "It is not proper to linger at the gate, neither should you ask him to the porch at a late hour."[9] The same writer had asked about getting married. She was eighteen and her boyfriend was nineteen. Vincent answered that they were too young and likely not truly in love. Her advice to most teens was to wait and see a variety of people so that they would be sure of their feelings when they finally did marry and settle down.

Sometimes writers just wanted to vent their feelings about the opposite sex. One young man complained about "girls who are all made up and perfumed."[10] Vincent said there were plenty of nice girls in Winnipeg, and "if he wished to find one he could."[11] A female letter writer complained about stylish fellows who "go around with one of those things—some call them moustaches—their hair in a pomp [pompadour] and soaked in perfumed hair oil, and other oddities of their race including the eternal cigarette."[12] The same writer, who seemed disgusted with everyone, complained that one seldom saw a "dolled up" girl without a few boys to dance with her "at the beaches or the dance places or anywhere."[13]

The shadow of the war hung over some of the letters Vincent received. One man, a veteran whose funds "are low just now," wrote in 1922, wanting to know what a wedding would cost. The chances are good that he was unemployed or working only part-time because many returned men were out of work. Vincent told him that a simple wedding in the minister's house would cost fifteen dollars for the licence, ring, and the clergyman's fee. If he married in a church, the ex-soldier would need to rent a car for about ten dollars, and wear a dark suit and black shoes. As for the cost of setting up house, she said it was a topic too complicated to go into in the column, but renting and furnishing a house would likely cost close to $1,000.

Another returned soldier, who had been invalided home, said he sometimes saw a woman he had known before enlisting and of whom he was fond. He wanted to get married but he was waiting to ask her. Vincent told him she would never know he loved her if he did not tell her, and warned him not to wait too long.

A war widow who was getting remarried wrote to ask if it would be correct to wear white. Her first wedding had been very simple, but now she wanted a proper wedding dress and had been told that that was wrong. Vincent answered that any light colour would be acceptable and that she should wear a hat and

Assiniboine Park, 1925. One of the many Winnipeg places young people could meet. City of Winnipeg Archives, A53 File 11 Item 1.

could have two attendants. Then she added, with unusual feeling that suggests she may have lost someone in the war, "Don't efface the memory of your husband entirely—you had in your first wedding, with your soldier husband and wartime romance, something that must have been infinitely more worthwhile than orange blossoms and white dresses."[14]

"Spooning" or necking was a frequent topic in Vincent's columns and in popular journalism in general. Public kissing and hugging in parked cars, city parks, or other places was more common than it had been before the Great War, and it probably took place in public because it would not be tolerated by the parents of most young women in their own homes or even on the front porch. Answering a young man who felt disillusioned by "petting parties" or house parties where couples "necked," Vincent wrote that girls who think their popularity depends on their being a "good sport" and men who spend their evenings kissing women they despise "both lack character and are a good match for each other."[15]

The daily Winnipeg papers reported some complaints about the spooning going on. In June 1924 some of the homeowners on St. Mary's Road complained to the police about people parking their cars in front of their houses at night to spoon. They wanted a bylaw to prevent this but the St. Vital municipal council refused. The local chief of police reported that spooners always saw him coming and drove off before he could approach them. Portage Avenue west of Deer Lodge Hospital was another favourite spot to park, and police in St. James received complaints about parked couples smoking and drinking and necking. Lovers who went to River Park at the foot of Osborne Street encountered a familiar Winnipeg problem. In the "Pet Peeves" column of the *Tribune*, someone asked: "Why oh why do the mosquitoes stick around you when you're out spooning with your best girl in River Park?"[16]

People became quite inventive in finding a place to spoon. In January 1924 it was reported in the paper that it was now a common practice for young couples to sit in the CNR station waiting room as though waiting for a train to leave. When the train was called, they would go to the stairs to the platform and kiss and embrace warmly as though one of them was going away. A few minutes after the train pulled out, they would be back in the waiting room, waiting for the next opportunity to legitimately smooch in public. The railroad staff said that this was a very common practice. The strategy was effective because the station saw as many as seven passenger trains a day.

In 1922 a sixteen-year-old described to Vincent what was for her a difficult problem. She had a boyfriend and her father caught them kissing on the front porch. He was very angry and told the young man to never come around again. She said that "this boy said he wouldn't go with a girl unless she let him spoon and that nowadays if a girl is such a prude no one can kiss her, no one will go with her." Vincent emphasized the girl's right to decide for herself and tried to strengthen her self-confidence. She also appealed to the reader's assumed social prejudices when she wrote: "What this boy told you is probably true of his class, but it is not true of all young people."[17]

Vincent wrote for the *Tribune* until 1930 but after 1927 the column did not appear every day. This coincided roughly with the time she began to do handwriting analysis based on the script in the letters she received. People might not have been as interested in that form of advice. However, there is no doubt that she had some impact in the lives of many young people struggling with how to relate to the opposite sex in the changing world of the 1920s.

Prohibition

One of the most significant reforms instituted by the Norris Liberals had been the introduction of Prohibition in Manitoba in 1916. Yet, on June 22, 1923, just seven years later, Manitobans voted overwhelmingly to abandon Prohibition and institute a system of government-controlled liquor sales. A month later, on July 25, the new Manitoba Liquor Control Act was passed, ending the Prohibition era in Manitoba. The anti-Prohibition movement that developed in the early 1920s was a symptom of the fundamental changes that were taking place in the province.

In the provincial elections of 1914 and 1915, the Liberals had allied themselves with a number of groups that supported Prohibition, including the Social Service Council, various Temperance organizations, and representatives of pro-Temperance churches such as the Methodists and Presbyterians. After their huge victory on August 6, 1915—they won forty of forty-seven seats—the Liberal Party asked the Social Service Council to draft temperance legislation. The Social Service Council set up a committee that soon recommended using Conservative Premier Hugh John Macdonald's Prohibition Act, passed during his brief time in office in 1900. Macdonald's successor, Premier Rodmond Roblin, had never passed the bill into law. His policy was to instead control the liquor trade with licensing and regulations and leave the individual municipalities to decide whether to completely ban liquor by using the so-called local option. Roblin always claimed he was a temperance supporter who respected the freedom of individuals to decide whether to drink or not.

Early in 1916 Tobias Norris's government followed the Social Service Council's advice and resurrected the Macdonald legislation, and passed it into law as the Manitoba Temperance Act.[18] Under the Act it was possible to buy alcohol for religious and medical purposes, and doctors were allowed to prescribe it. Alcohol did form a legitimate part of a doctor's resources in the years when the pharmaceutical industry was still in its early stages. Some doctors, however, took advantage of this provision and issued hundreds of prescriptions to people who were not necessarily sick. In 1920 the Temperance Act was amended to restrict doctors to issuing a total of 100 prescriptions per month for twelve ounces of hard liquor or a twenty-four-ounce bottle of wine or a case of malt beverages. Physicians were provided with a booklet of 100 prescription forms to be used each month. Some doctors did not comply, and during 1920, after the amendment passed, sixteen medical doctors, one of whom had issued 10,000 prescriptions for liquor to his patients in a single month, had their licences suspended for various periods of time. But the newly amended Act did not end the sale of liquor by prescription in drugstores. In January 1922 alone, 16,381 legitimate prescriptions were issued for 1,406 gallons of liquor. Many doctors were unhappy about what they called their "bar tender" role, and the College of Physicians and Surgeons referred to the situation as "an embarrassment."[19]

Support for Prohibition was tested in 1920 in a referendum vote on whether the ban on importing liquor into Manitoba should be extended. In 1917 the federal government had passed a wartime order-in-council prohibiting the importation of liquor into provinces with a Temperance Act like Manitoba's, interprovincial trade being the responsibility of the Dominion. This ban, which sought to prevent people from circumventing the law by ordering liquor through the mail, lasted from April 1918 until December 1919. The Federal Temperance Act was amended to give the provinces the power to extend this ban if public support was demonstrated in a referendum. In Manitoba, a referendum was held on October 25, 1920, and the extension of the ban on imported liquor was approved with a majority of 13,000 votes. But the victory seemed suspect because only slightly more than half of the eligible voters bothered to cast a ballot. The ban simply did not affect many people: only the wealthy could afford to import cases of liquor or wine.

Following the 1920 referendum there were signs of a new attitude toward Prohibition. At a meeting of the Great War Veterans Association (GWVA) in January 1921, a motion was passed supporting the establishment of a Moderation League. This new group, modelled on similar organizations in British Columbia and Ontario, would work for an end to Prohibition. League supporters wanted to replace complete Prohibition with a regulated liquor trade carried on through government stores. The league was organized at a meeting in the Royal Alexandra Hotel later in January 1921. Those present passed a resolution to "support all legislation designed to advance the welfare of the community which does not interfere unduly with or curtail personal liberty, legitimate social customs and recreation for the people."[20]

The secretary of the new group and the man who, more than anyone, made it a success, was J. Kensington Downes. Born in England, he had a career there as a teacher, headmaster, and professional football player. He had come to Winnipeg in 1912 and he served in the Great War as an officer in the Canadian 11th Railway Battalion. After the war he became an active member of the Great War Veterans Association. In 1922 he would win one of the ten Winnipeg seats in the provincial Legislature and sit as an independent.

Downes became the secretary of the Moderation League when it was founded, and by the fall of 1921 he had already enrolled 16,000 members. He placed ads in the daily papers with a membership form people could clip and mail in with their one-dollar membership fee. Echoing the resolution passed by the GWVA, the ad stated that the Moderation League stood for "true temperance and personal liberty and against prohibition, class legislation, undue interference with legitimate activities, habits, customs and recreations of the individual."[21]

The argument that Prohibition infringed upon personal liberty must have resonated with many of the young men who had just fought a war, they believed, to safeguard that very thing. The mention of "class legislation" was aimed at working-class people who often were not strong supporters of Prohibition and were aware that, unlike them, people with money could always get a drink.

In January 1922, at the first annual meeting of the league, President Colonel William Grassie reported that a petition calling for an end to Prohibition had 18,000 signatures. The executive was aiming to have in the region of 50,000 names to prove that Manitobans were "absolutely tired" of the current liquor legislation. Other speakers said that the law was inefficient because it was not stopping the liquor trade carried on by bootleggers, while it was making criminals of honest citizens. Downes reported on his work and made the point that most of the people breaking the existing law were actually in favour of temperance in the form of moderate drinking. The question, he said, was a moral, not a legal, one, and abuse of liquor should be tackled with education, not law enforcement.

These were not new arguments but they had never been made so forcefully in the past by people not obviously connected to the liquor industry. The Temperance movement fought back by forming a Better Citizenship League in the fall of 1921 to campaign in favour of maintaining the existing law. Shortly after their annual meeting, the Moderation League's petition calling for a referendum on the question was presented to the Legislature with 53,000 signatures. Joseph Bernier and Joseph Hamlin, both former Conservative members sitting now as independents, presented the document. Bernier, in a speech that lasted for an hour and a half, made all the classic arguments against Prohibition, saying the proposed change to a government-controlled system of liquor stores would drive bootleggers out of business and provide a new source of income for the government from liquor taxes.[22]

However, MLAs had a good deal to say about the heavy-handed administration of the Act. One member said the evidence suggested that the Temperance Act was oppressive: "You see small districts paying 10 or 12 thousand dollars in fines in the space of a month." Many people were being charged under the Act. In Winnipeg there were weekly prosecutions for infractions under the Temperance Act on the day referred to as "hooch day" in City Police Court. In the month of October 1921 alone, 201 cases were tried and $10,741 in fines were collected. Individuals were picked up on the street for carrying liquor. The papers carried the story of Larry Dolan, who was caught in the CPR station on New Year's Eve with a bottle in his pocket. "Stool pigeons framed up on me," was his defence.[23] The fine for most infractions was $200, an amount that would not discourage a real bootlegger but one that could amount to a week's wages for many drinkers.

The Act was enforced by a small staff in the Temperance Department and by the Manitoba Provincial Police, established in March 1921 and commanded by Colonel John G. Rattray. They were a force of sixty-four men, fifty-five of whom were returned soldiers. Rattray's men were responsible for enforcing not only the Temperance Act but also the Game, Motor Vehicle, School Attendance, and Public Health acts. Local headquarters under the command of inspectors were established in Brandon, Minnedosa, Portage, Dauphin, and Morden, and individual constables were stationed in many smaller towns.

In 1921 the chief inspector for the Temperance Act, then in his fifth year of operations, reported that in the previous twelve months there had been 740 convictions under the Act, resulting in $121,826 in fines. This was compared with 610 convictions in 1919 with fines of $105,465. These enormous amounts are equivalent to between $2 and $3 million in today's money. The addition of the Provincial Police constables seemed to be having an effect.

The beginning of Prohibition in the United States in January 1920 opened up a vast new market for Canadians. As early as April of that year the Provincial Police arrested three men in the Turtle Mountain area for importing fifty cases of liquor into Manitoba from Saskatchewan, where wholesale liquor warehouses were still legal. The men brought the booze into Manitoba with the intention of taking it across the border and selling it in North Dakota. The Turtle Mountain area became a regular route for smuggling. Most drivers were armed, as were their American customers, and the police in the United States took to using machine guns.

One group of smugglers included W. Ironsides, whose father had been a partner in the Gordon Ironsides & Fares meat-packing company. Ironsides had sixty cases of liquor delivered to his house at 94 Roslyn Road during a brief period when liquor imports were legal in 1918 and he and a "ring" of collaborators had been selling it off. Ironsides himself was stopped by United

Still at 251 Boyd Avenue, 18 September 1922. Archives of Manitoba, L.B. Foote fonds, 662, N2262.

States officials at the border when he tried to drive an automobile loaded with cases of whisky into the United States. All Ironsides's colleagues pleaded guilty, something that Provincial Police commander Colonel Rattray said he regretted, since a trial with cross-examinations might have revealed more names.

A good deal of the liquor smuggled into the United States was homebrew. In June 1920 alone there were 180 prosecutions for operating stills, many in Winnipeg. In October 1920 a local man was charged with having a still in his house on Machray Avenue and with storing liquor for sale. At the same time seven other men were fined a total of $2,300 for operating stills in the city and at Ridgeville.

Bootlegging was sometimes a family business. In September 1921, Police Magistrate Robert Noble complained that "the docket has been choked with Galsky cases for the past month."[24] Mrs. Moses Galsky, her husband, son, and two sons-in-law had all been charged with selling liquor from their house at 312 Selkirk Avenue. At one of the trials Charles Galsky was also charged with assaulting a witness who had informed on Charles's mother.[25]

City hotels were routinely fined for selling liquor or beer with more than 2.5 percent alcohol content. The Sutherland, Sherman, City, Leland, and Royal Albert hotels were all fined for having liquor for sale on their premises in September 1921. It was said that the large hotels like the Fort Garry and the Royal Alexandra were not often fined even though they, too, would sell a guest a drink.

By December some of Rattray's men were accused of taking bribes. There was a lot of money to be made in bootlegging, and bribes were no doubt cheaper than paying the fines. Several constables were fired at the time. Multiple charges of bribery had also been laid against M.L. McPhail, a former inspector for the Temperance Office.

During the 1921 estimates process in the provincial Legislature, the Temperance Act was reviewed. The enforcement staff did not seem to enjoy strong support from MLAs. The charges of corruption probably played a part in this. As well, the methods used by the Provincial Police seem to have been heavy-handed, and Rattray had to answer questions about individuals being searched in the street without a warrant. Some MLAs were also alarmed at the large amounts of money being taken out of rural districts in the form of fines. They showed their displeasure by cutting the combined $245,000 budgets of the two offices by $36,000, an amount equal to the total budget of the Temperance Department.[26] Rattray was forced to lay off constables, and in the fall of 1921 he closed the Portage la Prairie and Morden offices.

Colonel Rattray got into a different sort of trouble in January 1922 when, during a speech made at a Lion's Club meeting, he expressed the opinion that the crime rate was increasing in Manitoba because so many "middle Europeans" had settled here. He said that 95 percent of bootleggers were Jews and that the Jews, the Japanese, and the Prussians—a novel group of allies— were engaged in a sinister conspiracy to undermine the forces of right. A *Free Press* reporter attended the luncheon meeting and published a report of the speech. At first it seemed that Rattray would not suffer any consequences for his comments. The *Tribune* did mention the speech in the editorial on January 7. Under the title "Race Prejudice," the editor wrote, "The outburst of Colonel Rattray though highly unbecoming in an official may be passed over." It was likely, said the *Tribune*, that Rattray was sore about being outwitted by some Jewish or Japanese criminals.

Then on January 10 a delegation from the Anti-Defamation League of the B'nai B'rith went to see Premier Norris to ask what the government's attitude was toward these statements about Jews made by a public servant. The next day the *Tribune* published a very different comment on the issue: that theories about Jewish conspiracies should be "upheld by a police official is an alarming thing." The Jews, said the paper, were persecuted by the police in Russia and Prussia, but "to have a British law enforcement officer hint at suspiciously similar standards is unprecedented, and a reassurance must be given that it is not the policy of those who have administration of the law to arouse class hatred that may result in insecurity of public peace."

MLAs took up the case during meetings of the Public Accounts committee. John Queen asked Attorney General Thomas Johnson if Rattray had been taken to task for his comments. Johnson said Rattray was interviewed and it was concluded that the newspaper report of his talk was not accurate. But the Labour members did not allow the matter to drop, and at the end of February George Armstrong moved that Rattray be summoned to be questioned by the committee and that the *Free Press* reporter be subpoenaed to appear.

Rattray, faced with determined questioning from Queen and Conservative MLA John Haig, finally admitted that the *Free Press* account was accurate. When asked for his source for the 95 percent figure, he said his claim was that 95 percent of liquor wholesalers in North America were Jewish and his source was private. Rattray agreed he might have used the phrases "sinister world wide conspiracy" and "sons of Abraham."[27] The *Free Press* reporter, a man called Spencer, said his story was based on shorthand notes and was accurate. Some committee members defended Rattray, and after the meeting had "gone around in circles" for a while, the matter was dropped.[28]

On February 6 *Canadian Finance* agreed with Rattray that the crime rate was increasing because of the number of "foreigners" in the country. The paper then repeated some old and well-worn arguments about immigrants. Many foreigners had no feeling for Canada, said the paper, but were living here strictly for economic reasons, earning money that they would then take home. In their minds they were still at home in their countries of origin. The answer to this was the school, "the only possible melting pot" where children and their parents could learn to become Canadians.[29] The incident revealed the extent of anti-Semitic feeling in the city.

Rattray was not disciplined for his speech, but a few months later he was fired for different reasons. Southern Manitoba had been suffering from a series of bank robberies perpetrated by American gangs who crossed the border to commit the crimes and then returned the way they had come. In October the Provincial Police got a tip that a gang from Minot was on its way to rob the bank in Pipestone. Rattray could not be located to organize a suitable reception for the robbers because he was at a meeting of the board of the Elmhurst Golf Club. A lone constable was able to stop the robbery, but the gang escaped. Rattray and one of his senior inspectors were dismissed following an inquiry.

In the midst of this, Prohibition remained a topic of dispute. In the provincial election of July 1922, the Liberals were defeated and the United Farmers of Manitoba succeeded in electing the largest number of members. The Moderation League had gotten all city candidates to support their call for a referendum on the Prohibition question. During the election Downes campaigned in support of a referendum. There was support among working-class people for abolishing Prohibition, and Labour politician and temperance supporter William Ivens was booed at a Labour meeting during the election when he spoke in favour of a continued ban on liquor. The Moderation League had one Labour MLA, Matthew J. Stanbridge of St. Clements, on their executive. It was heavily supported by ex-army officers—it also had three colonels and one major on the executive.

In January 1923 the Moderation League submitted yet another petition, this time with 76,000 signatures, to the Legislature. The petition included a draft bill establishing government control of liquor trade. The League proposed a three-person commission appointed by the government to supervise the sale of liquor through government liquor stores. Any persons over twenty-one who purchased a one-dollar permit could shop in the stores and, once paid for, the liquor would be delivered to the buyer, wrapped in brown paper, by commission staff. If a municipality held a local vote and the result was to not have a government liquor store, none would be opened there. Residents of that municipality would purchase liquor elsewhere. Penalties for infractions would be not less than fifty dollars, and the surpluses produced by the commission would be divided equally between the Province and the municipalities. This proposed legislation is essentially what was later passed into law.

As a Progressive, Premier Bracken believed in politicians' carrying out the will of the people, and so even though he and many of the United Farmers members were temperance supporters, he agreed to a referendum to be held on June 22, 1923. Bracken campaigned for the "no" side in the period leading up to the vote. At the same time a separate group, said to represent "the liquor interests," began to campaign for a second referendum on the question of allowing hotels to sell beer and wine in their restaurants. Bracken decided to hold two separate referenda on these two questions, and July 11 was set for the beer and wine vote.

On June 15 there was a large Prohibition meeting that filled the Walker Theatre. James H. Ashdown, a Methodist and long-time temperance campaigner, said that businessmen like him wanted to see money spent on clothes and food rather than wasted on liquor. Clergy spoke about their own experiences as pastors, dealing with homes that were now free of drunkenness and children who had never seen a parent intoxicated. Just as the Moderation League argued that personal moderation in drinking was a British trait, the prohibitionists argued, "We are all proud to be British and ready to claim our rights," but that it "was the true British spirit to sacrifice personal liberty when it came to standing in defence of the weak."[30]

About the same time there was a women's meeting at St. Stephen's Church on Broadway Avenue. The hall was filled to capacity to hear Jesse Kirk, a teacher who, the year before, had been the first woman elected to Winnipeg City Council. She spoke in favour of the Moderation League's bill. On the negative side was Mildred McMurray, who had recently been called to the bar and would have a long career as a lawyer in private practice and then as an attorney for the Child Welfare Division of the Manitoba government.

Mildred McMurray, 4 January 1951. Winnipeg Tribune photo. She was the first female lawyer in Manitoba.

Jesse Kirk congratulated those religious groups that had stayed out of the debate—the Jews, Roman Catholics, and Anglicans—and criticized the Methodists and Presbyterians who were deeply committed to the temperance cause and seemed to feel that they were therefore better Christians. This brought a laugh from the audience. She told of a man who was sent to jail because he could not pay the fine for having two bottles of homebrew in his house. She asked if anyone on the platform at the meeting had not had two bottles of homebrew at some time or other. She did not get an answer, but there was more laughter from the audience. Kirk had some harsh words for the officials who were administering the Temperance Act and the vast amount of fine money they were extracting from Manitobans.

Mildred McMurray spoke against the proposed change. She stated the real and only important issue was that the Moderation League was intending to reintroduce liquor into the province for the purpose of sales. Women had to decide if that would improve the quality of Manitobans' homes because that was the standard by which the province would be judged. She said she had experienced life with liquor and without, and she felt that the Temperance Act was working well. She questioned the statement that the Moderation League proposal would restore personal liberty to Manitobans. McMurray argued that the income that was promised the government would make under the new system was illusory because millions of dollars would be drained out of the Manitoba economy that might have been spent on more necessary things. The average home was getting along very well without liquor, and had many comforts that would otherwise not be possible if money was being spent on liquor.

The lively meeting, which had been punctuated with interruptions from the audience, came to an end with the chairwoman, Liberal MLA Edith Rogers, declaring that she had been convinced by the temperance arguments.

Voters gave overwhelming support to the Moderation League's proposal for government-controlled liquor sales—107,609 for and 67,879 against. The support was strongest in St. Boniface and Winnipeg, where only a few polls in the Wolseley area—Chestnut Street, Home Street, Basswood Place—voted to maintain Prohibition. In Brandon the vote was for government control in 1922. In Portage la

Edith Rogers, 1921. Archives of Manitoba. She was the first woman elected to Manitoba's legislature.

Prairie and the rural areas south and west of there, the vote was strongly in favour of continuing the ban on liquor sales. But even in the rural areas, the dry vote was not as large as it had been in 1916 when Prohibition was first approved.

The new Liquor Commission was appointed soon after. Former mayor Richard Waugh was the chair and would remain in that job until his death in 1938. Waugh was an experienced public servant, having worked on the construction of the Shoal Lake Aqueduct and, after the war, as one of the Allied commissioners appointed to administer the territory of the Saar Basin in Germany. The two assistant commissioners were William P. Dutton, a lawyer who had owned several different lumber companies and had been president of the pro-Bracken Winnipeg Progressive Association, and William J. Bulman, owner with his brother of a large printing company and former president of the Conservative Association of Manitoba.

Temperance leaders were dismayed by the result. William R. Wood, the leader of the Prohibition campaign, said the results were "very disappointing," and he maintained that "where it has been adequately enforced it [Prohibition] has been of inestimable value to the community . . . it has created conditions at least 80 percent better than they were before 1916." Wood, a Presbyterian minister, was a Liberal MLA and secretary of the United Farmers of Manitoba. He maintained that the results would teach Temperance people that only "sleepless and eternal vigilance can defend us from the invasion of the liquor power." He said that he was sure the Temperance movement would "never disband and never rest till the province is freed from the curse."[31]

But this kind of strong conviction clearly no longer struck a chord with the majority of Manitobans. Times had changed and even some of the Temperance leaders were resigned to the new situation. Reverend Robert S. Laidlaw of Knox Church said that although he regretted the results very much, they were "decisive enough, and there is nothing for it but for the people to make the best of circumstances."[32]

This change was significant and interesting in that it overturned the decision of only six years before. Much had changed in that time. Veterans also had an influence. Men returning from the front had learned to drink in the army, if they had not had the habit before. It was the practice in the Canadian Army to pass out a rum ration every morning—something that even Temperance leader Reverend Charles Gordon came to recognize, during his time as a chaplain, as an important way for the men to keep their spirits up.

In 1916 many people had considered that support of the Temperance referendum was patriotic and would help the war effort. This motivation no longer existed in the early 1920s. In general there was less support for the social gospel ideals like Temperance that had done so much to get the Liberals elected in 1915. Many of the important things the social gospel movement wanted to achieve had been accomplished. The influence the Protestant churches and groups like the Temperance movement had had was slowly diminishing. One example of this change can be seen in the work of George Chipman, editor of the *Grain Growers' Guide*. He and the writers he employed had tremendous influence in the western farm community, championing various social gospel causes. Yet in the 1920s there was less support for the ideas Chipman supported. Historian Ian McPherson, writing about Chipman, said, "As the twenties progressed the causes of the social gospel, the labour movement, prohibition, the women's movement, and progressive education declined, achieved limited objectives, or found progress difficult to achieve. Continuing poverty for some people, consumerism for a few, the fading of post-war idealism, and the rebirth of widespread cynicism reduced enthusiasm for these causes."[33]

Portage Avenue in 1920, looking west from Donald Street, showing Eaton's and Dunlop's Drugs. Archives of Manitoba, McAdam fonds, 440.

CHAPTER 9

New Entertainments

In the 1920s social life in Winnipeg began to change, influenced by changes taking place in the outside world. Movies, radio, and magazines brought news of what was happening in the great cities such as New York, and a transition began. New kinds of social events, quite different from the dances and entertainments Winnipeggers had enjoyed, marked the changes. One of these non-traditional diversions was the Gyro Club Mardi Gras, which was held as a fundraiser at the Royal Alexandra Hotel each year from 1925 until 1929. Just like Mardi Gras or "fat Tuesday" celebrated in other cities, the Winnipeg version took place just before the beginning of Lent as a last chance to have fun before the pre-Easter season. Many people did still acknowledge Lent, with its expectation of less fun and frivolity.

The Gyro Club was one of the relatively new men's service clubs that, like Kiwanis and Rotary, attracted many new members during the 1920s. Many were younger men who were war veterans. They worked on raising money for good causes like the Fresh Air Camp—a summer camp on Lake Winnipeg for underprivileged children—and providing for needy families of returned soldiers. The club had its headquarters in the Royal Alexandra Hotel and the hotel turned over its facilities for their major annual fundraising event.

The Gyro Club Mardi Gras Carnival was a way to brighten up the long Winnipeg winter and have some fun as well as support the club's charities.

Because Winnipeg was at one end of the Pine to Palm highway that had the city of New Orleans at its opposite end, it was felt that a Mardi Gras celebration held at the same time as the famous one in the southern city would support Mayor Webb's campaign to attract more American tourism. In 1926 some club members travelled to New Orleans to see what features of the New Orleans event could be duplicated in Winnipeg. They specifically tied their event to the "Pine to Palms" tourism promotion in their advertising. In some years, executives from other Gyro clubs in the United States visited during the Mardi Gras, and the international president was in Winnipeg in 1926. Winnipegger Gordon Stovel was elected as international president at the end of the 1920s, and at least one Gyro convention took place in the city in the early 1930s.

The Mardi Gras in Winnipeg represented a shift in what younger Winnipeggers found acceptable and entertaining. It put an emphasis on chorus lines and entertainment by young women in slightly risqué costumes. In the weeks leading up to the first annual event in 1925, the society pages of the *Tribune* carried tasteful photos of attractive young women who would be performing as dancers. These were local women, wives, or friends of the Gyro members. The idea of participating in a fundraiser was not new, but the chorus lines were a little more daring than the sort of entertainments usually seen at social events. The dancing symbolized not only the liberation young women were experiencing in the 1920s, but also the increase in the objectification of female bodies that was also a feature of the decade.

Ned Wayburn, the New York producer who directed many of the Ziegfeld Follies productions, was the author of *The Art of Stage Dancing* (1925), a guide to all aspects of professional dancing as taught in his dance school. In his introduction, he wrote:

> The Follies, the Frolics, the Scandals, the Music Box, the Vanities, the Passing Shows—by whatever name the modern revue is spread before an eager public, the basis of its appeal is always the same. And when the Junior Leagues—the various charity organizations and the social and college clubs of our cities stage a performance that shall appeal to the interest of their public, and consequently gather in the shekels to their coffers, these amateur organizations turn naturally to music and dance and spectacle as the mediums with the widest appeal; an appeal to both the performer and the spectator.[1]

It is possible that the organizers of the Mardi Gras had Wayburn's book or one like it to help in training the dancers.

The main dining room of the Royal Alexandra was reserved for stage shows like the routine of the debutante chorus, who were described as being like dancers at a Greenwich Village Frolic or a Midnight Frolic. A Greenwich Village Frolic was a show put on by artists' models as a fundraiser, and "Midnight Frolic" was the name given to floor shows at the nightclub on the roof of New York's Amsterdam Theater, presented by Florenz Ziegfeld using his Ziegfeld Follies showgirls. These references to faraway New York likely demonstrate the results of people's listening to radio broadcasts from the large American cities and watching Hollywood movies about the Follies like *The Follies Girl* (1919), *Pollie of the Follies* (1922), and *Pretty Ladies* (1925). As well, many of the club's members had served overseas and would have enjoyed big musical shows with plenty of chorus girls while on leave in Paris and London. The Ziegfeld Follies were elaborate stage shows with young women dressed in

Winnipeg Tribune *from 26 February 1927, showcasing Gyro Club's Mardi Gras events. It displays the shift in the type of entertainments that were newly acceptable to young Winnipegers. University of Manitoba Archives,* Winnipeg Tribune *fonds.*

fantastic costumes, with a fair amount of nudity. The association of young women from Winnipeg with the Follies girls definitely introduced something new to the social life of the city.

In 1928 the Mardi Gras added a beauty contest to the event. The contest itself took place at the Capitol Theatre, a large movie house on Portage Avenue and Donald Street. For several nights, contestants would appear on stage in elegant gowns, and the winner would be the woman who received the loudest audience applause. The grand prize was a $100 gown from Holt Renfrew. Other prizes included admission tickets to the Royal Alexandra event and tickets for the automobile draw. A 1926 Studebaker Erskine 6 sedan was given away. Ellsie Meade was chosen as Mardi Gras Queen and she was crowned by Edmund Kagy of Cleveland, the international secretary of the Gyro clubs, at the opening night of the Mardi Gras.

The Gyro Mardi Gras had a number of committees, and the wives and girlfriends of the members were involved in planning and putting on the event. In most years a professional dance teacher was involved in preparing the dancers. The Mardi Gras was all indoors for obvious reasons in February. There was a Mardi Gras parade in the hotel with people in costume following Rex, the King of Misrule. He was preceded by women of all ages throwing flowers in his path. There was a casino where people could gamble with Gyroubles that could be purchased at a rate of 10,000 for a dollar. Gyroubles could not be cashed in—the money exchanged for them went to charity. Thousands of Gyroubles were won and lost, but people were warned not to try to use them to pay for the taxi. The games included Housie Housie, an Australian game similar to Bingo. It was one of many gambling games played by soldiers during the Great War, and the young men in the club who had been in the army in France would have recognized it. There were booths with different kinds of midway games operated by the Gyro members and their wives and girlfriends, who were known as Gyrettes. People won Kewpie dolls, electric lamps, and boxes of candy, and a fortune teller read palms. The Mardi Gras also offered a regular dance with the music supplied by the Canary Cottage and Country Club orchestras. Two weeks later the club held a cabaret in the Royal Alexandra dining room where the performers from the recent Mardi Gras entertained again and were all given compacts in appreciation.

The young men who belonged to the Gyro Club and the young women who took part in the entertainments were some of Winnipeg's "sophisticated youth," as Betty Vincent would have called them. Interested in having fun, they also had a social conscience and raised money for good causes. But the

Mardi Gras was a very different event from the usual balls and charity dances traditionally held at the Royal Alexandra and is an indication of the tastes and attitudes of a new generation of the Winnipeg elite. The Mardi Gras attracted 11,000 people in its first year and similar numbers in subsequent years. In 1929 the event was changed and had a rodeo theme but was equally popular. The onset of the Depression undoubtedly made successful fundraising events much more difficult, and after 1929 the club did not hold another fundraiser until 1932, when they sponsored a real rodeo at the Amphitheatre.

Fashion

Two hallmarks of the 1920s—short or bobbed hair, and short, simple dress-es—were in evidence in Winnipeg. Voluptuous curves and swirls of beautiful hair piled on the head were definitely passé. Dresses were simple and had simple lines to show that the woman's body was the "same all the way down," as one fashion writer put it. Another researcher describes the dresses as "gauzy, strappy, short flapper costumes that bared the chest, shoulders and back, designed to twirl scandalously in motion, revealing legs all but naked in the new flesh-coloured rayon stockings."[2] Stockings were worn rolled down to reveal the knees. "Flappers" were said to be the first women to have shown their knees in public since the time of the Roman Empire.

The flapper style was immortalized by magazine illustrator John Held, who put flappers on the cover of *Life* and in the pages of the *New Yorker*. It was an urban style suitable for women who were working and active. Long, flowing dresses and complicated corsets that took a long time to put on were manageable for women who spent a lot of time in their homes. But women's lives were changing in the 1920s. Many women had worked during the war and took on responsibilities outside the home. Not all of them gave up their jobs when the men came home, although many were forced to do so. They needed comfortable, simple clothes in which to work.

The new simpler styles lent themselves to mass production, and fewer women sewed their own clothes or employed a seamstress to fit dresses to their bodies. Standard sizes were the result of the mass production of clothes. Suddenly women were motivated to be slim so they would fit into one of the six available sizes. A more active, sporty life and dieting began to be the norm. North American styles still originated in Paris and the reigning French de-signers turned out clothes that they then sold to U.S. clothing manufacturers to be mass-produced. The new designs appeared in department stores like Eaton's and Hudson's Bay and in their mail-order catalogues.

Women walking down Portage Avenue, 1923. Archives of Manitoba, McAdam fonds, 10, N17771.

But the flapper style was more than fashion; it was a deeply valued symbol of the new freedom women were feeling in the 1920s. When Paris decided in 1924 and again in 1929 to change back to longer skirts, American women rejected the new designs. They had the skirts shortened in the store. One woman reacted in this way: "We are scarcely worthy to have the vote or other hard-won modern liberties" if women give up the simpler clothes and the freedom they give. "Ankle length skirts and confining waists belong to the middle ages or the harem."[3]

Jazz

A revolution was also taking place in music and social dancing. In newspaper notices about dances and parties, bands were usually described as playing the "latest music," but not much more detail than that was given. In the 1920s jazz was certainly the latest music and the latest jazz records were available in many stores. Winnipeg's big movie theatres, like the Capitol and the Allen, were beginning to feature jazz bands as well as their theatre orchestras to accompany the movies. Young people in Winnipeg were dancing to jazz tunes and doing some of the new dances like the Charleston, which had emerged around 1923. The Black Bottom was first seen in 1926. The two-step was a standard dance at the time, and young people danced it to jazz tunes.

While jazz, for the most part, originated with Black musicians who are now well known to us—Fletcher Henderson, Duke Ellington, and Louis Armstrong, for example—these men and their bands would probably not have been known to many young people in Winnipeg in 1925. It was only toward the end of the decade when they made their first appearances in Hollywood movies that white audiences became familiar with them, and it would be another few years before audiences in Winnipeg actually got to see them live. Of course, their bands were featured on radio programs that people in Winnipeg could pick up. Jazz bands in Winnipeg in the 1920s were white and played their own version of jazz filtered through the arrangements played by other white orchestras on the radio or on records or published as sheet music. They played piano, banjo, trumpet, trombone, and saxophone.

The fashions young people were wearing in the 1920s and the music they danced to caused a good deal of worry among some clergy and other opinion makers. A "noted British surgeon" was quoted in the February 14, 1920, *Winnipeg Tribune*: "The frivolous, scantily-dressed jazzing 'flapper,' irresponsible and undisciplined, to whom a dance, a new hat, or a man with a car is more important than the fate of the nation, must be converted into a sensible young woman. This type is physically very attractive to men and has strong reproductive instincts. We must save them from ruin." This sounds very like a preacher who warned his listeners in Guelph, Ontario, in 1921 about the dangers of the current dance craze. Dance halls, he said, had a "reeking atmosphere and cause inevitable stirrings of sexual passion."[4] This connecting of dancing and jazz with sexual licence was a constant theme throughout the 1920s. Queen Mary tried to set an example when she refused to have jazz music played at any of the dances she organized. Her son, the Prince of Wales, on the other hand, was a "jazzer" and loved to dance the new dances, just as he apparently loved to engage in sexual licence with flappers. In fact, it appears that on at least one of his trips to Canada he had the Canary Cottage jazz orchestra travelling with him.

In 1927 in Ottawa there was an example, among many others, of the reaction to jazz. A local Presbyterian minister, E.B. Wyllie, began a newspaper campaign against the Ottawa Collegiate Institute where his son was a student. He charged the school was a "cesspool of sin." Students attending unsupervised dances were learning to engage in drinking and sex and to acquire "undesirable habits." The premier appointed Judge R.A. Orde to look into the allegations. Orde dismissed them, saying Ottawa Collegiate was no different from other schools and that there were always instances of bad behaviour when teenagers got together.[5]

Winnipeg Little Theatre

During the 1920s the rich and diverse theatre world of Winnipeg carried on as it had in the past with the difference that motion pictures played an increasingly important role. On one weekend in February 1922, for example, the city had a long list of entertainments from which to choose. At the Walker Theatre *The Beggar's Opera* was playing, to be followed the next week by a new three-act play, *The Unloved Wife*, starring Ruby Norton. Norton was also appearing in the vaudeville review nearby at the Orpheum on Notre Dame, where she was billed as the "Little Big Star of Song." Pantages was the other vaudeville theatre in town. At the Winnipeg Theatre a repertory company presented plays, and their current offering was *Charlie's Aunt*. The biggest of the many movie houses, the Allen, later called the Metropolitan, and, just down Donald Street, the Capitol, both offered the latest motion pictures together with some stage acts. Both had orchestras, and the Capitol also featured singing and dancing on its stage. The theatre organist at the

Portage Avenue at night between Donald Street and Smith Street, decorated for Christmas, showing the Capitol Theatre, c. 1935. Archives of Manitoba, McAdam fonds, 457.

Allen presented a recital at the end of each evening's program. There were many smaller movie theatres and a few of them had live entertainers as well.

Most of this live entertainment would come to an end with the advent of talking pictures. *The Jazz Singer* was released at the end of 1927 as the first full-length movie with at least some sound: synchronized dialogue sequences as well as the songs and music numbers. It took time to rewire theatres and perfect the technology for making "talkies," but by mid-1929 the studios in Hollywood were no longer turning out silent features and the stages of many movie theatres began to fall silent except for the soundtrack of the movie.

In the midst of the ads for all this professional entertainment, in February 1922 the Winnipeg Community Players inserted a simple notice for their first performances at the Dominion Theatre on Portage Avenue East. They announced they would be presenting, later in the month, three one-act plays, *The Little Stone House, Squirrels,* and *Suppressed Desires.*

The Winnipeg Community Theatre, a predecessor of the Royal Manitoba Theatre Centre, had been founded in 1921. At the time, a community theatre movement was spreading in Britain, the United States, and Canada, although in this country only Winnipeg, Montreal, and Toronto had companies in the early 1920s. Winnipeg had a long history of amateur theatre stretching back to the Red River Settlement. But the Winnipeg Community Theatre had fairly high-minded goals, pledging itself to putting on plays of a better class "without making box office receipts the primary consideration." The theatre was seen as a place not to just have fun, but to learn and develop one's artistic taste. In 1922 the *Tribune* praised the group: "It is all done for the good of the cause, the final objective of which is greater refinement."[6] Both the amateur performers and their audiences, then, were interested in increasing the sophistication of the Winnipeg theatre world, making it more like the theatre of larger cities.

With all the competing entertainment available in Winnipeg theatres, it was just as well that the box office was not the Winnipeg Community Theatre's prime consideration. The group would be giving members a chance to learn about all aspects of theatre work: acting, directing, stage design, and writing. The community theatre movement has been satirized over the years, but there is no doubt that it was the starting place of many professionals and helped build an audience for live plays. The Winnipeg Community Theatre would function until 1936 when, heavily in debt, it was closed down. It was revived after the Second World War and would merge with Theatre 77 in 1958 to form what is now the Royal Manitoba Theatre Centre.

The theatre's doings were reported in the *Tribune* and *Free Press* society pages, and the actors, crew, and directors were local people with a fair representation from the city's wealthier families. Gordon Craig and his wife, Irene, were among the founders and worked in theatre for many years. Craig was an engineer but he became interested in theatre in Winnipeg and worked with the Winnipeg Community Theatre as a volunteer and then as its director.

The first play produced by the Community Players, staged at the Dominion Theatre in December 1921, was John Galsworthy's *The Pigeon*. The cast all gave the papers their resumés. Leslie Lambe, playing a returned soldier, worked as an agent for a motion picture company. M.F. Wardhaugh, another veteran who had been part of a little theatre group in England, was also involved with another Winnipeg company called the Western Players. Everett Stovel said he had extensive stage experience and was also a member of the Western Players. Rowena Brownstone, a recent graduate of the University of Manitoba, had studied dramatics and claimed to have gained some stage experience in New York. Phyllis Matheson had acting experience and had appeared on the professional stage. Colonel W.K. Chandler was another veteran and had been the organizer and director of the Strollers theatre company when they won the Earl Grey Trophy for drama. Wooton Coodman had experience as a member of the local Horner Opera Company, and he worked during the day in the

Winnipeg's Little Theatre production of Pirandello's Henry IV, *1928. (L-R)*
W. McGuillen and G. Waight. Archives of Manitoba, McAdam fonds, 475.

treasurer's office of the CPR. Gibson Gunn had also had experience with the
Horner Opera, and worked as the treasurer of a local insurance company.[7]

While the first productions of the Community Players were in the
Dominion Theatre on Portage Avenue East, the group soon purchased their
own venue, called the Little Theatre, a former movie house at 959 Main Street.
The theatre had 250 seats, most of which were sold by subscription. Members
from the university faculty were involved and the University Women's Club

was a supporter of the group. A list of donors from these early days includes names such as James Richardson, Robert Rogers, and Arnold Brigden, and many of the same people who were often mentioned in the society columns. In 1928 Lady Tupper directed a production of *The Importance of Being Earnest*. The celebrated Winnipeg artist Walter J. Phillips designed sets and local volunteers sewed costumes.

The group was fairly sophisticated in what it chose to present in the Little Theatre on Main Street. There were plays by Edmond Rostand, Alan A. Milne, George Calderon, John Galsworthy, George Bernard Shaw, Philip Marlowe, and John Synge. Some of the plays chosen had only recently debuted in New York. For example, in 1922 Rowena Brownstone directed *Six Who Pass While Lentils Boil* by Stuart Walker, a new play performed for the first time the year before in New York. In February 1923 she directed *The Potboiler*, with a cast made up of members of the University of Manitoba Menorah Society, a Jewish students' group. The one-act play, by Alice Gerstenberg, a young woman active in the Chicago Community Theatre, became a classic. It satirizes playwrights and their foibles. Plays were chosen in part by asking the members of the group what they would like to see the following year. During the winter season, on Saturdays when there was no production, the group workshopped one-act plays and presented readings.

Rowena Brownstone was the daughter of a middle-class Jewish family. Her father was involved in several businesses and her mother volunteered for the Red Cross and the Liberal Party. Rowena was involved in drama at university and directed several plays for the Community Players. But she also travelled to Toronto, where she was involved with a dramatic production at Hart House. She visited New York as well, and in 1925 she married New Yorker Michael Kley. He was an insurance company executive and they had two daughters. She lived in New York for the rest of her life and died in the 1990s.

As to the quality of any of the productions, local critics like Professor William F. Osborne, who taught French and Modern Languages at the university, published reviews in the daily papers that ranged from very critical to glowing. When someone complained to the paper about a bad review, the answer came back that if one gave only good reviews, then a truly good one means nothing.

The Little Theatre group participated in fundraisers for other causes in the city and to support their own efforts. In 1925 they put on a street fair on Gertrude Street, closing the street between Wellington Crescent and Daly Street to raise funds for the theatre. In November 1925 a group of young women borrowed the Little Theatre to put on a *Humpty Dumpty Review*, a pantomime-type entertainment for children. They were all members of the Humpty Dumpty Club, a group of teenaged girls formed in 1918 by Ellen Code and Mary Machray. The group decided at their first meeting that they would work to raise funds for the children who were patients at Winnipeg General Hospital. One of their regular fundraising events was the *Review*. The club remained in existence for many years, always with teenaged members. Ellen Code was the director of the *Review* in 1925 and her sister Lorraine was one of the players. The Codes were the daughters of Abram Code, who was an inspector for the federal Department of Inland Revenue, and his wife, Gertrude, who was one of the daughters of Edward Drewry, the owner of the Redwood Brewery. Mary Machray, their cousin, was the daughter of lawyer John Machray and also a granddaughter of Edward Drewry.

An aspect of the Little Theatre that was quite different from other Winnipeg theatres was that it was a place where people of different backgrounds worked together on plays. While most of the works put on by the group were by British authors, members like Rowena Brownstone introduced a wider variety of material. For example, in 1930 *The Dybbuk* was performed by a cast of forty, mostly members of the Menorah Society at the university. The director was Winston McQuillin, who worked for the Cockfield Brown Advertising Agency. That same year a Scandinavian classic, *Eywind of the Hills*, was performed. Winnipeg audiences were thus being exposed to drama from a variety of traditions. The group was heavily supported by members of the city's elite and the cosmopolitan nature of some of the plays probably indicates that attitudes were changing when it came to non-British cultures.

Horse Racing

One enterprise that grew from literally nothing to a solid success in the 1920s was thoroughbred racing. James Speers created the new industry for the city. Amid all the examples of decline in the early 1920s, Speers's activities can be seen as one of the great success stories of the decade and an example of the contributions a new generation of business people began to make at the time.

Horse racing has a long history in Winnipeg, but the sport was not organized or properly regulated until the 1920s. There had been horse racing at the annual Industrial Exhibition, held at the Exhibition Grounds, beginning in the 1890s and ending in 1914. There was also a racetrack at River Park, the Street Railway Company's park at the south end of Osborne Street, where harness race meets were held as well as the saddle horse races.

Horse racing at Whittier Park, 1924. Archives of Manitoba, McAdam fonds, 193, N15951.

R. James Speers, known as "Jimmie," was born in Peel County, Ontario, in 1882. He first came west, like thousands of other young people, as a harvest excursionist in 1900. He stayed in the West and settled in Battleford, Saskatchewan, in 1908, becoming a cattle buyer and an auctioneer, and the owner of a line of country grain elevators. He ran for the Conservatives in the 1911 federal election and lost, Saskatchewan being one of the few provinces where the Liberals held back the Conservative landslide. During the First World War, Speers travelled around western Canada and the United States, buying horses for the French Army. While on a buying trip to the United States, he was seriously injured in a train wreck, and Richard B. Bennett, then a young barrister in Calgary, won him a $40,000 settlement from the railroad. With this money he came to Winnipeg in 1920 and set up shop as a commission agent at the St. Boniface stockyards with a partner, Jerry Dohan, buying and selling livestock. He was successful in the cattle business and would eventually be the president of the Winnipeg Livestock Exchange. Speers, Dohan, and the other cattle buyers at the stockyards spent their days in the saddle, moving among the cattle pens. At off times they liked to race on the dirt roads in the area.

James Speers was one of the new men who became prominent in the city during the 1920s. He might not have been quite respectable in the minds of some of Winnipeg's social leaders, but he had the support of many prominent people for his business enterprises. He also created a lot of economic activity in the city, employed people, and provided entertainment. He continued with his work for many years until his death in 1955.

Historian James Gray, in his book *The Roar of the Twenties*, gives us a portrait of this colourful Winnipegger. Speers loved to gamble and he was part of at least three regular poker games. Gray writes: "He was equally attracted to the $1.00 limit Thursday night poker game at the Manitoba Club; to the no-limit table stakes at the Fort Garry Hotel Saturday–Sunday game with Squinchy Loeb, Frank Fowler, Frank Shae and Don Grant; to the kibitzing, joke-telling, wassailing game with Bill Connelly, Jerry Dohan and his stockyards cronies at the Empire Hotel."[8]

His love of poker meant that he was often broke. He once lost his house in North Battleford in a poker game. He borrowed from his friends, but he always paid his debts and was always ready to lend. We can only assume his wife must have had nerves of steel. Jim Coleman, a sports writer, wrote that James Speers's wife, understandably, hated his gambling. Then he made this interesting comment: "She declined to accept the fact that it was his ability to gamble boldly which established the family fortune. Indeed it was Speers' reputation as a good gambler which set him apart from lesser men and which caused him to be revered as one of the truly colorful and successful pioneers of Western Canada's business community."[9]

It was at River Park in 1920 that James Speers and Jerry Dohan organized their first race event, a trotting and running race meet with both sulky and saddle horse races. The Winnipeg Driving Club had been sponsoring races at the park for a few years, and Speers managed the event for them. Sports writer Jim Coleman lived in Winnipeg as a boy and went to the races with his parents. He remembered River Park as being bare and dusty, "but to me it was glamorous and exciting."[10]

In just five years Speers would transform racing in Winnipeg by introducing regular thoroughbred races. He built his first racetrack at Whittier Park in 1924, and opened the Polo Park racetrack in 1925. He bred thoroughbred horses on his St. Boniface farm close to the Whittier Park track. He was involved with racing throughout the remainder of his life, breeding and racing his own horses and bringing owners and trainers from all over Canada, the United States, and Mexico to run their horses on Winnipeg tracks. He managed race meets in other cities such as Calgary, where he owned the Chinook racetrack, and organized the racing and supplied horses at the Calgary Stampede and for the summer fairs in Edmonton, Regina, Saskatoon, and Brandon. Speers also made sure that the races were presided over by experienced officials—the

Winnipeg Tribune *ad for Polo Park horse races, 14 June 1929. It lists R. James Speers as the Winnipeg Jockey Club Manager and advertises the Pari-Mutuel System he introduced. University of Manitoba Archives,* Tribune *fonds.*

stewards, secretaries, starters, and veterinarians who would enforce the rules and made the races as safe and fair as possible.

Speers introduced parimutuel betting to River Park in 1922, the year after it became legal in Canada. Parimutuel betting was not a new idea but it had become widespread in the United States and Canada because of public outrage over a number of recent gambling scandals at American tracks. With parimutuel betting, instead of allowing bookies to take bets on the races, the management of the track, using parimutuel machines, provide the opportunity to gamble. The machines record bets, calculate winnings, and deduct percentages for the track management and for taxes. The money put on each individual race forms a pool for that race. All those who bet on the winning horse share equally in the winning pool of money. It was considered to be a fairer method of gambling than leaving the bettors in the hands of bookies, and it also produced a steady stream of income for the track.

There were still bookies in Winnipeg. James Gray tells us there were at least twelve operating in the city in the 1920s, taking bets on races in other cities in Canada and the United States. They were not involved in the betting at Winnipeg tracks; the police morality squad made sure of that.

Speers did not allow touts to operate at his tracks. Touts, for a small commission, share privileged information about sure things with gamblers. Coleman describes how, early in Speers's career managing races in Winnipeg, a group of racetrack touts from Chicago showed up at the race meet. They soon found themselves in Speers's office, where the local morality squad police had delivered them. Speers told them to go home but gave them their train fare and money for expenses. His charitable act made him famous, and he was held in high regard by touts all over the racing circuit.

In 1924 Speers leased a piece of land from the CNR between their main line in St. Boniface and the Red River. He called it Whittier Park, after the American poet John Greenleaf Whittier, who wrote, referring to St. Boniface Cathedral, "The bells of the Roman mission— / That call from their turrets twain / To the boatman on the river / To the hunter on the plain." Gray tells how Speers involved many of his business associates and friends in the enterprise. He got Gus Creelman, a road contractor, to build the track, and Dan McDonald, a lumber dealer, built the grandstand, clubhouse, and stables, all on credit. The buildings were white clapboard with green shingles, giving the place a trim, respectable look to reassure the customers. Speers convinced Jack Lee of Green River Bottling to loan him $15,000 interest-free in return for the exclusive right to sell soft drinks at the track. He raised more money by establishing the Manitoba Jockey Club and selling $100 memberships. He added a note of respectability by having Lieutenant-Governor James Aikins open the track along with Premier John Bracken. With crowds of 6,000 people at the opening day in June and 12,000 on Dominion Day, the track was soon in the black.

There had been, however, some anxious moments during construction. On one memorable day the crew building the track buildings had not been paid and might have walked away from the job. Luckily there were races at River Park that day and Speers arranged to have all the cash from the parimutuel betting rushed over to St. Boniface so the men could have their money.

Whittier Park opened on Tuesday, June 24, 1924. The *Free Press* was enthusiastic:

> Brilliant in every way was the formal opening of the seven days' race meeting of the Manitoba jockey club yesterday afternoon when the splendid new Whittier Park opened its gates for the first time. Lieutenant Governor Aikins, Premier Bracken and hosts of others prominent in the business, political and social life of Winnipeg were in attendance. The jockey club has reason to be proud of its new plant. . . . There were 6,000 spectators. The club house was packed and the green lawns were beautiful. The track has wide turns and stretches so there was no crowding even when the field consisted of 12 horses. . . . The grandstand was decorated with colored streamers and a dozen flags were flying in the breeze from the river.

The *Free Press* writer said that considerable time was spent "watching the jockeys getting mixed up with the scenery and (CNR President) Sir Henry Thornton's trains coming in on the railway track and the horses we were backing not coming in anywhere."[11]

Jim Coleman later wrote:

> If I were granted a return into the past for another day of my life, I believe that I would choose to relive an afternoon at Whittier Park. There we would be again on the grass lawns in front of the white club house. From where I sat on a garden bench, secure between my father and my stepmother, I could see those two regal old ladies, Mrs. G.V. Hastings and Mrs. Patrick Shea, sitting in their adjacent black limousines beside the clubhouse fence. [These ladies were the wives, respectively, of one of the owners of Lake of the Woods Flour Milling and Shea's Brewery.] "We'd sit there watching the horses run again—Duchess of York, Cappy Ricks, Son o Unc, McGonigle, Formic and Little Joey, and when the last race had been run, we'd get into the waiting taxi for the leisurely ride home.[12]

He remembered how the ladies of the St. Agnes Guild provided tea every afternoon. The guild was and is a group that raises money for the Children's Hospital. Selling tea at the races helped them make money and it cemented a relationship with a "powerful element in the community which, under less fortuitous circumstances might have been inclined to inveigh publicly against horse racing as an abomination of the devil."[13] Speers did not believe in selling liquor at racetracks but there was a room in each of the clubhouses where male club members "retired at regular intervals" to console themselves over lost bets.

The next year James Speers borrowed money from his friends brewer Patrick Shea and his son Frank Shea to buy land at Polo Park for another racetrack. Unlike Whittier Park, which was owned by the shareholders, Polo Park belonged to James Speers himself. Speers's bank, the Dominion, was nervous about the rapid expansion of his business and called in his $100,000 line of credit, refusing to lend him more. He turned to individuals he knew, such as Shea and former Conservative Cabinet minister Robert Rogers, to tide him over. Walter Kane, the contractor for the Polo Park buildings, did $100,000 worth of work on credit.

In May 1925 the city was preparing for the racing season, which would take place at the city's three tracks: River Park, Whittier Park, and the new Polo Park, where the stables were under construction, the grandstand was half done, and the track was coming along. Horses were coming from the United States and from Mexico for the Calgary race meet, beginning on May 23 and then on to Winnipeg in June.

Polo Park race track, Labour Day, c. 1930. Archives of Manitoba, McAdam fonds, 31, N22277.

Friday, June 12, 1925, was the first day of racing at the brand-new Polo Park track. It was a warm day with clouds in the sky. Although it had been raining for several days, the park looked wonderful and there was no mud or water anywhere. The lawn was newly sodded. Five thousand people heard a short opening ceremony with a speech by Mayor Webb, who said the track was a credit to the city of Winnipeg. The entrances were on Portage Avenue, where police were directing the heavy traffic.

The *Free Press* covered horse racing in some detail, perhaps because John Sifton, an executive at the paper and the eldest son of the owner, Clifford Sifton, was president of the Jockey Club. The reports were sometimes humorous, especially when they dealt with betting. One *Free Press* reporter said he "made a little money on the fourth race as we were out eating a hot dog during the betting and didn't have anything up, but on the fifth took a chance on something listed in the program as 'she will,'. . . as it turned out it was a case of she didn't."[14]

Enormous amounts of money were wagered at the three tracks. In 1924, $750,000 passed through the parimutuel machines at Whittier Park and, just two weeks before, $647,000 were bet at River Park. These figures are roughly equivalent to $18 million dollars in today's money. The profits must have been substantial: in January 1926 Speers announced that because of the successful racing season of 1925, prizes for the races in 1926 would be doubled and two new handicap races would be staged, one at Polo Park and the other at Whittier Park. They would each have prizes of $2,500.

Complaints began to be heard about the amount of money being wagered at the racetracks. Landlords, retail stores, and groups like the Board of Trade and the Women's Christian Temperance Union claimed that people were gambling away their salaries and not paying their rent or other bills. In February 1926 Attorney General Richard W. Craig took action. Gambling was a federal matter covered by the Criminal Code, so Craig took aim at something he could control: the number of race days licensed per year. He introduced a bill to limit the number of days of racing in any Manitoba city to two weeks a year. He was careful to say the bill was no reflection on the men who were currently managing racing; they had kept the sport clean. But it was in danger of becoming commercialized in a way that might destroy the sport itself. The new regulation effectively gave Speers a monopoly on thoroughbred racing already established at his City of St. Boniface and City of Winnipeg tracks. It ended racing at River Park or any other location within the boundaries of Winnipeg.

The bill was debated on February 15. William D. Bayley, the Labour member from St. Clements, made a gloomy prediction about what would happen.

He said he was against racetracks that often start out being run by associations and attracting the best people in society, as in England, because then they begin to move toward the situation in Germany, where the government takes a share of the profits, or to the American situation, where unscrupulous owners had made racing into a business and reaped enormous profits. He said he did not want to see the tracks become gambling dens, but "in my judgement, Winnipeg tracks will follow the same course despite the good intentions of the present management and shareholders. Gradually the one share respectable citizens will disappear and a tempting offer from a race track promoter of the bad type will complete the evolution."[15]

These predictions did not influence racing fans, and the attendance at the tracks remained high. Local stores profited from racing by promoting the idea that people had to dress up to go to the races. On June 10, 1924, the Hudson's Bay Company advertised "captivating 2 piece sport suits for women" attending the races. The Bay assured women that "you'll feel confident of your fashionable appearance if you choose one of the newly arrived, distinctly better grade productions as sketched." The ad said: "Soon the bells of St. Boniface will be ringing a welcome for you to come to Whittier Park and enjoy the 'sport of kings' at the summer race meets at River Park and Whittier Park ... society in its gayest mood will be dressed in its gayest, smartest apparel. Hudson's Bay specialty shops and ready to wear departments have exclusive, fashion right apparel and accessories for just such festive occasions." In March 1929 Eaton's placed an ad for new blouses—"these are the little blouses that 'go places'— golf at the St. Charles, races at Polo Park, tea at the Lower Fort." Similar ads appeared before every race meet.

Going to the races was considered an event that should be covered by the society columns in the newspapers. On Saturday, June 12, 1926, a fashionable crowd was present at the opening of the Polo Park season. The *Free Press* described the dresses of the society ladies seen—for example, Lady Macdonald, Mrs. George Carruthers, and Mrs. Heffelfinger—and the wives of grain merchants, lawyers, politicians, and judges.

The organizations sponsoring racing were also places where the Winnipeg elite was involved. The Winnipeg Jockey Club's 1929 annual meeting was held in May in the boardroom of the *Free Press*. John Sifton was re-elected president. General Ketchen was the honorary president, and other board members were Colonel Price Montague; Donald W. Dingwall, owner of Dingwall Jewellers; and D'Alton C. Coleman, Jim Coleman's father and western vice-president of the CPR.

PART 4

The Developing City

PARLIAMENT BLDG. AND CARNIVAL AT NIGHT, WINNIPEG

Looking north at the 1922 Winnipeg Winter Carnival grounds on the west side of the Manitoba Legislative Building. Postcard from a photo by Meyers. Past Forward: Winnipeg's Digital Public History. Postcard collection of Martin Berman.

CHAPTER 10

Amusements Parks and Winter Fairs

Winnipeg's Industrial Exhibition had been held every year since 1891 when, in the summer of 1914, it was cancelled because of the Great War. Organizers felt that it would be unseemly to hold a fair when the nation was getting down to the serious business of fighting.

Conceived as a large regional fair, the Industrial Exhibition was in its day the largest summer fair in the West. In its last few years it had normally gone on for ten days in July, with a midway consisting of rides, games, and stage shows, and a nightly grandstand show. The exhibition was also an agricultural fair with cattle and horse shows, flower, baking, sewing, and many other contests, as well as displays of the latest products of local industry. There were horse races and car races. The railroads offered special exhibition fares, and thousands of people came from all over Manitoba and further away for a day or two at the exhibition, staying in hotels or boarding in private homes. Winnipeg's economy received a boost as people coming to the fair spent money in Winnipeg stores, hotels, and restaurants.

In 1912 the Winnipeg Exhibition Board and community leaders had launched an ambitious campaign to secure $1 million in federal funding to transform the fair into a centennial celebration of the Selkirk Settlement. They envisioned a world's fair that would attract attention all over North America. They were not successful in getting federal support, and the exhibition

proceeded pretty much as usual with a few Selkirk-related events. Some identified this failure as proof that Winnipeg had overreached. But the ambitious
plan is also evidence of the importance with which community leaders in the
city endowed the exhibition.

In 1913 the city decided to turn the exhibition, which had been losing
money, into a giant rodeo, calling it the Winnipeg Stampede. The stampede also
lost money and was not repeated in Winnipeg. During the war the buildings
and the grounds were used to house troops, and the stables, large grandstand,
and display buildings were not maintained. As they deteriorated they were
slowly torn down, the final demolitions taking place in 1920.

The old Exhibition Grounds stretched from Jarvis Avenue north to Selkirk
Avenue and from McPhillips Street east to Sinclair Street, in more or less the
same location occupied by the old Exhibition Park today. It was city-owned
land and it lay just over the fence from the main CPR yards. By the 1920s the
yards contained multiple sidings, coal bunkers, repair shops, and roundhouses
besides the main line. The activities of the busy railroad yard produced constant
noise, smoke, and smells.

In 1912 City Council had made the decision to move the exhibition to
a more attractive treed area north of Kildonan Park on the banks of the Red
River, and the land was purchased by the city. The move was supported by
local community leaders like Edward L. Drewry, a long-time member of the
Parks Board, who felt the city was falling behind other communities with its
twenty-year-old fairgrounds beside the smoky rail yards, and needed a more
beautiful location with new buildings. Since it was not immediately used for
the fair, the city decided to use the area for a municipal golf course, which
opened in 1921.

During the 1920s attempts were made to revive the exhibition. There was
support for the idea, and both City Council and the Board of Trade identified
the exhibition as one of their priorities. It was seen as one of the events that
symbolized Winnipeg's pre-eminence among prairie cities, and its revival
was to be a way to help revive the city's fortunes. The Board of Trade had an
Exhibition Committee to work on the issue, and at various times during the
decade, City Council also appointed a Civic Exhibition Committee. Charles
Vanderlip, a local businessman, worked throughout the decade with his private
company, the Winnipeg Exhibition Association, trying to revive the exhibition
as a business enterprise. But all the attempts failed, largely because the various
groups and individuals engaged in the project could not agree to compromise
and work together.

Vanderlip made his first proposal to City Council and the Board of Trade in 1921. He wanted to mount a "Made in Canada" festival to be held on the vacant land on Portage Avenue between Vaughan and Colony streets. This area belonged to the Hudson's Bay Company and it was where their store would be built a few years later. Vanderlip's plan was to erect two long display buildings to showcase local products and also to book the Wortham Shows, one of the largest travelling midways in North America, to provide rides, vaudeville shows, games, and amusements. Wortham Shows already travelled to many fairs in Canada, including Toronto's Canadian National Exhibition.

The plan to use the Hudson's Bay property fell through, and Wortham Shows was booked to set up on vacant land on the north side of Portage Avenue between Sherburn and Garfield streets. This open area had been used before for circuses. Wortham Shows were to be at the Brandon summer fair before coming to Winnipeg.

Shortly before their engagement for the week of August 8, Vanderlip was informed that they would not be allowed to use the space on Portage Avenue. The reason, as Mayor Parnell informed the show's solicitor, was that the city had very recently revised its fire regulations, and attractions like the Wortham midway were no longer allowed to operate in the built-up part of the city. That there may have been more to the issue than fire regulations is suggested by Alderman John O'Hare's comment that it would be a disgrace to allow the midway to come to Winnipeg. He seemed to feel the sideshows and gambling games were vulgar and not the sort of thing that was wanted at the Industrial Exhibition, although the pre-war exhibitions had always included a midway. There seemed to be some animosity toward Vanderlip throughout the 1920s among some members of Council and of the Board of Trade, who thought that Charles Vanderlip's efforts were well below the standard they hoped to achieve and that he should therefore not be encouraged.

Vanderlip had already proposed putting on the Industrial Exhibition himself, an offer he had made more than once during the years after 1914. Council seemed to have reservations about his ability to handle such a big event. He had been involved in trying to get permission for Barnum and Bailey's Circus to come to Winnipeg as well as the Johnny Jones Midway. None of his proposals was approved and the objections seemed to stem from worry about his failing and leaving the city with a large loss to cover, as well as the feeling that midways and circuses were disreputable enterprises that were not the sort of entertainment Council wanted to encourage. Vanderlip owned a poolroom, which may have made him seem suspect to the aldermen.

In 1921 Alderman Abraham Heaps came to Vanderlip's rescue, proposing an amendment to the fire bylaw that would allow Wortham to use the Portage Avenue site for one week only. Heaps argued that the midway and its attractions provided popular entertainment at low prices and so were a benefit to Winnipeg's working-class people. Heaps won approval for his solution from a majority of aldermen, although one member of Council was quoted as saying this stopgap measure should never be repeated. The show opened, one day late.

Attendance was very high; clearly, people in Winnipeg liked vulgar entertainment. There was an added benefit to the visit of the Wortham Shows: an old romance was rekindled. A local secretary, Nellie Hoogevan, who had immigrated to Winnipeg from Holland, found an old school chum working on the midway. He was the seven-foot, five-inch Jan van Albert, featured as the "Dutch Giant." The eighteen-year-old Miss Hoogevan decided to elope with her friend, and she travelled with the show to Fort William, where the young couple was married.

Perhaps motivated by the difficulties he had had in the summer, Vanderlip decided to run in Ward 2 for Council in November 1921. His main election plank was the revival of the Industrial Exhibition. He lost to Labour candidate Thomas Flye, who would be an alderman for many years.

At the end of 1921 planning began for a different sort of fair, a winter carnival on a scale similar to the old Winnipeg Exhibition. Horace Chevrier, a pioneer Main Street merchant and member of the Exhibition Committee, linked the event to the revival of the Winnipeg Exhibition, saying that the surplus from the carnival could be used to help finance the summer fair. He said that there would be a saving if the same grounds could be used for both events. Chevrier said that the purpose of the carnival "was to give the people of Winnipeg and surrounding towns an opportunity to get out and enjoy themselves, to loosen up and crack a smile. Following a period of depression and gloom, which was but the natural reaction from the stimulated 'boom' of the war days, the idea of injecting a little new life into the community was an admirable one. The carnival was started with this idea in mind and was unquestionably a success."[1]

The legislative grounds were turned into the carnival site, surrounded by an ice-block wall decorated with evergreens. There was a toboggan slide down to the river, a ski jump, and a skating rink on the river ice. A Hicksville Comedy Centre on the grounds presented comedy acts and a jazz band. There were dog races, one of which began at Selkirk and proceeded down the river to the finish line at the carnival. There was also a twenty-four-kilometre ski race, and

Winnipeg Winter Carnival, 1922. A sketch of the 1922 Winnipeg Winter Carnival attractions on the grounds of the Manitoba Legislative Building. Past Forward: Winnipeg's Digital Public History. Postcard collection of Martin Berman.

ski jumping off a ramp that sent skiers sailing through the air above the ice of the Assiniboine River. The annual bonspiel, a car show, and other events all took place in the city during carnival week. The tone of the advertising was very positive and there was a lot of talk about "pep." Bonds had been sold to finance the event. Anyone who bought a bond had the right to vote for the Carnival Queen.

The Winter Carnival had strong support from Winnipeggers, who purchased $37,000 worth of bonds. The bond sales, along with gate receipts and admission to the toboggan slide, produced a $6,000 surplus. The two main promoters of the event were both members of the Elks Lodge. Dr. Edgar Bricker and Royal Burritt were men in their forties and both were involved not only with the Elks but other similar clubs like the Gyro Club, the Kiwanis Club, and the Masons. Burritt had been a staff officer in the Great War and his organizational skills were clearly excellent. The Board of Trade and City Council were not officially part of the organization that put on the event; perhaps we can assume that some members of these bodies objected to the tone of the carnival.

The official opening on Monday, February 6, began with a big parade moving through the streets from Central Park to the Legislature. The 2,500 people in the parade included members of various sports clubs; staff from Eaton's and

Winter Carnival. The large archway at the Manitoba Legislative Building is advertising "Winnipeg Hydro-Electric." Postcard collection of Martin Berman.

Twenty-four oval-shaped portraits of the 1922 Winnipeg Winter Carnival Queen, Princesses, and other contestants. Past Forward: Winnipeg's Digital Public History. Postcard collection of Martin Berman.

Winter Carnival Winnipeg. Ice blocks and skating rink. Building with faux columns and a gazebo. Union Jacks fly from both. Past Forward: Winnipeg's Digital Public History. Postcard collection of Rob McInnes.

Winter Carnival, 1923. Archives of Manitoba, Events, 227–28, N5889.

the two railroads; members of the Lions Club, Rotary, and Kiwanis; and the 100th Winnipeg Grenadiers Band. When they reached the carnival grounds, 20,000 people were present to watch the coronation of the Carnival Queen, Miss Hazel Tompkins, of the CPR administration offices. She had been supported by a big vote from CPR staff. Her first official act was to flip the switch that turned on the thousands of lights illuminating the site.

The carnival was judged a big success and some people said it should be an annual event. About 65,000 people attended, buying $5,400 worth of entrance tickets and spending more money on the site. Many people came from outside the city. The CPR and CNR both reported that more cars had to be added to their trains bringing people from rural points during the week. Both companies had special carnival fares. The Royal Alexandra and the Fort Garry hotels were completely booked, as were other hotels, and the Winnipeg Street Railway reported that it had carried more than 1.5 million passengers, a record for any single week.

And yet the carnival was never repeated. Possible explanations might be that the people of the City could not be counted on to purchase bonds every year and the City could not afford to fund the event. Neither could the members of the Elks Lodge be expected to take on such a massive task every year. The absence of Board of Trade involvement and the strong support of the various service clubs might well indicate some sort of split in the business community that would have made repeating the carnival difficult. But the success of the carnival proved there was a market for such events; the City simply had to find a way to present them.

In 1923 Council's Public Works Committee began negotiations with the Winnipeg Electric company to lease River Park, the company's property at the foot of Osborne Street, as the site of the Industrial Exhibition. The general manager of Winnipeg Electric, Andrew McLimont, agreed to give the property to the city free of rental to use as a park, playground, and exhibition grounds with the option of buying it. In return, the company would no longer have to pay taxes on the property.

River Park, at the south end of Osborne Street on the Red River, dated from 1889 when Albert Austin, owner of the city's first street railway system, bought three lots to create a park. He was hoping to create an attractive destination to which customers would ride on board his trolleys, a common strategy employed by urban streetcar companies. The street railway reached the park in 1891, and additional land was acquired in Elm Park across the river. In 1894 Austin sold his company, including the parks, to his rivals the Winnipeg Electric Street

Railway, owned by Sir William McKenzie, who would build the Canadian Northern Railroad.

At the time River Park was taken over by the City in 1923, it was home to a carousel, an open-air dance hall, a baseball field, and a racetrack where annual race meets were held complete with parimutuel betting. But the park was no longer remote. Indeed, neighbouring streets were lined with middle-class homes, virtually ensuring that there would be friction over noise and traffic.

In November 1923 a referendum on the exhibition was on the civic election ballot. Because the question did not involve the expenditure of money, all voters, not just ratepayers, were able to vote on whether the exhibition should be revived. They were also asked which of three sites—River Park, the Old Exhibition Grounds, or the Kildonan Park golf course—they would prefer as a location for the fair. Support for the fair in general was overwhelming, the vote being 24,293 for and 7,242 against. The recent success of the Winter Carnival probably helped build support. The preference in terms of the site was not so clear. River Park came first with a 3,102 margin over the next most popular choice, the Old Exhibition Grounds. Kildonan Park golf course was virtually "out of the running," in the words of the *Winnipeg Tribune*.

Council engaged a firm of exhibition designers, the Pearse Robinson Company of Chicago, to design new buildings and landscaping for the River Park grounds. The plans called for a number of display buildings, and a new grandstand and racetrack, all attractively arranged on the beautiful property stretching along the Red River. However, nothing was done as a result of the plans or the vote. One reason was undoubtedly that Winnipeg was still in the grip of the postwar recession and there was little money for new construction.

Charles Vanderlip was still in business and he sent a proposal to Council, saying he would be willing to develop the Old Exhibition Grounds and wanted to lease the site. Council's Exhibition Committee recommended that he be given the site for free. Alderman Flye did not agree and moved that the committee negotiate a formal agreement with Vanderlip, which was done. Some felt Vanderlip should not use the term "summer fair" because it might mislead people outside the city to believe that the Industrial Exhibition was being revived. William L. Parrish, a Winnipeg grain company owner and president of the Manitoba Livestock Improvement Association, agreed and said the absence of a livestock section would make the proposed fair less attractive to visitors. He said he hoped to one day revive a "real" exhibition.

This attitude was again in evidence at a special meeting that Mayor Webb called to discuss Vanderlip's proposal with the Board of Trade. Board of Trade members said the fair he would put on was too small and would have too many sideshows, and might prejudice the revival of an exhibition comparable to Winnipeg's size. It was also pointed out that the fair was scheduled for the same time as the Brandon Fair and Council did not want to compete with their western neighbour.

Vanderlip was never deterred by such sentiments. He said he planned to mount a fair with a lot of displays from local businesses but that at the moment there was no place for a cattle show, the barns having been torn down. He and his partners were planning to spend $75,000 on buildings on the site. He was given a lease to hold a fair at the Old Exhibition Grounds in the years 1925 and 1926.

In June 1925 Vanderlip's summer fair attracted thousands of visitors. At the grandstand they watched a pageant called "The Coming of the Selkirks," a presentation about the Selkirk Settlers. There was a fireworks display, and the crowd visited the display buildings and packed the midway. There were tourists in the crowd, including attendees at a convention of weekly newspapers taking place in the city.

The following year Vanderlip asked for a grant to put on a one-week summer fair in August. Despite his past successes Council agreed to support him only up to a maximum of $3,000, the support to be in the form of waived fees, and free power, water, and police protection.

Vanderlip's 1926 show had displays of Canadian manufactured goods and minerals from Manitoba mines, as well as the latest automobiles and trucks. There was also an all-terrier dog show. Vanderlip hired the Johnny J. Jones Shows to provide the midway attractions. At this time Jones's show was second only to the Barnum and Bailey Circus in size and required a fifty-car train to transport its equipment. The grandstand show featured a local Ukrainian choir of 100 voices, a ballet put on by Winnipeg dancers, and vaudeville acts booked by Vanderlip with the Keith Orpheum Theatre Circuit. There were evening fireworks on opening day and a Miss Winnipeg beauty contest.

At the end of the week Charles Vanderlip announced that his Summer Fair and Trade Exposition had been a success. All contracts were fulfilled and all bills were paid. In his press release, however, he expressed some frustration that unfortunately there existed a group of manufacturers whose opposition proved strong enough to make the displays of "Made in Canada" goods less interesting. He spoke of the undercurrent of destructive criticism that prevented Manitoba's being represented by "a truly impressive display of goods" in the exposition. He claimed to have attracted larger numbers than in past years and said the midway was very popular with thousands of visitors. If it was decided to mount an

Industrial Exhibition in 1927, he would certainly support the effort, but if that did not happen he would build and direct a Summer Fair and Trade Exposition that would be still greater than the 1926 show.

In 1927 it was once again Charles Vanderlip who provided Winnipeggers with a summer fair. In contrast with some of his colleagues, Mayor Webb had become a supporter of Vanderlip's, and he came to the Old Exhibition Grounds to drive in the first nail for the construction of the fairground buildings Vanderlip was erecting. A fair with a midway was a good draw for tourists, and Webb was always looking for ways to increase tourist traffic.

In 1927, a few days before the fair began on August 8, Webb published an open letter in the *Tribune,* calling on the people of Manitoba to support it. He said the people, the government, and City Council should unite to revive the Industrial Exhibition, which would attract the world and be a catalyst for the development of industry in Winnipeg. Not having an exhibition caused a loss not only to business but to the workers as well. He praised Vanderlip for trying to "arouse the people, especially manufacturers, to the awareness of the need for an exhibition."

On opening day everything was ready. The Thearle–Duffield Fireworks Company of Chicago had built a special stage, forty-nine metres in length, for their production "Our Nation's Glory" in front of the grandstand. Eight different circus acts also performed as part of the grandstand show. The Johnny J. Jones midway was also back again. As was customary, Vanderlip made the first day of the 1927 fair "children's day" with a special ten-cent admission to the grounds and to all the rides and attractions for children. All the money taken in on the first day was donated to the *Tribune* Newspaper Fresh Air Fund to pay for poor children to have vacations at the "fresh air camp" on Lake Winnipeg. On the previous Saturday most of the exhibiters had moved their merchandise and products into the display buildings. Vanderlip was pleased with the response this year, and all the display space had been sold. There was a free parking lot for visitors. Acting Mayor Dan McLean got into the spirit by parading from City Hall to the Old Exhibition Grounds, accompanied by the visiting Australian National Band dressed in military uniform and "digger" hats.

Once again the fair was a financial success, but in spite of this, when Vanderlip went to City Council in October, asking for an extension of his lease and for permission to rearrange the buildings he had put up and rebuild the racetrack, he met with opposition. Alderman Alexander Leonard, a businessman who owned a successful car dealership, said that "without questioning Mr. Vanderlip's good faith," it would not be wise to turn the site over to him permanently because the grounds were a prime location for industrial concerns. This use for the site had been included in the recommendations of the City Planning Commission report of 1912.[2] This was an argument that the Board of Trade would use in the late 1920s to discourage use of the Old Exhibition Grounds as a site for a fair. Alderman John O'Hare moved that Vanderlip's lease be extended by thirty days to give him time to remove his buildings from the site.[3]

But Charles Vanderlip was not discouraged by the consistently cool reception given to his ideas by some aldermen. A few days later he was reported to be negotiating with the Winnipeg Driving Club to hold harness racing events on the Old Exhibition Grounds. This would not have been popular with many aldermen and Board of Trade members. In response to complaints about how much money people lost at the races, the provincial government had limited Winnipeg to one race meet a year and Polo Park was already the location for that. Nevertheless, in December City Council extended his lease and Vanderlip headed for Chicago to line up entertainment for the following summer.

The following July he printed an announcement in the *Tribune*, saying that he had leased River Park as manager and anyone wishing to book the facilities could contact him at his office in the Paris Building. Vanderlip moved the summer fair to the River Park grounds in 1928. It once again featured the Johnny J. Jones midway, displays, and a grandstand show presented by the Schooley and Collins Review from Chicago. The show opened with Stroud's Singing Band performing the "Anvil Chorus" as the climax of their act. There was also a tableau called "Canada: The Melting Pot of the World," during which dancers portrayed many of the ethnic groups making up the population and performed folk dances from Russia, Ireland, Italy, and Holland, among other places.

When the fair opened the paint had barely dried on a spectacular new attraction: a large wooden roller coaster known as the "Deep Dipper." Vanderlip had engaged American roller coaster builder John A. Miller, who also designed the "Giant" roller coaster at Winnipeg Beach, to create the Deep Dipper. It was built with Winnipeg materials and machinery under the supervision of Chicago engineers Edward and William Pratt, who oversaw all the work Vanderlip had done at the park that summer. The roller coaster cost $30,000 and it had eleven drops to thrill the customers. The highest was 18.6 metres, from which the cars plunged to eight centimetres from the bottom. Five of the drops had bottoms below ground level, hence the "Dipper" name. There were two trains of three cars each. Long lines waited every evening to ride the Deep Dipper.[4]

River Park and its "Deep Dipper" roller coaster, 1925. City of Winnipeg Archives, i02136.

All this entertainment generated a lot of noise, and even before the fair was over there were complaints from people in the neighbourhood about the screams of people on the roller coaster and the general hubbub from the midway. On August 9 Council discussed the matter. A recommendation had come from the Licensing Committee that the roller coaster be shut down between 11:00 p.m. and 9:00 a.m. Despite a reminder from Alderman Frederick Davidson that Vanderlip had paid $30,000 for the roller coaster and must be allowed to earn money from it, a bylaw was passed, setting the park's closing hours between 11:00 p.m. and 9:00 a.m.

Parking during the fair on the side streets was a big irritant for area residents. The park had made the former racetrack available for free parking, but there was only one entrance. This resulted in traffic jams when people tried to leave, so they parked on the streets instead. Homeowners claimed that the park and the undesirable sorts of characters it attracted would reduce the value of their homes. "Something has got to be done about it," said one resident. "They talk about protecting the investment of the exhibition company, but how about protecting the thousands of dollars invested by home owners in this district?"[5]

Charles Vanderlip reminded everyone that the fair lasted for one week and that after Labour Day the park would be closed for the winter. He had paid out $27,000 in wages since taking over the park, and he had made a large investment in the new buildings and attractions on the grounds. Surprisingly, Alderman O'Hare, who had previously been critical of Vanderlip, came to his defence, saying that a great improvement had already been made and more could be accomplished by education than by compulsion. He argued that the parking area on the old racetrack should be advertised and the entrance and exit clearly marked. Police Chief Christopher Newton said he did not have enough constables to control street parking in the area. When Alderman Charles Kennedy suggested calling the police to deal with offenders, Chief Newton said it was difficult to prove an offence and people had to be willing to show up in court when they had made a complaint, something they seldom did.

On August 20, 1928, a petition with 1,500 names was presented at a Council meeting, demanding the prohibition of circuses, carnivals, and similar shows at the park; regulation of noise from machinery, bells, horns, drums, bands, and shouting; and the restriction of the roller coaster to the hours of 7:00 a.m. to 11:00 p.m., an opening time two hours earlier than the one in the bylaw. At the meeting the gallery in the council chamber was packed with Fort Rouge residents. Three homeowners, S.S. Patchell of Balfour Street, Professor M.C. Herner of Jubilee Avenue, and Fred G. Thompson of Rosedale Avenue, were the spokesmen for the petitioners. Speaking on the other side were Vanderlip, J.D. Suffield, and R.K. Eliot. Suffield argued, among other things, that Winnipeg was seen as a backwoods sort of place because it did not have an exhibition and the summer fair was helping to prepare the ground for re-establishing one. There does not seem to have been a resolution to the problem at the time. The roller coaster stayed in place until 1942, when it was torn down and River Park was subdivided into building lots for housing.

In December 1928 Ralph Webb, who was not the mayor at the time, took the initiative and sent a memorandum to Council's committee on re-establishing the exhibition on the Kildonan Park site. Webb had been meeting with a group that was interested in forming an association, distinct from Vanderlip's company, and selling stock to get start-up money. They would need $800,000 to put up display buildings and other structures on the Kildonan golf course site. It was City land, so Council would be represented in the management of the site.

The group that Webb had been talking to and had very likely called together included John Queen, at this time a Labour MLA; grain dealer William Parrish; and Wesley McCurdy, the business manager of the *Winnipeg Tribune*. The inclusion of a Labour member is an example of Webb's trying to build a coalition to get the project underway.

The *Tribune* was consistently supportive of the exhibition revival, which was listed day after day in the paper's civic "to do" list on the editorial page. McCurdy and the other men in the group were convinced of the economic benefits of an exhibition. R.G. Pearse, the American exhibition designer now located in Alabama, was also listed as one of the directors of the association, likely included as an expert consultant.

Yet another debate about the choice of a location occurred in the first half of 1929. By this time, there were as many as nine possible sites. The Council committee of ten, chaired by Alderman O'Hare and composed of representatives from City Council, the Parks Board, and Vanderlip's group, examined all the options. Kildonan Park, the land bordering Polo Park racetrack on the east and north, an area along the Red River in Fort Garry, and another plot at Silver Heights were some of the possibilities.

City Council decided to put the question to the ratepayers, and in mid-March 1929 a vote was taken on two questions. First, a bylaw was placed before the ratepayers, proposing a debt of $850,000 "to erect the necessary buildings for the re-establishment of an agricultural, industrial or other exhibition."[6] Second, voters were asked to choose between the Old Exhibition Grounds and the Kildonan Park site as the location for the exhibition.

The money bylaw passed easily, receiving 1,210 votes more than the required three-fifths majority. Clearly, there was still strong support for the idea. In a rare show of unity, it received a majority in all three wards. On the question of the site, however, the consensus broke down. The Kildonan site received 4,574 votes and the Old Exhibition Grounds received 1,099. The majority for the Kildonan site was 1,157 in Ward 1 in the south end of the city; 350 in Ward 2; and in Ward 3 in the North End there was a 983 vote majority for the Old Exhibition site. Apparently, rate payers wanted the exhibition but not in their back yards.

Although the Kildonan site was clearly the choice of the majority of voters, the golf course was heavily used, so there was a ready-made group who could be expected to oppose putting the exhibition grounds there. A humorous piece in the *Tribune* on July 19, 1929, described an imaginary debate on the course, suggesting that opinions could be fluid:

> Then there is Bill. . . . "It's a darned shame," he said: "there are all sorts of sites in the city they could use without tearing up a perfectly good golf course. Why can't they go to River Park or Selkirk Avenue or some place like that?" He continued in this mood till he came to the fourth hole. "Who in heck built that railway embankment right across the fairway?" he asked. "It's a cutoff," Freddy said. [Bill proceeded to drive his ball into the side of the embankment and lose it. He did the same thing when playing back in the opposite direction.]

Bill swore as he put down another new ball. "The sooner they put their darned exhibition here the better," he said. "The man who built a golf course round a railway was crazy."

River Park was not on the list of sites voted on, but in July Charles Vanderlip wrote an open letter to the papers, reminding everyone of his various efforts to revive the Exhibition and pointing to the investment he had made at River Park as proof of his dedication to the cause. He suggested the reason River Park was not on the list of possible sites had to do with personal animosity toward him, and this may well have been true. But he added that if anyone else was able to put the exhibition on, he would give them his full support and concentrate on making River Park a first-rate sports and entertainment area.

In September Alderman O'Hare, who was chairing the site committee, responded to Vanderlip by announcing that River Park had been offered and was in the running. He reminded people that it had been chosen in a referendum back in 1923 over the Kildonan and Old Exhibition sites. He thus reopened the question when he already had the March 1929 referendum in his pocket. By not moving forward immediately with the Kildonan site, O'Hare virtually ensured the revival would fail.

In 1930, with the dark clouds of the Depression forming over Winnipeg, the Board of Trade and other groups made a concerted effort to resolve the matter. In February Herbert M. Tucker, an Eaton's vice-president and manager of Eaton's enterprises in Winnipeg, had Eaton's staff build an enormous model of an imaginary new exhibition site built and put it on display in the store annex. The model was fifty-three by twenty-six metres and showed display buildings, a midway, crowds of fairgoers, and even miniature cattle in a show ring.

Tucker had the model built to give people a chance to "grasp the scope and possibilities of the Exhibition." Tucker was also president of the Civic Progress Association, the current iteration of the Citizens' Committee of the early 1920s, and a leader in the city's business community. He hosted a luncheon in the Eaton's store boardroom before the official opening of the exhibition model on February 4. Speakers at the lunch were in a positive mood. Mayor Webb complimented Tucker on the model and said it would stimulate interest. William Dutton, chair of the Winnipeg Exhibition Association, the group Webb had been meeting with and may have organized, said it looked as though the exhibition was at last going to be built. Duncan Cameron, president of the Board of Trade, said that the "efforts of the Winnipeg Board of Trade to get an

Exhibition for Winnipeg seemed to be on the verge of being a success," taking undeserved credit for the Board of Trade. It was an old-fashioned booster event of the type Winnipeg had once seen often: given positive thinking, a beautiful model, plenty of positive speeches, and the thing was bound to happen.[7]

Only ten days later Alderman Herbert Andrews attempted to nail the decision down when he gave notice that he would move that Council lease the Kildonan site to the Exhibition Association so they could begin work on construction of buildings. The motion was debated at the February 17, 1930, Council meeting. Before the meeting, it was clear there would be a battle over the motion. Three Council members, aldermen Jack Blumberg, Ralph Maybank, and Leroy Borrowman, had postponed a trip to an out-of-town meeting so that they could be present. Discussion on the motion lasted until 2:30 a.m., demonstrating just how fractured opinion was in the city: there were groups opposed to each of the sites. The North Winnipeg Rate Payers Association had protested locating the fair at the North Kildonan site and said that the Old Exhibition Grounds on Selkirk Avenue was their choice. The Polish Fraternal Aid Society also wanted the Selkirk Avenue site. These groups could see benefits for North End businesses as well as a source of jobs for unemployed people in their area. The Board of Trade expressed itself as "categorically opposed" to the Selkirk Avenue site, arguing once again that it was prime real estate for new industrial concerns. The board's executive had reaffirmed its support for the Kildonan site at a meeting on February 10. The Civic Progress Association had sent in a resolution that no further action should be taken until all the costs and plans could be laid before the citizens, further reducing the chances of a timely resolution.

The Labour aldermen representing the North End attacked the choice of Kildonan Park. As long ago as the 1924 election Abraham Heaps had argued that the Selkirk Avenue site would cost the least to refurbish. Alderman Thomas Flye said that there were additional costs at the Kildonan site that had not been budgeted for. He pointed out that the site was prone to flooding and yet there had been no provision for storm sewers. Flye said that supporters of the Kildonan choice merely wanted a way of introducing another two weeks of racing in the Winnipeg area in addition to the race meets at Polo Park in Winnipeg and Whittier Park in St. Boniface.[8] Flye considered the Kildonan plan "absolutely ridiculous." He favoured the Old Exhibition option, as did fellow Labour aldermen John Blumberg and James Simpkin, who argued that 17,000 golfers enjoyed the Kildonan golf course every year. In this case the

Labour aldermen were acting not so much on ideological grounds as that they were trying to get something—the exhibition—that would benefit their ward.

Some of the non-Labour members were also against the Kildonan site. Alderman Thomas Boyd said that North Main Street was very crowded with automobiles heading for the beaches in the summer, and this would make access to the exhibition grounds difficult. He also mentioned that the Exhibition Association wanted to promote horse racing, something many people did not support because of the enormous amounts of money lost betting on the races. He confused the issue further when he introduced the Polo Park area into the debate, arguing that it had the advantage of better rail access, since the CPR line ran right past it.

Both Mayor Webb and Alderman James Barry warned that the public was getting sick of Council's "toying around" with this issue. When Alderman Maybank moved an amendment to Anderson's original motion, calling for yet another referendum that would include Polo Park as a possible site, Webb warned that voters had already approved the Kildonan site less than a year before. Council could not now go back and ask about Polo Park. Voters would never approve it and political support for the exhibition would disappear as a dead issue. Ward 2 representatives spoke up for Polo Park, located in their ward, as a choice that should be considered.

The meeting was deadlocked with equal numbers for and against Andrews's motion that the Kildonan site be leased to the Exhibition Association. Aldermen Thomas Boyd and Fred Palmer, the six Labour councillors, and the Communist alderman, William Kolysnyk, were all against. The newly elected members of the Civic Progress Association were all in favour. At 2:30 a.m., a motion was made and carried to refer the question back to the Council Exhibition Committee and everyone went home to bed.

That committee did not meet again until March. They decided to review all the sites again and by May they had decided, based on reports from the City Surveyor, the Parks Board, and the Exhibition Association, that the Old Exhibition Grounds were the best choice. On May 12, 1930, Council was able to agree on this site with only two dissenting votes. The site was turned over to the Exhibition Association that Webb had begun meeting with at the end of 1928.

In June the association responded positively but gave Council a list of conditions that had to be met in order for them to proceed. They wanted a half-mile racetrack, a parking lot, drainage for the site, and the acquisition of the nine hectares between Sinclair Street, Arlington Street, and Selkirk

Avenue to provide more room for buildings and attractions. Ignoring the opposition on Council to a racetrack, the association also wanted the income from parimutuel betting in order to avoid deficits in the rest of the exhibition operations. Council refused to agree to the track, but approved all the other conditions. Mayor Webb, desperate to keep the project going, said that providing drainage for the grounds was already in the city's budget and the purchase of the extra land could be proceeded with, although it would take some time to come to terms with all the landholders. The total value of the land was estimated to be $371,000.

On July 4, 1930, the association was reported to have agreed to the City's terms, not insisting on the racetrack and declaring they could wait to acquire the nine hectares. But by the end of the month they had again changed their minds and formally withdrawn from the deal, stating that a racetrack was essential to their plans. In a last-ditch effort to resolve the problem, Webb stated that the City could go ahead by itself and operate the exhibition. He attempted to avoid the problem that the racetrack would create, arguing that horse races would attract only a few tourists from outside Winnipeg, and that Toronto's Canadian National Exhibition did not include horse racing. He said the essentials for a successful event were good management and cooperation by all interests concerned, the very things that were completely missing.

Council's Exhibition Committee reported that their relationship with the Exhibition Association was at an end. They asked for authority to "enquire into establishing the Exhibition along other lines" and employ an expert to make recommendations on layout and buildings. This request received unanimous support. Mayor Webb had already begun working on the new plan, and announced that he had engaged someone but would not release the person's name for fear that he would be lobbied from all sides before he could complete his work. Soon it was announced that he had hired none other than R.J. Pearse, now of Birmingham, Alabama, to consult on the site. Pearse's firm had created the original plan for River Park in 1924 and now he did another plan for the Selkirk Avenue site, which he pronounced to be the best site in the city. He would repeat this at several public speaking engagements.

Pearse's report was released to the press on September 18. It showed buildings not unlike the ones that had stood on the site in 1913: grandstand, display buildings, and concessions. Parking was the major new issue and Pearse suggested people's cars could be parked on vacant land west of McPhillips Street.

Pearse's report gave rise to another outbreak of bickering. In spite of the Old Exhibition Grounds site having received close to 100 percent support, and Pearse's high praise for the location, there were complaints over Polo Park not being considered. Webb remained enthusiastic, and the North Winnipeg ratepayers once again urged Council to go ahead with the Selkirk Avenue site, saying it would help alleviate unemployment in the North End. The Trades and Labour Council and the Builders Exchange also tried to push Council to act so that unemployed men could get work over the winter.

The Board of Trade refused to give up on Kildonan and continued to be opposed to the Old Exhibition Grounds site, announcing the results of a poll of its members in August. The result was 694 for Kildonan and only 64 for the Old Exhibition site on Selkirk Avenue. The Civic Progress Association contributed their opinion that ratepayers were confused—a very real possibility—and that another referendum was needed. The previous year voters had approved Kildonan, and the Exhibition Association had been put forward as the management group able to guarantee $250,000 to cover any losses. They argued that ratepayers needed to be shown the new plans and to be told who would now be responsible for running the exhibition.

Ralph Webb could see his goal of re-establishing the exhibition slipping away. At his request Pearse continued to speak to groups like the Kiwanis Club. He argued, "An Exhibition is one of the greatest means of advertising a city ever conceived. It is necessary to have one in Winnipeg and it should be established in spite of controversy."[9]

Pearse spoke to the Board of Trade executive and to the Young Men's Section of the Board of Trade. He received a cool reception from the Board of Trade: President Duncan Cameron moved a resolution expressing the Board's "unutterable opposition to the revival of the Exhibition on the Selkirk Avenue site." Then he added the fateful words: "The Board further doubts the advisability of re-establishing the Exhibition on any site at the present time" in view of the changed economic conditions. Unwilling to compromise, the Board was moving to scuttle the project if it could not get its way.[10]

Ralph Webb took the initiative and pushed hard for the Old Exhibition site. In this he was supporting the point of view of the Labour group on Council, breaking with his usual allies at the Board of Trade. This could explain the Board's direct opposition, embodied in their motion to abandon the exhibition project immediately after Pearse's visit to them.

Not only did the Board of Trade not successfully control and win on this issue, at the end of the day, they effectively killed the revival of the Industrial Exhibition by saying it should be abandoned because of the Depression. The Civic Progress Association, under President Herbert Tucker, the Eaton's vice-president who had had the model built, met at the Marlborough Hotel on October 1 and supported a different point of view, agreeing that another referendum was needed with a concrete proposal on which ratepayers could vote. But the exhibition was not on the ballot in November 1930. Webb had expressed his concern that going back to the ratepayers with yet another new proposal would cause a negative reaction against the project. As he predicted, it was once again on the shelf.

The exhibition struggled on during the 1930s, still without a permanent home and without unanimous community support. In 1934, the year Charles Vanderlip died, the fair was held at River Park, complete with the large Royal American Shows midway. Local residents raised a protest and some city aldermen attended their protest meeting and sympathized with them. In 1935 the fair was cancelled and in 1936 it took place at Polo Park and featured a rodeo. The exhibition was revived in 1952 with the name "Red River Exhibition." The first year it was held at the stadium on Osborne Street where the Great-West Life building now stands. Then it moved to Polo Park and stayed there until 1997, when it was moved to the present site beside Assiniboia Downs, on the western edge of the city.

The failure of City Council, the Board of Trade, Mayor Webb, and the long-suffering Charles Vanderlip to come to an agreement reveals how divided Winnipeg had become. In trying to restore the exhibition, a powerful symbol of the city's past success, the various groups involved were unable to compromise or give up their strongly felt opinions and, in some cases, their desire to take credit for finding a solution. Citizen interest groups seemed unwilling to make any kind of concession for the good of the city. Even Ralph Webb, who was generally popular with a large part of the population and had been willing to make common cause with Labour aldermen, was unable to secure agreement on the issue. Part of the problem was certainly the structure of City Council, which gave the mayor no real mechanism—in the form of a group like the current Executive Policy Committee—to ensure that his program was adopted. While there was agreement that the exhibition was important and worthy of being revived, the various groups in the city that had a part to play in that revival were unable to work together to ensure it. Winnipeg was not yet accustomed to the more complex decision making and political deal making that had now become necessary. Some people, such as Ralph Webb and some of the Labour aldermen, were willing to work at compromise, but the culture of the city was still quite confrontational and it had not yet adapted to fit itself to the changed political situation.

The jumble of streets between Vaughan and Colony streets that would eventually be transformed into Memorial Boulevard. Hudson's Bay Company Archives, 1987–31–180.

CHAPTER II

Building Memorial Boulevard

The Manitoba Legislature, completed and officially opened in 1920, was a proud achievement for the province and the city. As early as 1913 there had been planning and discussion about an appropriate setting for the building. It was agreed that a grand formal approach from the north was needed. This proposed approach road was referred to as the "Mall" and, after the Great War, it was proposed that it be designated as "Memorial Boulevard" to commemorate the contributions of Manitoba's soldiers.

The 1913 report of the City Planning Commission included a very detailed description of a mall that would provide a grand avenue leading to the new Legislative Building, on which construction was just beginning. The commission presented a comprehensive plan for a "civic centre" with a widened Vaughan Street connecting the new Legislature with a new City Hall to be constructed on Ellice Avenue. Vaughan Street was not used in the final design, but Memorial Boulevard would extend from the front entrance of the Legislature. The envisioned modern City Hall on Ellice Avenue would not be built.[1]

The other part of the Memorial Boulevard project that was described in the Planning Commission document was a cross-city highway to improve the flow of traffic and reduce congestion. In the 1913 version, this highway was to run along the west side of the legislative grounds and past the proposed City Hall property to provide good access to these two government precincts.

Once again, this exact plan did not come to pass, but the cross-town highway was included in the 1925 version.

So we can see the Memorial Boulevard project of the 1920s as a return of the earlier plan: the revival of an urban improvement from the days when the city had faith that the pace of growth in population and size would continue. Memorial Boulevard is therefore linked to Winnipeg's past but it is also a project, along with the other major projects of the 1920s—the Amy Street Standby Plant, the revival of the Exhibition, and the Housing Commission—that can be seen as one of the new initiatives that aimed to rejuvenate and continue the city's growth. Not all these initiatives were successful, but the construction of Memorial Boulevard was, and it proved that at times the City could still achieve important things.

It was not until 1925 that the redevelopment of the land between Vaughan and Colony streets north of the Legislature was finally approved by City Council. With the passage of the necessary bylaw, Council embarked upon what was arguably the most complex urban renewal project attempted in Winnipeg up to that time.

In her history of the Legislative Building, Marilyn Baker tells of the early discussions about the mall.[2] Baker gives credit for the idea of the Vaughan Street Mall to Leo Warde, a young engraver working at Stovel's Printing. Warde was listed in the Planning Commission report, perhaps as a staff person, and it is possible he had some input. He did, however, become a vocal advocate for the 1925 version of the mall and the cross-town highway and contributed a great deal to getting the project started.

Warde was well known in the city as a great all-round amateur athlete, playing hockey and baseball. In Winnipeg this was an important asset for an aspiring politician. He was a North Ender and one of the founders of the North End Athletic Club that produced many fine athletes, including 1912 Olympic Team runner Joe Keeper. Warde had fought in the Great War, receiving a head wound at Passchendaele. He awoke from a coma to find his left side paralyzed. The paralysis gradually disappeared but he was invalided home, and he seems to have suffered some continuing disability. One of the generation of young veterans who became community leaders of the 1920s, he was the provincial president of the Great War Veterans Association and the director of War Services for the Manitoba Red Cross. A Conservative, he had written for the *Winnipeg Telegram,* and between 1928 and 1930 he was active in politics as reeve of St. Vital. These credentials ensured him a hearing with Council and the Winnipeg establishment.

Warde became an advocate of the cross-town highway as a solution for some of the city's growing traffic problems. This highway was envisaged as a route that would follow what is now Route 62 through the city from St. Vital to the northern boundary. In the 1920s it began at the Red River at the end of Osborne Street and proceeded north to Broadway Avenue. Here, a new section of street was built to connect Broadway and Portage Avenue. Then the route would continue north to the CPR yards, where a bridge or an underpass would be necessary to cross into the North End to continue down Salter Street to the northern boundary of the city.

Before the extension of Osborne between Broadway and Portage was made, all traffic from south of the Assiniboine River turned east on Broadway at the end of Osborne and then north on Kennedy Street to Portage Avenue. Traffic jams were common in this congested area.

Warde promoted the idea of the highway. He told a January 1922 meeting of Council that "the trans city highway would afford a more comprehensive and adequate system of inter communication, following the general geographic center line of the City, and affording easy accessibility to various sections of the City."[3] The highway became an important part of the overall mall project and was a crucial factor in winning support for it.

Once planning and a design competition for the new Legislature got underway in 1911, discussion about a suitable approach to the building began anew. In 1913 Winnipeg architect John Atchison developed his version of the approach. Atchison's Mall, or "Capitol Approach," similar to what was eventually built, ran south from Portage Avenue along a straight line ending at the main entrance of the Legislative Building. Atchison's plan included an extended Osborne Street and envisaged a mall lined with dignified sandstone buildings.

There had been some work on the mall idea in pre-war Winnipeg. It was established that the cost of the development was to be borne by the City, and Council passed an expropriation bylaw in 1912 in preparation for acquiring the land. City Council began to make plans in 1913, identifying streets that would be closed. The estimated cost was $241,156. When the Great War intervened, the mall project was dropped until the early 1920s.

The area north of the Legislature and south of Portage Avenue, bounded on the east by Vaughan Street and on the west by Colony Street, was a jumble of streets formed by the junction—perhaps "collision" would be a better term—of the downtown Winnipeg street grid and the street grid west of Colony. There were many individual houses along these streets, as well as some terraces or rows of houses joined together. The remnants of Colony Creek, once the western boundary of the city, still meandered from north to south, east of Colony Street, its shallow course little more than a ditch.

The greatest challenge facing the proponents of the mall was the assembly of the land. There were a number of property owners in the area, the five largest being the University of Manitoba, the Hudson's Bay Company, All Saints' Church, and two Winnipeg business pioneers. The first of these businessmen, Alexander Macdonald, was the owner of Macdonald's Consolidated grocery wholesale and of a pickle factory and some residential properties in the area. The second, William H. Cross, a Winnipeg real estate investor, also had residential properties. Both had been in the city since its early days and had acquired a good deal of real estate over the years.

The University of Manitoba occupied a good portion of the space between Broadway Avenue and what is now York Avenue. This was land that had been granted by the federal government to the province in 1898 to be used for university purposes. Finding its facilities overcrowded in the postwar period, the university erected a long "temporary" building, with three wings linked to the original Science Building built in 1901 on the site of the fountains in the modern Memorial Park. By 1922 these structures occupied most of the present-day Memorial Park, partially blocking the intended path of Memorial Boulevard.

At the southwest corner of the area, the old All Saints' Church and Rectory partially overlapped the proposed route of the northward extension of Osborne

Construction of new All Saints' Church, 16 October 1926. Archives of Manitoba, Winnipeg Churches, N3424.

Street. On the north side of the area, the Hudson's Bay Company owned a rectangle of land bounded by Vaughan Street and Portage Avenue. This property had been assembled in 1912 as the site of a new Hudson's Bay store. The war had delayed its construction, but now the company stated that once the Memorial Boulevard project was planned and underway, the new store would be constructed. The store and the development it would bring became an important argument in favour of the mall, since the store would be one of the dignified sandstone buildings lining the mall.

The postwar revival of the mall project began slowly, and it became an issue during the civic election of November 1920. Labour candidates said they were not against building a memorial mall but felt that housing was much more important at the moment. Edward Parnell, soon to be elected mayor, said he, too, saw the need for more housing and planned to embark on an extensive program. But he also wanted to proceed with the mall and promised to do all he could to bring about its construction. Worried that the Hudson's Bay store would not be built, he said it would be "criminal neglect" to allow this opportunity to be lost.[4]

A year later, on January 2, 1922, Edward Parnell started his second year as mayor with an address at the first Council meeting of the year. He introduced the City's mall plan, which now carried a price tag of $600,000. He mentioned the long-planned Hudson's Bay store, which he hoped would now be built at a cost of not less than $5 million dollars. He said most property owners had agreed to the idea and a bylaw had been drafted. He wanted the first reading of the bylaw to be passed unanimously without discussion so it could be sent to committee for further work.

Parnell was experienced in City and Board of Trade politics, and he wanted to avoid opening up a long discussion of the mall before Council had a chance to debate it. But the fact that the mall bylaw would be given first reading at this Council meeting had been mentioned in the papers, and as a result the galleries were crowded with people wanting to speak. The bylaw did not get its first reading that evening, but all sorts of alternative plans, objections, and complaints were aired, foreshadowing the controversies that lay ahead.

The first speaker was lawyer Alfred J. Andrews, who said the mall would be a $1 million eyesore. He called the extension of Osborne "ridiculous." Andrews was a former mayor and a prominent lawyer who was an investor in property with property owners as clients. He focused on the risk of increasing taxes. Theodore Hunt, who had been the city solicitor but was now in private practice, also had some comments. He said getting final agreements with landowners would push up the price and he warned Council that they needed a signed agreement with the Hudson's Bay Company. The rest of the evening was much the same, with plenty of doomsayers attacking the plan and offering advice.

One positive voice was that of Leo Warde, who defended the plan that Parnell had outlined. Warde would be the first vice-president of the Young Men's Section of the Winnipeg Board of Trade when it was established in December 1923. We can assume, then, that his ideas were in alignment with those of Mayor Parnell and the Board of Trade.

In spite of the support of the mayor and others, the mall project by-law introduced later in January 1922 was voted down by Council. Many Winnipeggers shared Alfred Andrews's negative reaction and expressed worry in letters to the editor over an increase in taxes at a time when the economy was in recession. It was not the time to embark on ambitious new projects.

The Hudson's Bay Company was also hesitating. Council received a letter from the London board of the company early in 1922, saying the store would be delayed, given the current economic conditions. The Hudson's Bay board also knew that the mall had not been approved by Council and that there was still confusion about exactly what route it would take. The mall did eventually run through the western edge of the Hudson's Bay Company property. The company gave a strip of land to the city in exchange for additional land south of their existing property.[5] Augustus Nanton, who chaired the Hudson Bay's Canadian advisory board, returned from London in March 1922 and confirmed that the construction of the store was on hold.

Undeterred, the Board of Trade supported Parnell's and Warde's plan and also began to push for a civic auditorium, envisioned as one of a number of monumental buildings that would eventually line the mall. The auditorium, also the subject of fierce debate, was finally built ten years later in 1932.

Many other local groups were pushing for the project to begin. In September 1922 Margaret McWilliams, speaking for the Great War Memorial Committee of the Women's Canadian Club, said that indecision about the design of the mall was holding up planning on what sort of monument to erect and where to erect it. There was a temporary war memorial in front of the Bank of Montreal, which had granted use of its property at Portage Avenue and Main Street for two years in 1920. The bank had given an extension but action was required. But Council was slow to move the whole mall project forward. The city was still in the midst of the postwar recession and had more basic problems like housing and unemployment to worry about.

Osborne Extension and Broadway. Hudson's Bay Company Archives, 1987-32-3.

By May 1924 conditions had begun to improve and supporters of the mall once again began to move. Leo Warde brought a plan to the City Improvements Committee in which he estimated the City could acquire the necessary property for $100,000, and he outlined the street closures and openings that would be required. Mayor Farmer had also met with Hudson's Bay Company representatives and confirmed that they were still willing to cooperate with the creation of Memorial Boulevard.

In December 1924 Travers Sweatman, president of the Board of Trade, also began to urge immediate action on the mall. Newly elected Mayor Ralph Webb agreed that the mall was of paramount importance and should have been started long ago. In a rare show of unity, all the aldermen, both Labour and Liberal/Conservative, agreed with Webb that the project should get underway. On January 5, 1925, Council appointed a Special Committee on Opening Memorial Boulevard. The committee was chaired by Alderman Dan McLean and included Mayor Webb; aldermen Robert J. Shore, Thomas Flye, and John G. Sullivan; City Surveyor Richard H. Avent; and City Assessment Commissioner J.G. Hay. The value of the property still needed to complete the plan was now estimated to be $364,000.

About this time the *Tribune* published a summary of the property that would be needed. The Memorial Boulevard route would run north across university land for 213 metres from the entrance to the legislative grounds to a short street called "University Place." This would necessitate the demolition of some of the university's "temporary buildings." Then, after the gravel road at University Place, it would come to Cross Terrace, a series of attached houses that would have to be demolished. Then came Alexander Macdonald's property with several houses and storehouses, and then St. Mary's Place, a curved set of terrace houses. One of these belonged to the Hudson's Bay Company and the rest to individuals. On the other side of the area, the Osborne Street extension would require the demolition of All Saints' Church and Rectory and the adjustment of some of the rear property lines of houses on Colony Street. Where Colony Street and Memorial Boulevard intersected at Portage Avenue, a triangle of land would be left and could be used for the cenotaph.

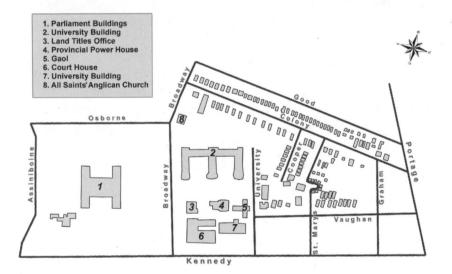

Memorial Boulevard Pre-Construction. Map by Larry Laliberte.

To keep the momentum up at the beginning of 1925, Leo Warde spoke to groups such as the Gyro Club and the Blackstone Club, a luncheon club for lawyers. With Warde and Sweatman backing the issue, the Board of Trade was playing a key role.

When Council finally passed the bylaw on July 31, 1925, the mall project was officially set in motion. The *Tribune* summarized the project's benefits for its readers: "The construction of a new department store of the Hudson's Bay Company, the building of a memorial avenue from Portage Avenue to Broadway, the extension of Osborne street as the first link in a cross-town highway, the extension of York Avenue from Kennedy Street [where it ended at the time], all the way to Colony and the beginning of the first big building boom since pre-war days." The Hudson's Bay Company's governor, Sir Charles Sale, confirmed the same afternoon that the company intended to start construction on a new store on the Portage Avenue site "as soon as arrangements with the City regarding Memorial Boulevard are completed."[6]

The *Tribune* called the mall bylaw "Winnipeg's 15 year old stormy petrel." Indeed, the plan would continue to lead to strife, as was clear during the acrimonious debate at the July 31 meeting of Council. In a rare cooperative effort Liberal/Conservative Alderman John A. McKerchar and Labour aldermen Herbert Jones and William B. Simpson all spoke against the new bylaw. They moved an amendment that would have delayed the bylaw and argued for a vote of the ratepayers before proceeding with the expenditure of money involved.

William Simpson commented that other parts of the city had improvements in need of funding, and Alderman John McKerchar raised his usual objection of the possible increase on taxes. All the arguments put forward by the three aldermen were met by the other councillors, who emphasized the benefits of the project. Abraham Heaps estimated that the new Hudson's Bay store would generate $60,000 a year in taxes. Mayor Webb said that the construction of the store would revive confidence in the city as a place with payrolls that could support such a business. Others said a vote of ratepayers was not needed because the project had been debated for over a decade. The bylaw passed by ten votes to three.

When the vote had been taken Mayor Webb and Alderman Robert Shore sent a telegram to Leo Warde, who was staying in the Red Cross Convalescent Hospital in Winnipeg Beach, resting after his non-stop promotion of the mall project. The telegram said: "Congratulations to you old boy, City Council today passed by-laws covering the Warde Plan for Memorial Boulevard and the Hudson Bay Company are going to build. Best wishes for a speedy recovery and return to the job."[7] The message generously gave Warde the credit he deserved for keeping the issue alive.

Although the project was approved, the work of assembling the land remained. The rest of 1925 and part of 1926 was spent negotiating with land-owners. All Saints' Church on Broadway Avenue was right in the path of the proposed extension of Osborne Street. The vestry, or governing board, decided to build a new church. To raise money for this, they had asked $147,000 for the existing church and land. City Council had countered with an offer of $82,000. The vestry turned this offer down, and finally in April 1926 the city offered $103,000, about $1.24 million in today's money, plus two lots on the west side of the new Osborne Street extension. All Saints' Church agreed, saying that construction of their new Tyndall stone church would commence immediately and be finished by October.

On the east side of the area, a parcel of land belonging to real estate investor William Cross also took some time to acquire. The Cross property included St. Mary's Terrace, with ten attached houses. Cross had asked $91,000 for the property, arguing that the houses netted him $4,900 a year after taxes and repairs. The city offered $54,000. By January 1926 the matter had gone to arbitration before Justice Thomas Mathers, who awarded Cross $77,000, a figure exactly halfway between the asking price and the City's offer. Alderman Dan McLean, chair of the Mall Committee, said that this figure was a glaring injustice and that the City was being "soaked." The City appealed the arbitrator's award but was unsuccessful.

The other large property owner on the east side of the mall area was Alexander Macdonald, who had several houses and lots on Vaughan Street and the White Star pickle factory with its outbuildings and more houses west of Vaughan Street. Macdonald had given some of this property to the City on the understanding that they would purchase the buildings on the lots and pay for moving machinery from the old pickle factory to its new location on the corner of Higgins Avenue and King Street. He also sold the City a triangle of land bounded by Osborne Street, Memorial Bouldevard, and York Avenue for the very low price of $8,000. Other property belonging to Macdonald on Vaughan Street would be purchased later when land was being assembled for the civic auditorium.

The last large landowner in the area was the University of Manitoba. An agreement with the City was complicated by the unsettled question of whether to further expand the university in the Broadway area or move it somewhere else.[8]

University of Manitoba, Broadway site, in 1922. Archives of Manitoba.

Premier Bracken had appointed a Royal Commission on Education in Manitoba in 1923 and they issued their report in January 1924. William S. Learned of the Carnegie Foundation consulted with the commission on the issues of higher education, and wrote a report with recommendations on what should be done about the university. Learned favoured amalgamating the Manitoba Agricultural College with the university, claiming it would save $200,000 a year. This was done, the office of president of Manitoba Agricultural College being abolished and replaced with that of a dean. He also said that the university and the church colleges should move to the Fort Garry campus of the Agricultural College. There was, however, no money to construct new buildings on the Fort Garry site in 1924, and so the move spread over many years, beginning in the 1930s and finishing in the 1950s.

Because of this uncertainty over the university's location, the Province and university were reluctant to sell any land, and this had an impact on the development of the mall. In April 1926 the Mall Committee met with William Clubb, the minister of public works in the Bracken government, and representatives of the university. At this meeting it was agreed that the proposed two-lane mall or Memorial Boulevard would have to narrow down

The foundations of the Hudson's Bay store, 9 March 1926. University of Manitoba Archives, L.B. Foote photograph.

Construction of the Hudson's Bay Company store on Portage Avenue, 1926. University of Winnipeg Archives, Western Pictorial Index, Delza Longman Collection, A0776-23323.

to one lane between York and Broadway avenues to avoid the "temporary buildings." Only after 1961–62, when the buildings were finally demolished, did Memorial Boulevard assume its present width with lanes on either side of the central boulevard.[9]

❖

The Hudson's Bay Company had finally begun excavating the basement of its new store on Portage Avenue in the fall of 1925. An attempt was made to ensure that building materials and fixtures used in the new store were made in Manitoba. The exterior was to be of Manitoba Tyndall stone instead of the terra cotta used in the company's other western stores in Vancouver, Edmonton, and Victoria. This was suggested by the contractors, Carter Halls Aldinger, and it was an appealing idea because the local Tyndall stone was cheaper. All the bricks used were manufactured in the province, and the steel reinforcing rods used in the concrete walls and floors came from Manitoba Rolling Mills in Selkirk. The 60,000 barrels of concrete used in the building were manufactured by Canada Cement at Fort Whyte. The 600,000 metres of wood used in the forms for the concrete was Manitoba white spruce.

The actual construction proceeded very quickly. Erection of the steel frame took ten weeks, and shifts worked around the clock to pour 380 cubic metres of concrete every day. At night giant spotlights were used to illuminate the areas under construction.

At 9:00 a.m. on November 18, 1926, George Galt, the Winnipeg grocery wholesaler and a member of the Hudson's Bay Company's Canadian Advisory Board, used a golden key to open the main door of the store in the middle of the Portage Avenue facade. The crowd surged into the new building and was greeted by the manager, W.H. Cooke, and his staff. People passed first through an arcade with vaulted ceilings and beautiful lamps built across the north side of the main floor. The arcade was to be left open until 11:00 p.m. at night, after the store was closed, so that people could wait for their streetcars there. In the store proper, the main aisle of the first floor stretched before the shoppers, affording a 122-metre view past the elevator lobby, all the way to the mezzanine at the rear.

Because of the solid concrete construction, the supporting columns could be placed 8.5 metres apart, producing unusually wide aisles. This, combined with the great height of the ceiling, gave the first floor a monumental quality. The contrast with the Hudson's Bay store on Main Street, opened in 1881, was staggering. Ever since the opening of Eaton's in 1906, the previous Hudson's Bay store had seemed overcrowded and old-fashioned, and it would soon be

Hudson's Bay store's main floor looking south, 21 November 1926. Hudson's Bay library photograph collection 1937/363–W-316/40.

Dining room of the Hudson's Bay store, 27 August 1927. Hudson's Bay library photograph collection 1937/363–W-316/43.

demolished. Now Eaton's seemed old-fashioned and their twenty-year-old store was spruced up by replacing the brick on the first storey with Tyndall stone and installing new show windows with brass frames.

The interior of the new Hudson's Bay store was sumptuously decorated. The floor on the first level was terrazzo with brass binding between the slabs. The upper floors were wood. The display cases were all made locally in Winnipeg of solid rosewood and walnut with marble bases. All the iron and brass fittings had also been manufactured in Winnipeg. The cash registers were the latest design, and the salespeople could send parcels to a central sorting area for delivery via a spiral conveyor belt. Using the Ok Credit System developed by Charles Kettering, inventor of the electric cash register, staff were able to phone the credit department where the customer's credit was checked. If the account was in order, the credit department staff stamped the cash register slip "OK" by remote signal.

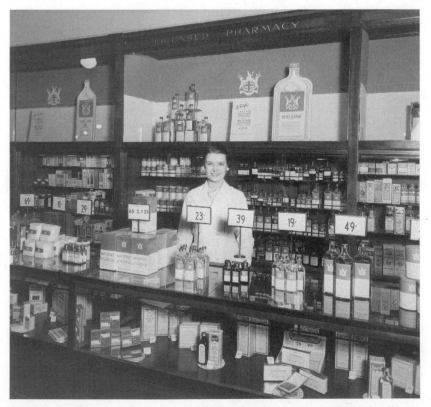

Drugstore in Hudson's Bay store, 1936. Hudson's Bay library photograph collection 1937/363-W-316/59.

The finished Hudson's Bay store. Hudson's Bay Company Archives.

The grocery department was located in the basement of the new store. The meat counter was especially well equipped with refrigerated display cases. Large storage freezers were located nearby. In the sub-basement were the huge boilers that heated the floors above, along with two giant refrigeration machines and three air compressors to force cool air through the store in the summer. The six elevators were of the latest type with automatic levelling devices. The operator could not start the car until the doors were safely closed, and if a car became stuck between floors, passengers could be evacuated through a side door into the car in the neighbouring elevator shaft.

The mezzanine at the rear of the first floor was where services like the post office and telegraph office were located, along with telephone booths, cloakrooms, and a lady's lounge. The circulating library and the Adjustment Bureau were also located there. The second floor was devoted to fashions, and a single carpet woven in Toronto covered its one acre of floorspace. When the fifth floor was finished later in 1927, it would feature what the Hudson's Bay Company promised would be one of the finest restaurants in Winnipeg. A cafeteria would be located on that floor as well. The idea of having first-class restaurants in department stores originated in Canada with Lady Eaton, who, inspired by Selfridges in London, had installed a luxurious dining room in the Eaton's Queen Street store in Toronto.

The predicted building boom did follow the opening of "The Bay" store with construction of a new Bank of Montreal branch and the Winnipeg Electric Company's Power Building east of the store on Portage Avenue. Unfortunately, the stock market crash and the beginning of the Depression in 1929 put further developments on hold for many years.

The Hudson's Bay store created construction employment and jobs inside the store. The increased income from taxes on the new store was estimated at a higher figure than Abraham Heaps's guess—$22,950 for the land and $99,000 for the building, plus business taxes of $30,000.

The new store was the sixth and last of the line of big urban department stores that the Hudson's Bay Company built in western cities, beginning with Calgary in 1912. The old store at Main Street and York Avenue had been the company's first urban department store when it opened in 1881. It was demolished as soon as the new store opened.

❖

June 1926 was when construction work on Memorial Boulevard had actually begun in the area. Alderman Robert J. Shore, a member of the Mall

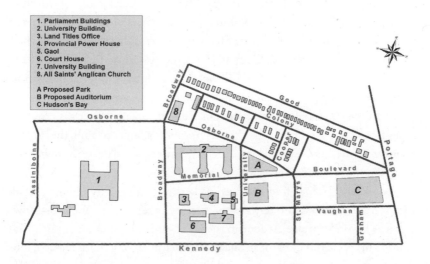

Memorial Boulevard Post-Construction. Map by Larry Laliberte.

Committee, said that the City wanted to "keep faith" with the Hudson's Bay Company by completing the Osborne Street extension with streetcar lines in place by the time of the store's official opening in the fall. Sewer and water lines had to be laid under the new streets and connected to existing lines, and then the surface of the streets was graded to make it ready for paving and streetcar lines.

The Osborne Street extension was now under construction, and fifty men and thirty teams worked levelling the area and filling the depression along the course of Colony Creek and the basements of demolished buildings with earth from the excavation of the Hudson's Bay store basement.

The Winnipeg Electric Company would lay tracks on the street after first installing complicated diamond junctions at Broadway and Portage avenues linking the new line with existing ones. The new tracks went down on the dirt surface of the street and concrete was poured into the bed between the rails. Then the Electric Company's contractor, Carter, Halls and Aldinger, paved outside the rails for forty-six centimetres on one side and thirty centimetres on the other. The city was responsible for paving the rest of the street out to the curbs. The tracks being laid north from Broadway had reached St. Mary Avenue when the weather forced work to stop on November 3.

The project inspired positive comments like those in a letter in the *Tribune* on October 5, 1926: "Walk up Broadway any afternoon and you will behold a very interesting sight. At the corner of Osborne Street 3 gangs of workmen are hard at work, one of them building the new walls of All Saints Church, the second busy with the Osborne Street extension, excavating the new thoroughfare to Portage Avenue, the third laying the new heavy track for the street railway where the Broadway and Osborne lines intersect." The anonymous writer said that while the church would be done before winter, the snow would soon halt the street railway construction. But "the dream of years is now only a question of a few months when the Mall will be a fait accompli, the greatest improvement Winnipeg will have seen in many years and destined to become more and more beautiful with the passage of time."[10]

Leo Warde, mindful of the need to keep prodding City Council, made a presentation that same day on the further extension of the cross-town highway beyond Portage Avenue to the CPR yards and on to the North End. Warde's proposal did not arouse much enthusiasm among the aldermen. John Blumberg, a Labour member, moved that Warde's plan, because it was a big project, should be held over for three months. He said there was no public demand and the cost of an underpass beneath the CP tracks would be enormous.

Warde agreed, saying that a bridge would be cheaper. The new Salter Street viaduct was not formally opened until 1932, spanning the CPR yards and completing the last link in the cross-town highway. Like the civic auditorium, the viaduct was a public works project intended to provide employment during the Depression and to be financed in part with federal money.

The mall project implemented some of the recommendations of the City Planning Commission report of 1913.[11] The commission had representative members from the city and provincial governments as well as a range of groups including the Board of Trade, the Board of Health, the Parks Board, the Trades and Labour Council, associations of architects, real estate companies, the university, and the Winnipeg Electric Railway. In addition to the various recommendations about problems facing the city, a general expression of support was provided for the role of comprehensive planning and the use of experts to ensure that developments and growth in the city were planned to fit together well and not create new problems. The city planning movement embraced by many large cities before the Great War had some influence, but in many cases development followed the same old haphazard course as in the past. Winnipeg had not used the commission report as the basis for a comprehensive plan for the city. Indeed, it seems that the commission was underfunded and that many of its research documents and maps have been lost over the years.

Winnipeg was not alone in western Canada in this regard. A rare example of a comprehensive city plan was the one created by the American firm of Harland Bartholomew and Associates for Vancouver.[12] In the 1920s planners like Bartholomew began to focus on making cities more efficient by such means as coordinating development projects. With the huge increase in the numbers of automobiles in the 1920s—there were 19,000 more cars in Winnipeg in 1929 than in 1920[13]—traffic control and traffic flow became dominant issues in city planning. There seemed to be less emphasis on aesthetics than there had been in the pre-war city planning movement, which had concerned itself with things like the psychological effect on citizens of the physical appearance of the city.[14] The focus was now on the "City Practical" or the "City Scientific."

In January 1926 Canon Bertal Heeney, the rector of St. Luke's Church and a member of the Board of Trade, spoke to the Young Men's Section of the Board of Trade about the need for city planning. Heeney was a novelist and an influential clergyman, having many of the members of Winnipeg's elite in his congregation. He told the Young Men's Section that the mall project needed centralized planning and coordination. He said care should also be taken to ensure that it was beautiful and would attract tourists, who did not necessarily come to Winnipeg only to visit the stores of the Manitoba Liquor Commission. Heeney was alluding to the fact that because the United States still had Prohibition while Canada had abolished it, many Americans came to Winnipeg for a drink. (Mayor Webb, for one, used this in attracting tourism. He said he wanted Winnipeg to be "the City of snowballs and highballs."[15]) Heeney had other criticisms. He said that the mall was in danger of simply becoming "just another street" instead of a memorial dedicated to the war dead. He also felt that the proximity of the provincial jail at the end of Vaughan Street, the site of any executions carried out in Manitoba, detracted from the mall. He felt the jail should be moved to some other less prominent location.

Alderman Dan McLean, the current chair of the Mall Committee, was angered by Heeney's comments. He said that his committee was in fact the central directing entity for the project that had negotiated all the land acquisitions and would oversee the construction work that would soon begin. Canon Heeney, McLean remarked, "would do well to familiarize himself to a greater extent with civic business before he undertakes such criticisms."[16]

McLean, however, clearly missed the point that a city plan would place the mall project in the wider context of the whole of Winnipeg. His angry outburst was a sign that the Council—Labour and business aldermen alike—was growing impatient with advice and criticism from the Board of Trade. While in the past Council and the Board of Trade had usually worked in tandem, this was no longer the case, as friction over the mall, the exhibition, and other projects suggested.

But Bertal Heeney's comments struck a chord with others. At the end of January the Manitoba Architects Association called for a governing commission to control building plans and approve the structures to be erected on the mall. The Young Men's Section of the Board of Trade agreed and in March endorsed Heeney's idea of a controlling body that, they said, could be established under the Town Planning Act to control the design, erection and use of buildings on the Mall. Several years before Leo Warde had published a pamphlet that said, "Much of the waste and inefficiency in our local improvements to date are due to the lack of relationship of one project with another. Every dollar spent on improvements should have in view the linking of the whole city at large and not merely those parts adjacent to the improvement."[17]

In February 1926, an article about town planning appeared in the *Tribune*, praising the mall as a good example. The reporter quoted Arthur Stoughton, professor of architecture at the University of Manitoba, who said that planning was now "regular accepted procedure in most places." In Winnipeg, however,

Stoughton complained that the City Zoning Committee, which had existed until the year before, had not been reappointed. When representatives of the Young Men's Section, including Leo Warde, pressed this idea during a presentation to Council, aldermen responded unenthusiastically, saying they would consider it. Labour alderman Thomas Flye revealed what was probably the main irritant when he said that "the Board of Trade has committees which duplicate every form of City government and if its members wanted to function in this sphere, the proper opportunity was at the polls when municipal election day arrived."[18]

Council soon confirmed everyone's worries by approving the construction of ten illuminated billboards along the mall. They were to have flowerbeds in front of them. There were protests and the decision was soon modified to allow billboards on Osborne Street but not Memorial Boulevard.

In October 1927 there was another controversy at Council, over a proposal to build a filling station at the corner of Osborne Street and Broadway Avenue. All Saints' Church was opposed, and Alderman Ernest Leech, a Conservative lawyer, said that they had already defaced the mall by allowing billboards to be erected and a filling station would make matters worse. It was "not in keeping with the general scheme of development in the area." But Council approved the construction by fifteen votes to one. The *Tribune* editorial of October 27 agreed with Leech, saying that approving the filling station was a mistake. It would have been a minor one, said the *Tribune*, if it were not a symptom of a general condition, which was that no attention was being paid to a "general scheme of planning for Winnipeg. Mistakes without number have been made for which Winnipeg will pay dearly in the future." The editorial went on to say that improvements like the mall were of little value if they were not related to one another in a "well considered and modern scheme of city planning."

In 1928 Council responded by creating a Special Committee on Town Planning, consisting of aldermen and the city surveyor, R.H. Avent, an idea supported by the Board of Trade, the Real Estate Board, and the Winnipeg Town Planning Institute. During 1928 the committee had twenty-eight meetings. They drafted a zoning bylaw, planned the extension of Wellington Crescent along the riverside to Assiniboine Park, and worked on the planning for the cross-town highway. They employed W.E. Hobbs as a consulting engineer. Zoning was a concept that was popular with real estate companies because it was a form of protection against changes that might reduce the value of nearby properties.

Winnipeg Auditorium. Archives of Manitoba, Celebrity Concert fonds, 1.

Civic Auditorium

As soon as construction of the mall began, lobbying for a new city auditorium began. The city had no large auditorium after the demolition of the Board of Trade's Industrial Bureau building at Main Street and Water Avenue in 1925. In March 1926 City Council had established a special committee to look into the question, and in June the members met with the City Finance Committee to make a pitch for an auditorium on Memorial Boulevard at the corner of St. Mary Avenue, exactly where the civic auditorium building was erected six years later. The auditorium committee members who spoke were Leo Warde, George Mathieson, and John N. Semmens, the architect who would eventually design the building. George Mathieson supported the new auditorium as a venue for musical performances. A grain company executive, Mathieson was also a long-time member of the executive of the Men's Musical Club and served on the board of one of the predecessors of the Winnipeg Symphony, which he helped to found.

The first step would be acquisition of the necessary land at the corner of Memorial Boulevard and St. Mary Avenue. The Finance Committee explained that because the arbitration of the price of the Cross property was still before the courts and the purchase of the Alexander Macdonald property was not complete, the auditorium project would have to wait. The Auditorium

Committee was disbanded. Never downhearted, Leo Warde went to visit Mayor Ralph Webb after his re-election to a third term in November 1926. He encouraged Webb to reappoint the special committee. Webb cautioned Warde that the project might take longer to get underway than they hoped. He pointed out that the necessary property was not yet in the hands of the City and getting Council support might be difficult.

Webb's instinct, developed during two years of working with Council, was correct. An acrimonious debate over the auditorium began early in 1927. Dan McLean, chair of the revived Mall Committee, had announced that the city was close to having a new auditorium on the mall. Some of the Labour alderman spoke against the idea. Thomas Flye stated that it would be a mistake to concentrate all the city's public buildings on the mall and that other areas of the city deserved consideration. He warned that there would be resistance if the matter was pushed through Council. Now that Memorial Boulevard was completed, Flye and other Ward 2 and Ward 3 aldermen were looking for new development in their own wards. The auditorium issue was one on which Council did not divide strictly on political lines. Rather, Flye and his colleagues were acting as ward politicians, defending the interests of their constituents. The position of the Mall Committee was that the location at the corner of St. Mary was ideal; there was parking nearby and there would be excellent streetcar service. They ignored Flye's warning and proceeded to draft a bill of incorporation and a charter for the new building.

The matter was on the agenda of a Council meeting late in May and various citizen delegations attended. One question was whether the auditorium project should be voted on by ratepayers immediately or as part of the civic election in November. Mayor Webb, Alderman Robert Shore, Robert G. Persse of the Board of Trade, and Alderman John Queen all favoured a June referendum. Once again the issue of the auditorium crossed the lines between the Labour and pro-business aldermen. Alderman John McKerchar was generally opposed to the project, as he was opposed to most new spending, and felt that the building should be paid for with private fundraising rather than money borrowed by the City. The Taxpayers Association was also in favour of waiting for the fall and it, too, was opposed to the estimated $800,000 expenditure required to build the hall and the taxes that would have to be levied to repay the loan. Aldermen Flye and Jack Blumberg objected to the expense as well but then argued for a North End location for the building.

Ralph Webb had one of his periodic losses of patience and accused the aldermen of a lack of backbone in not supporting this important improvement.

He said that industries were going to other cities because Winnipeg was showing no enterprise or initiative. McKerchar replied that Winnipeg might have a bright future "if it did not have to listen to hot-air artists." Presumably he had the mayor in mind.

The banker Hugh Osler spoke at the meeting, saying that if Winnipeg did not go forward with such projects, it would go backward. It was time, he said, to spend some money on a new auditorium. The Trades and Labour Council representatives at the meeting agreed with Osler and called for a June vote, no doubt thinking of the construction jobs that would result. At the end of the meeting, however, City Council voted for a referendum to take place in November 1927 at the same time as the civic election.

The decision frustrated many. In a letter to the editor of the *Tribune*, an impatient citizen advised Council to "get a move on. Don't listen to every contrary wind of criticism—for the most part it's nothing more than wind. Nothing right would ever be accomplished in this world if criticism and condemnation are pandered to."[19] Others wrote letters saying the auditorium and the whole mall project were things the city could well do without at the moment. On November 24, an ad paid for by Holt Renfrew and D. Dingwall Jewellers appeared on page two of the *Tribune*. It encouraged ratepayers to vote for the auditorium, arguing, "we need the convention business it will bring." The auditorium will "show the world that Winnipeg is a modern progressive city."

Alderman Shore was chair of the auditorium committee, and he brought a complete report on the issue to Council. A bylaw was drafted on which the ratepayers would be asked to vote. It gave a cost of $900,000 for the auditorium. When the bylaw was given first reading, McKerchar and Flye both spoke against the project. Flye called for an accounting of how much the mall project had cost to that point. The figure was $471,256, including the cost of the land that had been expropriated. The cost of the auditorium would be $1.6 million once it was repaid over a twenty-year period. These figures were guaranteed to scare off at least some voters.

Continuing their unusual alliance, the Taxpayers Association and Labour Alderman John Blumberg both spoke in favour of a North End location, and aldermen Flye and McKerchar—another unlikely pair of allies—put forward the idea that the ratepayers should be asked to vote on the location as well. Others pointed out that placing the auditorium elsewhere might help to maintain property values in the area around the building. Andrew R. McNichol, a real estate developer who had the distinction of having the city's largest tax bill, wrote a letter to the papers, throwing yet another option into the debate.

He supported the construction of an auditorium but thought it would make more sense as part of a new City Hall development on Main Street, something that would eventually happen in the 1960s. Alderman Shore, frustrated, said that every community proposal that came before Council was opposed by the "calamity howlers." He said that the auditorium was essential if the city expected to attract convention business, and he was uncomfortable about the way different areas of the city were being pitted against one another.

The *Tribune* supported Shore and the proposed building, and on October 5, 1927, told Winnipeggers that they should be guided in the voting by their "civic pride, enterprise and duty." Closer to the election the paper argued that the building would provide an up-to-date facility for the city, something that would express civic spirit, pride, and purpose, all things that play a role in the forward march of progressive cities.[20] The Trades and Labour Council intervened once again with strong support for the project. The antagonism between the international union representatives who dominated the Trades and Labour Council and the Labour aldermen came to the surface when Labour City Council officers claimed that Labour aldermen were "motivated by blind antagonism ... these men are against anything that is brought forward by the other group on Council."[21] This criticism was not actually true, as Labour and some business aldermen had formed an alliance to oppose the auditorium and the chosen site.

Things became even more confused in early November, just weeks away from the election, when the Board of Trade suddenly announced that it supported the idea put forward by McNichol: a new City Hall complex including a city auditorium. The Board expressed concern that the auditorium might be voted down because the cost of the land on the mall made the project more expensive. In reality the bylaw being voted on did not contain any mention of a proposed site. Nevertheless, the Board of Trade asked Alderman Ernest Leech to make a motion to rescind City Council's approval of the mall site. When this motion came up for a vote at Council, Alderman Blumberg blocked it by moving that the meeting adjourn before the motion was voted on.

The motion to rescind approval was later voted on at a special meeting of Council. It was defeated, and Council support for the mall location was maintained. The discussion at the meeting was a clear indication of the lack of unity among Council members as well as of the reduced ability of the Board of Trade to influence events. Mayor Webb tried hard to get a consensus among the aldermen present, but he failed. If the ratepayer voters were confused, it would not have been surprising.

Lawrence Tibbet concert at the Winnipeg Auditorium, 9 November 1932. Archives of Manitoba, Celebrity Concerts, 37.

On November 24, 1927, the day before the election, Webb, throwing his considerable prestige behind the auditorium project, published a three-quarter-page comprehensive defence of the auditorium in the papers, laying out in detail his answers to all the objections that had been raised to locating it on the mall. He rejected the new City Hall idea because of the immense cost of building a large facility to house both the city government and the auditorium. He said the auditorium would bring in money from ticket sales and rentals to pay a portion of the operating costs.

On election day the bylaw was defeated. The actual vote of 5,703 in favour and 6,433 against meant that supporters were 1,578 short of the three-fifths majority required for a money bylaw. Five years later, in 1932, the auditorium was finally built on what was by then called Memorial Boulevard. Like the Salter Viaduct and the federal building at Main Street and Water Avenue, the project was partly funded by the federal government as one of the many public projects intended to provide work for unemployed men.

The politics surrounding the auditorium vote were frustrating for the supporters of the project. But to look at it from a different perspective, the controversy indicated that a more mature democracy was developing in Winnipeg. Aldermen formed alliances that crossed the left/right line that divided Council. The public participated in the debate, and some politicians, like Ralph Webb, took strong positions and fought hard for them. Labour had established itself as a permanent political force in the city, and the Board of Trade no longer could expect unquestioning support for its positions.

The Music Community

Some of the main supporters of the auditorium project had been people in the music community in Winnipeg, who believed the building would help the development of the performing arts in the city. The 1920s were years when music lovers began to have much better access to classical music in their homes and at concerts. There had been concerts and travelling artists visiting the city for a long time, and the Women's and Men's Musical Clubs had, since 1894 and 1915, respectively, been sponsoring concerts featuring both local musicians and musicians brought in from elsewhere.

But during the 1920s greater access to piano rolls, acoustic recordings, and, after 1925, electric recordings brought the performances of great soloists into people's homes and greatly increased the interest in live concerts. The city had a number of churches that could be used for performances and rooms in hotels, such as the seventh-floor Concert Room in the Fort Garry, but the only large auditorium, the hall in the Board of Trade building at Main Street and Water Avenue, with a capacity of 3,000, was closed in 1925 because it did not meet the requirements of the fire code.

In the mid-1920s, gramophone recordings of orchestral works became more popular with the coming of electric recording, which captured the performance with a microphone and transferred it to the record as electrical impulses. This produced a sound closer to a live performance than had older techniques. With the widespread introduction of electrical recordings, anyone with a phonograph in their living room could enjoy the improved quality of sound recordings. As music historian Robert Philip writes, "In the long term it was recordings that spread the knowledge of what was best in orchestral performance. Increasingly, the great conductors were promoted by their recordings."[22] The same could certainly be said of famous soloists who began to tour to places like Winnipeg in the 1920s. In 1924, for example, Jascha Heifetz came to Winnipeg on November 27 for one of many local concerts he gave over the years. He played in the Board of Trade auditorium at Main and Water. He was already an important recording artist and his records were available in Winnipeg.

The music world in Winnipeg was enriched during the 1920s by the organists and choir masters in the big churches. Most of the large downtown churches had good-quality pipe organs and choir programs, and had

Maggie Teyte and Fred Gee, 15 March 1947. Gee was responsible for organizing celebrity concerts in Winnipeg, which were held at the Auditorium after it was built.

paid organists and choirmasters on staff. Hugh Ross was one example. An Englishman who came to Winnipeg to be the organist and choirmaster at Holy Trinity Church, Ross founded the Philharmonic Choir and led the Winnipeg Orchestral Club orchestra. He took the Philharmonic Choir to perform at Carnegie Hall in 1923. In 1927 he left Winnipeg to become the director of the Schola Cantorum of New York. He had a long, successful career in that city as a teacher at the Manhattan School of Music and choral director at the Tanglewood Festival.

Fred Gee, another organist, had come from Scotland to be the organist at Augustine Church on River Avenue. He also played as an accompanist for other musicians at concerts of the Men's Musical Club, and in 1921 he went on an eleven-week tour as accompanist for Canadian violinist Kathleen Parlow, who played a total of twenty-five concerts in the western United States. Gee went on another extensive tour with the émigré Russian tenor Vladimir Rosing in 1924. Gee also began to organize concerts in Winnipeg for visiting artists and in 1927 he founded the Celebrity Concert Series. At first he used the Central Congregational Church on Hargrave Street near Notre Dame Avenue. People could subscribe to the concert series or just buy individual tickets, usually at a store such as Winnipeg Piano. The 1927 series included singers Anna Case, an American soprano; six English singers from London; and Louis Graveure, an English baritone who lived in New York. In December 1928 Gee also organized benefit concerts for the Knowles Home for Boys and the Children's Hospital. The patrons of the concert were Mr. and Mrs. James Richardson, Mr. and Mrs. Hugh Osler, and Mr. and Mrs. Harold Gooderham, all wealthy social leaders. The performer for the concert was Kayla Mitzl, a brilliant Winnipeg violinist, thirteen years old at the time, who had studied in the United States and Europe. Unfortunately, she retired from playing when she was still quite young and went to live in California. Gee would continue to offer the Celebrity Concerts for over thirty years and, once the auditorium was built in 1932, his series performances always took place there.

The Cenotaph

On Sunday, June 13, 1920, Reverend Charles W. Gordon of St. Stephen's Church and Rev. Woods of St. Margaret's Church dedicated a temporary cenotaph, erected at the corner of Portage Avenue and Main Street in front of the Bank of Montreal. It was a project of the Women's Canadian Club. General Patterson and other army officers were present and Mrs. Aikins laid the official wreath. Many other wreaths in memory of individuals and groups were also laid. Mrs. Code spoke of the many crosses in quiet corners overseas, and of Winnipeg's need for a permanent cenotaph to commemorate the dead.

In 1927 the location and design of the Winnipeg cenotaph still had not been settled except for agreement that it would be placed somewhere on Memorial Boulevard. There had been controversy because the first winner of the design competition, Emmanuel Hahn, had been born in Germany, which apparently made his work unacceptable in spite of the fact that he had come to Canada as a child and had long been a naturalized Canadian. The committee

The unveiling of the Memorial Boulevard cenotaph, 11 November 1928. Archives of Manitoba, Events 344, N19831.

appointed to oversee the cenotaph had received communications from veterans' groups and family members of Canadian war dead who did not think it was appropriate for a memorial to Canadian soldiers to be designed by someone of German origin. A second call for designs resulted in Toronto artist Elizabeth Wyn-Wood's winning the competition. However, when it was discovered that she was Emmanuel Hahn's wife, her entry was also rejected. Committee members said they thought her design of a naked man with a sword was "too much for Winnipeg." In the end, the cenotaph we now have, designed by Wilfrid Parfitt, a local architect who had been born in England, was approved.

The Board had supported the wishes of veterans' and soldiers' family members about using Hahn's design, but it did not want this to be construed as being opposed in any way to naturalized Canadians. The statement said that "some of our best citizens are naturalized Canadians" and two presidents of the Board had been in that category.[23] This comment refers to Alvin K. Godfrey and William H. Carter, who were both born in the United States. The Board of Trade said they were aware Mr. Hahn was a loyal Canadian.

On Sunday, November 11, 1928, ten years after the end of the Great War, the cenotaph was finally dedicated. Memorial Boulevard was crowded with the largest Armistice Day congregation to date. They lined the area north of the new cenotaph and Lieutenant-Governor Theodore Burrows unveiled the memorial. There was a church service, and wreaths were laid by the mayor and representatives of different military units and organizations. Many individuals in the crowd also laid flowers at the memorial and some kneeled down to pray for loved ones. Winnipeggers at long last had a memorial that could be the focus of their memories and their grief.

Main Street, looking south, with Confederation Life Building on left, 1923. Archives of Manitoba, McAdam fonds, 431.

CONCLUSION

The 1920s in Winnipeg had begun under the shadow of the shocks of the General Strike, the First World War, and the influenza pandemic. The decade had also started with the grand opening of the magnificent new Legislative Building, an impressive symbol of the city's earlier optimism and sense of its own future. Throughout this difficult decade, the people of Winnipeg and their leaders fluctuated between these two poles of anxiety and ambition. Their confidence had been shaken by the events of the previous decade, but they still held onto much of their old optimism. If Winnipeg could no longer boast of being the Chicago of the North, it was still Canada's third largest city—at least until Vancouver's population overtook it by 1931—and a place that deserved large civic projects.[1] There were many ambitious public and private enterprises undertaken in the decade, from new hydroelectric plants to the beautiful new Hudson's Bay Company store and the development of Memorial Boulevard. The city, it seemed, was not going to be written off. The expansion of manufacturing that took place after 1925 resulted in more employment. The construction of new hydroelectric capacity provided power for the future expansion of manufacturing. The opening of the Flin Flon mine provided some benefits for Winnipeg, as did the construction of the paper mill at Fort Alexander.

In the late 1920s existing Winnipeg firms had expanded their facilities and new enterprises opened in the city. The garment industry expanded and

First page of The Winnipeg Evening Tribune *from 19 July 1929 showing James Richardson's proposed skyscraper. University of Manitoba Archives,* Winnipeg Tribune *fonds.*

began manufacturing a much wider range of products. A new slaughterhouse was constructed in St. Boniface and existing facilities were expanded. Even the fur business boomed because of the demand for luxury furs in the United States. The Industrial Bureau worked hard to promote Winnipeg products, and the Tourist and Convention Bureau promoted the city as a destination and a site for conventions. The continued development of hydro capacity on the Winnipeg River was driven by the needs of the expanding industrial sector for cheap power. All this activity began to slow down in 1929 and 1930, although the actual number of manufacturing businesses continued to expand as unemployed people set up enterprises.

By the end of the decade, another ambitious and optimistic new building was announced by a man who was becoming a leader of the city's business community. James Richardson had diversified his family grain business during the 1920s to become a leading stockbroker, and in 1926 had established Western Canada Airways, which would help make Winnipeg an important hub in air travel. In 1928, he assembled parcels of land at the corner of Portage and Main, and in October 1929 announced plans for a seventeen-storey skyscraper. Both Winnipeg newspapers featured drawings of the new building on their front pages. Designed in the popular Gothic Revival style, the Richardson Building would cost $2 million. It would be ten stories higher than the massive Grain Exchange Building on Lombard Avenue and would tower over the other buildings in the city's commercial centre. It would be topped by a huge clock face and revolving aircraft beacon, a kind of commercial counterpoint to the city's other symbol of progress and optimism, the Golden Boy. This skyscraper at the city's iconic corner was clearly meant to signal confidence and pride in the city's financial and commercial future. Construction started immediately, with the demolition of the existing buildings at Portage and Main and the excavation of the basement.

Only weeks later, however, the crash of the New York Stock Market started the chain of events that would become the Great Depression. It did not take long for its impact to be felt in Winnipeg. Richardson suffered losses, and in November 1929, as the extent of the crash became clear, he stopped work on the project. The basement was filled in and a gas station was built on the site. The cancellation of the proposed skyscraper more than anything else symbolized the effect of the stock market crash on Winnipeg. The optimism that had been slowly building in the last half of the 1920s was once again dampened.

Beyond the thwarted construction project, the impact of the U.S. stock market crash was manifested only slowly in Winnipeg. Many building projects started in 1929 proceeded, including the construction of a number of luxury houses in Tuxedo. Then, as 1930 progressed, building slowed and the value of construction in that year turned out to be about 50 percent of the total for 1929—$6.6 million compared with $11 million.

Although there was some building activity during the 1930s—federal grants made possible the completion of the Civic Auditorium, the federal office building on the corner of Main and Water Streets, and the Salter Street viaduct—there was little other construction for some time. For most of the decade of the 1930s, Winnipeg would struggle to provide relief for large numbers of unemployed and the city would experience a period of low growth or actual decline.

In Winnipeg the collapse of prices on the stock market was combined with the collapse of grain prices. After a crop of record size in 1928, the prairies produced a much smaller wheat crop in 1929. Grain prices fell because of oversupply from Argentina and Australia and the re-entry of Russia into the grain export trade. The wheat pools faced serious problems because they had paid their members an initial price of one dollar, only to see the market price drop below that figure. They had to turn to the provincial and then the federal governments for loans in order to prevent their collapse. Wheat prices declined from a peak of $1.57 a bushel in May 1928 to $1.13 a year later, and then on down to average prices of forty-nine cents a bushel in 1930, thirty-eight cents in 1931, and thirty-five cents in 1932.[2] Drought and low prices caused parts of the prairies to be abandoned by farmers. The effects of the Depression on Winnipeg businesses, dependent as they often were on sales to farmers, was devastating.

In 1920 Winnipeg was only fifty years away from its origin as a disorganized cluster of frame buildings on the edge of over 1,000 kilometres of prairie. During that half-century the city had metamorphosed into a modern city not very different from much older communities in eastern Canada and the United States. Along the way, it had transformed itself from a rowdy, brawling frontier town with saloons into a community with streets and buildings steadily taking on the look of a small Ontario city. It had been the first beachhead of the eastern Canadian invasion of the West, the place where speculators made and lost fortunes as the Dominion Land Survey transformed thousands of kilometres of prairie into neat, saleable farms and town lots. Winnipeg and its people participated in this land casino, and when the boom collapsed in 1882 and Easterners lost their shirts, many locals were ruined as well. The second great boom in the years leading up to the Great War ended similarly with speculators facing ruin and a few walking away as big winners.

By the 1920s most people slowly realized there would never be another boom, although there was controversy over this question during the mayoral election campaign in which Ralph Webb challenged Seymour Farmer. Webb's appeal was, in part, that he seemed to be the man who could bring back the boom years and set Winnipeg on the road to success once more. By the 1920s Winnipeg's dominant position had been eroded and the city, faced with increased competition from communities further west, continued to

View of Donald and Ellice, looking northwest, towards Old Knox Church and First Baptist Church, 1923. Archives of Manitoba, McAdam fonds, 426, N19832.

decline during the decade. There were energetic and determined individuals who tackled the city's decline and tried to halt it and turn it around. They had differing views on the matter, and this sometimes resulted in a failure to put remedies in place.

Winnipeg had been the headquarters for the eastern transformation of the prairies, and its people and institutions presided over constant change. It is fair to say that the city, too, changed constantly during its first half-century, but in some ways the same people remained in charge, the same groups maintained control of decisions about the development of the city, and so there was much that did not change. The 1920s were a time of transition in these areas and for the people who had had control in Winnipeg. All this produced conflict and chaos, but at the same time it began to lay the foundations of a more diverse and ultimately healthier city

During the Depression the old elite were forced to make the first small concessions, and the new groups learned the tactics and strategies of successful politics. They learned well, and the 1930s saw John Queen, a Labour mayor, win seven terms and Labour aldermen hold the majority on City Council for the first time. While Ralph Webb occupied the Mayor's Office at the beginning of the Depression, from 1930 to 1934, and then became a Conservative MLA. Former Labour mayor Seymour Farmer also sat in the provincial Legislature in the 1930s and was the leader there of the new CCF Party. Farmer was minister of labour in the short-lived coalition government in the 1940s.

There were many other changes that define the modern city of Winnipeg, and in the people and events considered in this book we can see the first glimpses of many of the things that would define Winnipeg in the future. There could be no doubt that Winnipeg had a future, and that the people of the city would once again rise to the challenge.

Winnipeg, 17 November 2018

Acknowledgements

Many people have helped me in the making of this book. I have presented parts of it in courses I taught at the University Women's Club, McNally Robinson Booksellers, and for the 55 Plus Program of the University of Winnipeg. I am grateful for those opportunities and for the support that staff and volunteers gave me in each place.

I have spent many hours in both the City of Winnipeg Archives and the Archives of Manitoba, and the staff in both places helped me immensely in finding documents and photos. City Archivist Jody Baltessen and her staff were patient with my requests and made suggestions. I am grateful to Jody for writing the Preface for this book. At the Archives of Manitoba, the staff were similarly helpful and patient. I am particularly indebted to Chris Kotecki for his suggestions and guidance. Thanks as well to Larry Laliberte, GIS Librarian at the University of Alberta, for creating the maps for this book.

The staff at University of Manitoba Press played, as usual, important roles in editing and improving my text. Managing editor Glenn Bergen and copy editor Pat Sanders corrected many mistakes and smoothed out my sometimes convoluted prose. The director, David Carr, gave encouragement and support during a very long writing process. Barbara Romanik did an outstanding job finding photos to illustrate the book and I am grateful to her for her work.

Family and friends have been hearing about this book for a while now and I thank them all for looking interested and listening to me. My father, who grew up in the 1920s, first got me interested in this decade. Even though they were a little outdated, his tips about the best places to neck and spoon around Minnedosa were interesting and I would thank him for his inspiration if he were still with us.

Notes

Preface

1 Council Communications, No. 11772, 1919 (A182), 3 March 1919.
2 H. Carl Goldenberg, "Report of the Royal Commission on the Municipal Finances and Administration of the City of Winnipeg, 1939," 17.
3 Council Minutes, 14 July 1924.

Introduction

1 *Winnipeg Tribune*, 15 July 1920, 2.
2 Maurice Genser was the president of Genser and Sons Furniture and supported Winnipeg's musical community by serving as the business manager of the Musicians' Union and president of the Winnipeg Orchestral Club. By the 1920s his three sons—Lawrence, Harold, and Percy—were also well-known musicians in Winnipeg.

Chapter 1: Hope Against Despair

1 Morton, "The 1920s," 205.
2 Durkin, *The Magpie*, 141-2.
3 *Winnipeg Tribune*, 17 March 1919, 12.
4 City of Winnipeg Archives, Housing Committee Files, letter in file A1369 f.8.
5 Aikins, "Address of the President."
6 Ibid., 541.
7 *Dixon's address to the jury in defence of freedom of speech and Judge Galt's charge to the jury in Rex v. Dixon*. [Winnipeg: Defence Committee], 1920, 9 and 22. Parts of the speech are quoted in the *Winnipeg Tribune*, 14 February 1920, 1 and 11.

8   Robson, "Report of the Royal Commssion," 6.
9   Ibid., 29.
10 Ibid., 27.

Chapter 2: The Postwar Depression and Its Effects

1   Thompson and Seager, *Canada 1922–1939,* 76–77.
2   The reasons for the drop in prices is discussed later in the section on the Winnipeg Grain Exchange.
3   Bliss, *Northern Enterprise,* 383–88, deals with the postwar depression.
4   Kryzanowski, "Canadian Banking Solvency," 366.
5   Riley, *Memoirs,* 85–86.
6   Ibid., 86.
7   *Canadian Finance,* 16 September 1925, pp. 505–6.
8   Winnipeg Board of Trade Annual Report, 1924/5.
9   Hedlin, "Edward A. Partridge," http://www.mhs.mb.ca/docs/transactions/3/partridge.shtml.
10 Acland, "Report of the Royal Grain Inquiry."
11 Patton, *Grain Growers' Cooperation,* 210.
12 See Levine, "Open Market."
13 Anderson, *Grain,* 148.
14 Ibid., 111.
15 Bellan, *Winnipeg First Century,* 73–74.
16 *Canadian Finance,* 1924, 297.
17 *Winnipeg Community Builder,* 1 December 1921, 5(58).
18 Hibbitts, "A Change of Mind," 96.

Chapter 3: Twenty-One Millionaires

1   The *Telegram* article is reproduced in Artibise, *Gateway City,* 117–30.
2   *Canadian Finance,* 1 August 1928, 451.
3   A rough calculation to establish the modern value of Canadian dollars for 1920 to 1930 is to multiply by twelve. http://inflationcalculator.ca/ (accessed 5 January 2017).
4   *Winnipeg Tribune,* 19 March 1926.
5   See https://www.dollartimes.com/calculators/inflation.htm.
6   Lowe, "All Western Dollars," 13.
7   Hanlon, "William Forbes Alloway," http://www.biographi.ca/en/bio/alloway_william_forbes_15E.html.
8   AM (Archives of Manitoba), Sanford Evans Correspondence, MG14 B28, letter to his aunt, 16 May 1921.
9   Ibid.
10 Ibid.
11 This business developed into the Sanford Evans Statistical Service, which for many years published grain statistics. Sanford Evans Research Group still exists at the time of writing and publishes the Gold Books that provide information on vehicle values.
12 AM, Sanford Evans Correspondence, MG14 B28, box 6.

Chapter 4: Unemployment and Unrest

1   See Blanchard, *Winnipeg's Great War*, 154–60.

2   *Winnipeg Tribune*, 28 January 1919.

3   Ibid.

4   *Winnipeg Tribune*, 8 February 1919.

5   *Winnipeg Free Press*, 11 April 1919.

6   *Winnipeg Tribune*, 15 August 1919.

7   As a federal Labour MP, Heaps played a major role in lobbying for an insurance system and he drafted the bill that became the Federal Unemployment Insurance Act passed in 1940.

8   City of Winnipeg Municipal Manual, 1921, 39.

9   Goeres, "Disorder, Dependency and Fiscal Responsibility," 51.

10 James Gray describes what it was like working in the same wood yard a decade later during the Great Depression. Gray, *Winter Years*, 15 and 16.

11 *Winnipeg Tribune*, 26 January 1921.

12 Goeres, "Disorder, Dependency and Fiscal Responsibility," 72.

Chapter 5: City Politics and the Trauma of the Strike

1   "Liberal-Conservative" was not a designation used at the time, but since most of the people in question would have been either Liberals or Conservatives it seems like a useful term to apply to them. This number was increased to six in 1882 and seven in 1906. The ward system and the property qualification for voters were, like most other aspects of Winnipeg city government, imported from Ontario. See Artibise, *Gateway City*, 27.

2   City of Winnipeg Municipal Manual, 1919, 11.

3   Ibid., 105.

4   Epp-Koop, *We're Going to Run*, 130–31.

5   *Winnipeg Tribune*, 21 February 1929, 13.

6   *Winnipeg Telegram*, 23 September 1919.

7   Hall, "Times of Trouble" is the best source for a description of this struggle.

8   Hall, "Times of Trouble," 74.

9   City of Winnipeg Archives, Election Records, A-800, 1919.

10 Ward 5 was a North End ward between Selkirk and Logan avenues.

11 *Winnipeg Tribune*, 19 November 1919.

12 In the event Gray won only 541 votes to Farmer's 2006 in Ward 5.

13 *Winnipeg Tribune*, 24 November 1919.

14 City Council Minutes, 19 January 1920.

15 A total of fourteen strike leaders were arrested in June 1919. Ten of these men— George Armstrong, Roger E. Bray, Abraham Heaps, Fred J. Dixon, William Ivens, Richard J. Johns, William A. Pritchard, John Queen, Robert B. Russell, and James S. Woodsworth—were charged with seditious conspiracy or seditious libel. The trials began in November 1919 with Russell, who was convicted and given a two-year sentence. The others received one-year sentences except for Heaps and Dixon, who were acquitted, and Woodsworth, whose charges were dropped. Some were released early.

16   *Winnipeg Free Press*, 17 August 1920. Sullivan was born in the United States and came to Canada in the 1890s to work as a professional engineer. He was eventually chief engineer of the CPR.

17   *Winnipeg Tribune*, 20 November 1920, 15.

18   Hall, "Times of Trouble," 77.

19   See http://westenddumplings.blogspot.ca/2010/02/elgins-bread-history.html (accessed 3 September 2017), for information about Speirs and Parnell.

20   *Winnipeg Tribune*, 27 November 1920.

21   *Winnipeg Tribune*, 11 November 1920.

22   Sutcliffe, "Economic Background of the Winnipeg General Strike," 22.

23   Quoted in *Seventh Census of Canada, 1931*, Volume XII, Monographs, H.F. Greenway, *Housing in Canada*, 435.

24   This was about 6 percent of the total appropriation. Manitoba, with 610,118 people, had about 6.9 percent of the country's population.

25   City of Winnipeg Archives, Meeting Minutes in Housing Committee, file A 1369, f. 8

26   *Winnipeg Tribune*, 22 April 1919.

27   *Winnipeg Tribune*, 3 May 1919.

28   *Winnipeg Tribune*, 25 July 1919.

29   *Winnipeg Tribune*, 10 July 1919.

30   Winnipeg City Council Minutes, 1919, p. 590. *A Report of the Special Committee on Housing*, dated 15 July 1919, is printed in the minutes.

31   Winnipeg Municipal Manual, 1924.

32   *Winnipeg Tribune*, 24 November 1921.

33   *Winnipeg Tribune*, 30 November 1920.

34   City Council Minutes, 9 June 1919.

35   Cited in Bumsted, *Winnipeg General Strike*, 41.

36   *Winnipeg Tribune*, 25 November 1922.

37   *Winnipeg Tribune*, 13 November 1924.

38   *Canadian Finance*, 3 October 1923, 577.

39   *Winnipeg Free Press*, 16 November 1923.

40   *Winnipeg Free Press*, 16 November 1923.

41   *Winnipeg Free Press*, 6 November 1923.

42   *Winnipeg Free Press*, 24 November 1923.

43   *Winnipeg Tribune*, 24 November 1923, 4.

44   *Winnipeg Free Press*, 24 November 1923, 13.

Chapter 6: Towards a New Consensus

1   *Winnipeg Free Press*, 23 November 1924, 6.

2   *Winnipeg Tribune*, 19 November 1924, 11.

3   *Winnipeg Tribune*, 19 November 1924, 11.

4   *Winnipeg Tribune*, "Civic Forum," 26 November 1924, 8.

5   The railway to Hudson Bay was revived in 1928 and finished in 1929, but the jobs that were created were poorly paid, as low as twenty-five cents an hour, and working

conditions were terrible, resulting in deaths among the workers. "The Coldest Site on the Web," http://www.zambonista.com/hbr/ (accessed 2 January 2017).

6   *Winnipeg Free Press*, 29 November 1924, 1.

7   Thompson, "Political Career of Ralph H. Webb," 1.

8   George Siamandas, "The WinnipegTime Machine," http://timemachine. siamandas.com/ (accessed November 2014). The Alhambra had opened first as the Coliseum in 1912 and changed its name in 1918. It was built for dancing. Dancing lasted from 8.30 p.m. to 12.30 a.m., and you could go early at 7:00 p.m. and take dance lessons.

9   *Canadian Annual Review*, 1925/6, 460.

10   *Canadian Finance*, 18 February 1921, 127.

11   AM, MG 10 A 21, Industrial Development Board of Manitoba files.

12   *Less Travelled: A Journey from Pine to Palm*, Highway Walkers Media, 2015, is a film about driving the Jefferson Highway in 2015.

13   *Canadian Finance*, 1925, 560.

14   *Winnipeg Free Press*, 18 November 1925, 2.

15   *Winnipeg Tribune*, 25 November 1925, 3.

16   *Winnipeg Tribune*, 24 November 1925.

17   *Winnipeg Tribune*, 19 February 1926.

18   *Winnipeg Tribune*, 19 February 1926.

19   *Winnipeg Tribune*, 23 November 1926, 17.

20   "All-weather roads" in 1920s Manitoba refers to gravel or, more rarely, paved roads that, unlike the more common dirt roads, could be used all year round.

21   *Winnipeg Free Press*, 29 December 1927.

22   *Canadian Finance*, 1927, 663.

23   For Bracken's role in northern development, see Mochoruk, *Formidable Heritage*, especially Chapter 8, "Premier Bracken's Struggle," 291–322.

24   *Winnipeg Tribune*, 22 November 1928.

25   *Reports Relating to the Development of the Seven Sisters Site on the Winnipeg River.* Province of Manitoba, 1928.

26   *Winnipeg Tribune*, 19 November 1929.

27   *Winnipeg Free Press*, 20 November 1929.

28   *Winnipeg Free Press*, 21 November 1929.

29   Ibid.

30   *Winnipeg Free Press*, 23 November 1929.

31   *Winnipeg Tribune*, 19 November 1929.

32   *Winnipeg Tribune*, 21 November 1929, 7.

Chapter 7: The Elite in an Unhappy City

1   *Winnipeg Free Press*, 17 November 1925.

2   Nanton, *Prairie Explosion*, 127.

3   Huck and Whiteway, *One Hundred Years at the St. Charles Country Club*, 9.

4   Gyro Club of Winnipeg, "History of Our Club," www.winnipeg.gyro.ws/history. html.

5   Levine, *Coming of Age*, 127.

6   Vincent, "Development of the High-Rise."

7   Levine, "Rise of American Boarding Schools."

8   AM, Sanford Evans Correspondence, MG14 B28, box 6.

9   Hungerford, *Planning a Trip Abroad*.

10 Ibid., 18.

Chapter 8: A Diminished Roar

1   Winnipeg Public School Board Annual Reports, 1919, 1920–1929. For the situation nationally, see Stamp, "Canadian High Schools."

2   *Winnipeg Tribune*, 25 May 1921.

3   *Winnipeg Tribune*, 28 June 1921.

4   *Winnipeg Tribune*, 4 August 1921.

5   *Winnipeg Tribune*, 28 March 1926.

6   *Winnipeg Tribune*, 3 January 1925.

7   *Winnipeg Tribune*, 24 November 1926.

8   Morton, "Women on Their Own"; Murray, "Governing 'Unwed Mothers'"; Chambers, "Adoption, Unwed Mothers."

9   *Winnipeg Tribune*, 19 August 1921.

10 *Winnipeg Tribune*, 4 August 1921.

11 Ibid.

12 Ibid.

13 Ibid.

14 *Winnipeg Tribune*, 2 March 1922.

15 *Winnipeg Tribune*, 5 April 1922.

16 *Winnipeg Tribune*, 28 July 1921.

17 *Winnipeg Tribune*, 21 September 1922.

18 See Thompson, "Prohibition Question."

19 *Winnipeg Tribune*, 5 March 1921.

20 *Winnipeg Tribune*, 26 January 1921.

21 *Winnipeg Tribune*, 29 January 1921.

22 *Winnipeg Free Press*, 25 January 1922.

23 *Winnipeg Tribune*, 3 January 1921.

24 *Winnipeg Tribune*, 21 September 1921.

25 Ibid.

26 *Winnipeg Tribune*, 9 April 1921.

27 *Manitoba Free Press*, 31 January 1922.

28 *Winnipeg Tribune*, 21 January 1922.

29 *Canadian Finance*, 6 February 1921, 245.

30 *Winnipeg Free Press*, 16 June 1923.

31 *Winnipeg Free Press*, 23 June 1923.

32 *Winnipeg Tribune*, 23 June 1923.

33 MacPherson, "George Chipman."

Chapter 9: New Entertainments

1   Wayburn, *Art of Stage Dancing*.
2   Comacchio, "Dancing to Perdition," 9.
3   Yellis, "Prosperity's Child," 60.
4   Comacchio, "Dancing to Perdition," 5.
5   *Montreal Gazette*, 8 January 1927.
6   *Winnipeg Tribune*, 9 December 1922.
7   *Winnipeg Tribune*, 3 December 1921.
8   Gray, *Roar of the Twenties*, 15. "Table stakes" means that players can only bet once in each hand and cannot raise during the hand.
9   Coleman, *Hoofprint on My Heart*, 76.
10 Ibid., 49.
11 *Winnipeg Free Press*, 10 September 1924.
12 Coleman, *Hoofprints on My Heart*, 50.
13 Ibid., 49.
14 *Manitoba Free Press*, 13 June 1925.
15 *Winnipeg Tribune*, 18 February 1926.

Chapter 10: Amusement Parks and Winter Fairs

1   *Winnipeg Tribune*, 13 February 1922.
2   "City Planning Commission Report," in Artibise, *Gateway City*, 226–64.
3   *Winnipeg Tribune*, 18 October 1927.
4   Coaster Enthusiasts of Canada, http://cec.chebucto.org/ClosPark/River.html (accessed 25 September 2015).
5   The homeowners of this neighbourhood had fought to protect their peace and quiet once before. In 1912, when Sir William McKenzie, president of the Canadian Northern Railway, had attempted to build a railroad line along the riverbank parallel to Jubilee Avenue and across the Red River to St. Vital, the residents campaigned successfully to stop him. See Blanchard, Winnipeg 1912, 103.
6   *Manitoba Free Press*, 7 March 1929.
7   *Winnipeg Tribune*, 5 February 1930.
8   After the construction of Polo Park and Whittier Park in 1924 and 1925, the provincial government, alarmed at the amount of money being gambled at the tracks, legislated that only one race meet a year could be held in any municipality. Polo Park was inside Winnipeg's boundaries and Whittier was in St. Boniface, but the North Kildonan site, being in a separate municipality, would be eligible for an additional race meet.
9   *Winnipeg Tribune*, 16 September 1930.
10 *Winnipeg Tribune*, 30 September 1930.

Chapter 11: Building Memorial Boulevard

1   "Joint Committee's Report on Proposed Civic Centre," in Artibise, *Gateway City*, 237–38.
2   Baker, *Symbol in Stone*.
3   *Winnipeg Tribune*, 2 January 1922.

4   *Winnipeg Tribune*, 2 December 1920. The opportunity Parnell referred to was the new Hudson's Bay store, to be built once the mall plan was completed.

5   HBC Files RG 2/2/52, Report of January 1922.

6   *Winnipeg Tribune*, 31 July 1925.

7   *Winnipeg Tribune*, 1 August 1925.

8   Johnson,"Broadway Site."

9   Ibid., 25.

10 *Winnipeg Tribune*, Tuesday, 5 October 1926, 4.

11 "City Planning Commission Report," in Artibise, *Gateway City*, 225–64.

12 *A Plan for the City of Vancouver, British Columbia*, Harland and Associates, 1928.

13 Winnipeg Electric Company Annual Report, 1929.

14 Van Nus, "Toward the City Efficient." Also Gordon, "A City Beautiful."

15 Thompson and Seager, *Canada: Decades of Discord, 1922–1939*, 67.

16 *Winnipeg Tribune*, 13 January 1926.

17 *Winnipeg Tribune*, 2 January 1922.

18 *Winnipeg Tribune*, 11 June 1926, p. 3.

19 *Winnipeg Tribune*, 27 May 1927.

20 *Winnipeg Tribune*, 22 November 1927.

21 *Winnipeg Tribune*, 5 October 1927, 5.

22 Philip, *Performing Music*, 21.

23 *Winnipeg Tribune*, 3 December 1927.

Conclusion

1   See Artibise, Table IV from census.

2   Bellan, *Winnipeg First Century*, 206.

Bibliography

Acland, F.A. "Report of the Royal Grain Inquiry Commission." Ottawa: 1925.

Aikins, James A.M. "Address of the President of the Canadian Bar Association, Winnipeg, August 1919." *Canadian Law Times* 39, no.10 (1919): 235–38.

Anderson, Charles. *Grain: The Entrepreneurs.* Winnipeg: Watson and Dwyer, 1991.

Armstrong, Christopher, and H.V. Nelles. "Contrasting Development of the Hydro-Electric Industry in the Montreal and Toronto Regions, 1900–1930." *Journal of Canadian Studies* 18, no.1 (1983): 5–27.

Artibise, Alan F.J. "Boosterism in the Development of Prairie Cities, 1871–1913." In *Town and City: Aspects of Western Canadian Urban Development,* edited by Alan F.J. Artibise, 209–35. Regina: University of Regina Press, 1981.

———. "City-Building in the Canadian West: From Boosterism to Corporatism." *Journal of Canadian Studies* 17, no. 3 (1982): 35–44.

———. "Divided City: The Immigrant in Winnipeg Society, 1874–1921." In *The Canadian City: Essays in Urban and Social History,* edited by Gilbert A. Stelter and Alan F.J. Artibise, 360–91. Ottawa: Carleton University Press, 1984.

———. *Gateway City: Documents on the City of Winnipeg, 1873–1913.* Winnipeg: Manitoba Record Society and University of Manitoba Press, 1979.

———. "Parties and Power: An Analysis of Winnipeg City Council, 1919–1975." *Social History / Histoire Sociale* 11, no. 21 (1978): 241–3.

———. "Patterns of Population Growth and Ethnic Relationships in Winnipeg, 1874–1974." *Social History / Histoire Sociale* 9, no. 18 (1976): 297–335.

———. "An Urban Environment: The Process of Growth in Winnipeg, 1874–1914." *Canadian Historical Association Historical Papers* (1972): 109–33.

———. "The Urban West: The Evolution of Prairie Towns and Cities to 1930." *Prairie Forum* 4, no. 2 (1979): 237–62.

Baker, Marilyn. *Symbol in Stone: The Art and Politics of a Public Building*. Winnipeg: Hyperion Press, 1986.

Bellan, Ruben. *Winnipeg First Century: An Economic History*. Winnipeg: Queenston House Publishing, 1978.

Bliss, Michael. *Northern Enterprise: Five Centuries of Canadian Business*. Toronto: McClelland and Stewart, 1987.

Blanchard, James. *Winnipeg 1912*. Winnipeg: University of Manitoba Press, 2005.

———. *Winnipeg's Great War: A City Comes of Age*. Winnipeg: University of Manitoba Press, 2010.

Bumsted, Jack. *The Winnipeg General Strike of 1919: An Illustrated History*. Winnipeg: Watson and Dwyer, 1994.

Burley, David G. "Immigrants in Prairie Cities: Ethnic Diversity in Twentieth-Century Canada." *H-Net Reviews in the Humanities and Social Sciences* (2011): 1–4.

———. "The Keepers of the Gate: The Inequality of Property Ownership during the Winnipeg Real Estate Boom of 1881–82." *Urban History Review / Revue d'Histoire Urbaine* 17, no. 2 (1988): 63–76.

———. "Rooster Town: Winnipeg's Lost Métis Suburb, 1900–1960." *Urban History Review / Revue d'Histoire Urbaine* 42, no. 1 (2013): 3–25.

Carstairs, Catherine. "Innocent Addicts, Dope Fiends and Nefarious Traffickers: Illegal Drug Use in 1920s English Canada." *Journal of Canadian Studies* 33, no. 3 (1998): 145–62.

Carty, Roland K. "The Electorate and the Evolution of Canadian Electoral Politics." *American Review of Canadian Studies* 26, no. 1 (1996): 7–29.

Chambers, Lori. "Adoption, Unwed Mothers and Powers of the Children's Aid Society in Ontario, 1924–1969." *Ontario History* 98, no. 2 (2006): 161–82.

Coleman, Jim. *A Hoofprint on My Heart*. Toronto: McClelland and Stewart, 1971.

Comacchio, Cynthia. "Dancing to Perdition: Adolescence and Leisure in Interwar Canada." *Journal of Canadian Studies* 32, no. 2 (1997): 5–35.

Cox, Heather M. "Drowning Voices and Drowning Shoreline: A Riverside View of the Social and Ecological Impacts of the St. Lawrence Seaway and Power Project." *Rural History* 10, no. 2 (1999): 235–57.

Desjardins, Pauline. "Navigation and Waterpower: Adaptation and Technology on Canadian Canals." *IA: The Journal of the Society for Industrial Archeology* 29, no. 1 (2003): 21–47.

Desloges, Yvon. "Behind the Scene of the Lachine Canal Landscape." *IA: The Journal of the Society for Industrial Archeology* 29, no. 1 (2003): 7–20.

Dreiman, Lawrence. "The Winnipeg Municipal Electric Utility: I. Rate Policy and Rates Charged." *Journal of Land and Public Utility Economics* 14, no. 4 (1938): 388–401.

———. "The Winnipeg Municipal Electric Utility: II. Financial History and General Conclusions." *Journal of Land and Public Utility Economics* 15, no. 1 (1939): 76–93.

Durkin, Douglas. *The Magpie: A Novel of Post War Disillusionment*. Toronto: University of Toronto Press, 1974.

Epp, A. Ernest. "Cross-Currents: Hydroelectricity and the Engineering of Northern Ontario." *Social History / Histoire Sociale* 33, no. 65 (2000): 204–6.

Epp-Koop, Stefan. *We're Going to Run this City: Winnipeg's Political Left after the General Strike*. Winnipeg: University of Manitoba Press, 2015.

Evans, Sanford. *St. Lawrence Deep Waterway in Relation to Grain Traffic*. Winnipeg: Dawson Richardson Publications, 1923.

Gidney, Catherine. "Dating and Gating: The Moral Regulation of Men and Women at Victoria and University Colleges, University of Toronto, 1920–60." *Journal of Canadian Studies* 41, no. 2 (2007): 138–60.

Gilpin, John. "The Dark Side of the 'Saskatoon Spirit': James F. Cairns and Power, Street Railway and Land Development in Saskatoon, 1908–1914." *Saskatchewan History* 45, no. 2 (1993): 15–23.

Goeres, Michael. "Disorder, Dependency and Fiscal Responsibility: Unemployment Relief in Winnipeg, 1907–1942." MA thesis, University of Manitoba, Winnipeg, 1981.

Gordon, David. "A City Beautiful Plan for Canada's Capital: Edward Bennett and the 1915 Plan for Ottawa and Hull." *Planning Perspectives* 13 (1998): 275–300.

Gordon, Michael. "Changing Patterns of Upper-Class Prep School College Placements." *Pacific Sociological Review* 12, no. 1 (1969): 23–26.

Grams, Grant. "The Deportation of German Nationals from Canada, 1919 to 1939." *Journal of International Migration and Integration* 11, no. 2 (2010): 219–37.

Gray, James. *The Roar of the Twenties*. Toronto: Macmillan Canada, 1975.

———. *The Winter Years*. Toronto: Macmillan Canada, 1966.

Gutkin, Harry, and Mildred Gutkin. *Profiles in Dissent: The Shaping of Radical Thought in the Canadian West*. Edmonton: Newest Press, 1997.

Hackett, J. Alan. *Manitoba Links: A Kaleidoscopic History of Golf*. Winnipeg: Gold Quill Publishing, 1998.

Hall, David. "Times of Trouble: Labour Quiescence in Winnipeg, 1920–29." MA thesis, University of Manitoba, Winnipeg, 1983.

Hanlon, Peter. "William Forbes Alloway." *Dictionary of Canadian Biography*, http://www.biographi.ca/en/bio/alloway_william_forbes_15E.html.

Hedlin, Ralph. "Edward A. Partridge." *Manitoba Historical Society Transactions*, Series 3 (1958/59).

Hibbits, Bernard. "A Change of Mind: The Supreme Court and the Board of Railroad Commissioners, 1903–1929." *University of Toronto Law Journal* 41, no. 1 (1991): 60–113.

Huck, Barbara, and Doug Whiteway. *One Hundred Years at St. Charles Country Club: A Centennial History*. Winnipeg: Heartland Associates, 2004.

Hungerford, Edward. *Planning a Trip Abroad*. New York: Robert McBride, 1923.

Jansen, Harold. "The Political Consequences of the Alternative Vote: Lessons from Western Canada." *Canadian Journal of Political Science* 37, no. 3 (2004): 647–69.

Johnson, Richard A. "The Broadway Site of the University of Manitoba: Origins and Demise." *Manitoba History* 51 (February 2006).

Jones, Esyllt W. "Contact Across a Diseased Boundary: Urban Space and Social Interaction during Winnipeg's Influenza Epidemic, 1918–1919." *Journal of the Canadian Historical Association* 13 (2002): 119–39.

————. "Politicizing the Laboring Body: Working Families, Death, and Burial in Winnipeg's Influenza Epidemic, 1918–1919." *Labor: Studies in Working Class History of the Americas* 3, no. 3 (2006): 57–75.

Kaplan, Harold. *Reform Planning and City Politics: Montreal, Winnipeg and Toronto.* Toronto: University of Toronto Press, 1982.

Kealey, Gregory S. "State Repression of Labour and the Left in Canada, 1914–20: The Impact of the First World War." *Canadian Historical Review* 73, no. 3 (1992): 281–314.

Kinnear, Mary. "Post-Suffrage Prairie Politics: Women Candidates in Winnipeg Municipal Elections, 1918–1939." *Prairie Forum* 16, no. 1 (1991): 41–57.

Kryzanowski, Laurence. "Canadian Banking Solvency, 1922–40." *Journal of Money, Credit and Banking* 25 (1993): 361–76.

Latham, Angela. *Posing a Threat: Flappers, Chorus Girls and Other Brazen Performers.* Middletown: Wesleyan University Press, 2000.

Levine, Alan. *Coming of Age: A History of the Jewish People of Manitoba.* Winnipeg: Heartland Press, 2009.

————. "Open Market or 'Orderly Marketing': The Winnipeg Grain Exchange and the Wheat Pools, 1923–1929." *Agricultural History* 61, no. 2 (1987): 50–71.

Levine, Steven B. "The Rise of American Boarding Schools and the Development of a National Upper Class." *Social Problems* 28, no. 1 (1980): 63–94.

Lightbody, James. "Electoral Reform in Local Government: The Case of Winnipeg." *Canadian Journal of Political Science* 11, no. 2 (1978): 307–32.

Lowe, Peter. "All Western Dollars." *Transactions of the Manitoba Historical Society,* Series 3 (1945–46).

MacLaren, James, and Associates. *Report on Waterworks Development in Metropolitan Winnipeg to 1981.* Winnipeg: City of Winnipeg, 1961.

MacPherson, Ian. "George Chipman and the Institutionalization of a Reform Movement." *Transactions of the Historical and Scientific Society of Manitoba,* Series 3, no. 32 (1975–76).

Macpherson, L.G. "Report of the Royal Commission on the Municipal Finances and Administration of Winnipeg, 1939." *Canadian Journal of Economics and Political Science* 6, no. 1 (1940): 68–72.

McCullough, A.B. "Winnipeg Ranchers: Gordon, Ironside and Fares." *Manitoba History* 41 (2001): 18–25.

McLaren, Angus. "'What Has This to Do with Working Class Women?': Birth Control and the Canadian Left, 1900–1939." *Social History / Histoire Sociale* 14, no. 28 (1981): 435–54.

Mills, Allen. "Single Tax, Socialism and the Independent Labour Party of Manitoba: The Political Ideas of F.J. Dixon and S.J. Farmer." *Labour / Le Travail* 5 (1980): 33–56.

Mitchell, Tom. "'Legal Gentlemen Appointed by the Federal Government': The Canadian State, the Citizens' Committee of 1000, and Winnipeg's Seditious Conspiracy Trials of 1919–1920." *Labour / Le Travail* 53 (2004): 9–46.

Mochoruk, Jim. *Formidable Heritage: Manitoba's North and the Cost of Development, 1870 to 1930.* Winnipeg: University of Manitoba Press, 2004.

Morrell, Kathy. "The Bronfman Family and the Yorkton Courts." *Saskatchewan History* 62, no. 1 (2010): 16–40.

Morton, Suzanne. "Women on Their Own: Single Mothers in Working-Class Halifax in the 1920s." *Acadiensis* 21, no. 2 (1992): 90–107.

Morton, William L. "The 1920s." In *The Canadians, 1867–1967,* edited by J.M.S. Careless, 205–35. Toronto: Macmillan, 1968.

Muir, James, and University of Manitoba, Faculty of Law. *The Demand for British Justice–Protest and Culture during the Winnipeg General Strike Trials.* Vol. CLHP-WPS-93-7. Winnipeg: Faculty of Law, University of Manitoba, 1993.

Murray, Karen Bridget. "Governing 'Unwed Mothers' in Toronto at the Turn of the Twentieth Century." *Canadian Historical Review* 85, no. 2 (2004): 253–76.

Nanton, Paul. *Prairie Explosion: The Life and Times of Augustus Meredith Nanton, 1860–1925.* Nanton Press, 2010.

Nelles, H.V. "Public Ownership of Electrical Utilities in Manitoba and Ontario, 1906–30." *Canadian Historical Review* 57, no. 4 (1976): 461–84.

Passfield, Robert W. "Construction of the St. Lawrence Seaway." *Canal History & Technology Proceedings* 22 (2003): 6–55.

Patton, Harold. *Grain Growers' Cooperation in Western Canada.* New York: AMS Press. 1969.

———. *Papers on the World's Wheat Trade.* Edmonton: Department of Extension, University of Alberta, 1925.

Penner, Norman. *Winnipeg, 1919: The Strikers' Own History of the Winnipeg General Strike.* Toronto: James Lorimer, 1975.

Peterson, Larry. "Revolutionary Socialism and Industrial Unrest in the Era of the Winnipeg General Strike: The Origins of Communist Labour Unionism in Europe and North America." *Labour / Le Travail* 13 (1984): 115–31.

Philip, Robert. *Performing Music in the Age of Recording.* New Haven: Yale University Press, 2004.

Pike, Robert M. "A Chequered Progress: Farmers and the Telephone in Canada, 1905–1951." *Journal of Canadian Studies* 33, no. 3 (1998): 5–30.

Purdy, Sean. "Building Homes, Building Citizens: Housing Reform and Nation Formation in Canada, 1900–20." *Canadian Historical Review* 79, no. 3 (1998): 492–523.

Rea, J.E. "The Politics of Class: Winnipeg City Council, 1919–1945." In *The West and the Nation: Essays in Honour of W.L. Morton,* edited by Carl Berger and Ramsay Cook, 233–49. Toronto: McClelland and Stewart, 1976.

———. "The Politics of Conscience: Winnipeg After the Strike." *Canadian Historical Society Historical Papers* 6, no. 1 (1971): 276–88.

———. "The Usable Urban Past." In *The Usable Urban Past: Planning and Politics in the Modern Canadian City,* edited by Alan F.J. Artibise and Gilbert Stetler, 155–65. Ottawa: Macmillan of Canada, 1979.

———. "The Wheat Board & the Western Farmer." *Beaver* 77, no. 1 (1997): 14–23.

———. *The Winnipeg General Strike.* Toronto: Holt, Rinehart and Winston of Canada, 1973.

Repatriation Committee. *General Survey of Canada's Repatriation Plans*. Ottawa: The Committee, 1919.

Riley, Robert T. *Memoirs*. The Author, 1928.

Robson, Hugh. "Report of the Royal Commssion to Enquire into the General Strike in Winnipeg." 1919.

Robson, Robert. "Manitoba's Resource Towns: The Twentieth Century Frontier." *Manitoba History* 16 (1988): 2–16.

Russenholt, Edgar S. *Heart of the Continent*. Winnipeg: McFarlane Communications, 1968.

Sangster, Joan. "The Communist Party and the Woman Question, 1922–1929." *Labour / Le Travail* 15 (1985): 25–56.

Segworth, Walter. *Retraining Canada's Disabled Soldiers*. Ottawa: King's Printer, 1920.

Seidman, Steven. "Sexual Attitudes of Victorian and Post-Victorian Women: Another Look at the Mosher Survey." *Journal of American Studies* 23, no. 1 (1989): 68–72.

Sendbueller, Matt. "To Produce the Highest Type of Manhood and Womanhood." *Urban History Review / Revue d'Histoire Urbaine* 26, no. 2 (1998): 42–55.

Seventh Census of Canada, 1931. Volume XII, Monographs, *Housing in Canada*, by H.F. Greenway, 411–578, http://publications.gc.ca/collections/collection_2017/statcan/CS98-1931-12-eng.pdf.

Sharp, Walter. "The Canadian Election of 1925." *American Political Science Review* 20, no. 1 (1926): 107–17.

Smith, Doug. *The Winnipeg Labour Council, 1894–1994*. Winnipeg: Manitoba Labour Education Centre, 1994.

Spragge, Shirley. "A Confluence of Interests: Housing Reform in Toronto, 1900–1920." In *The Usable Urban Past: Planning and Politics in the Modern Canadian City*, edited by Alan Artibise and Gilbert Stetler, 247–67. Toronto: Macmillan, 1979.

Stamp, Robert. "Canadian High Schools in the 1920s and 1930s: The Social Challenge to the Academic Tradition." Canadian Historical Society, *Historical Papers* 13, no. 1 (1978): 76–93.

Stevenson, J.A. "The Political and Economic Situation in Canada." *Edinburgh Review* 492 (1925): 209–29.

Strong-Boag, Veronica. "Canadian Feminism in the 1920s: The Case of Nellie L. McClung." *Journal of Canadian Studies* 12, no. 4 (1977): 58–68.

Sutcliffe, J.H. "The Economic Background of the Winnipeg General Strike." MA thesis, University of Manitoba, Winnipeg, 1972.

Taylor, Jeffery M. *"Fashioning Farmers: Ideology, Agricultural Knowledge and the Manitoba Farm Movement, 1890—1925*. Regina: University of Regina Press, 1994.

Thompson, John Herd. "The Prohibition Question in Manitoba, 1892–1928." MA thesis, University of Manitoba, Winnipeg, 1969.

———. "The Political Career of Ralph H. Webb." *Red River Valley Historian* (Summer 1976): 1.

Thompson, John Herd, and Alan Seager. *Canada 1922–1939: Decades of Discord*. Toronto: McClelland and Stewart, 1985.

Van Every, Margaret. "Francis Hector Clerque and the Rise of Sault Ste. Marie as an Industrial Centre." *Ontario History* 56, no. 3 (1964): 191–202.

Van Nus, W. "Toward the City Efficient: The Theory and Practice of Zoning, 1919–1939." In *The Usable Urban Past: Planning and Politics in the Modern Canadian City,* edited by Alan Artibise and Gilbert Stetler, 226–46. Toronto: Macmillan, 1979.

Vincent, David. "The Development of the High-Rise Apartment Complex in the Roslyn Road Area." MA thesis, University of Manitoba, Winnipeg, 1974.

Wayburn, Ned. *The Art of Stage Dancing.* New York: Ned Wayburn Studios of Stage Dancing, 1925.

Wichern, Philip H. *The Development of Urban Government in the Winnipeg Area: A Collection of Materials from Government Reports and Student Research Papers.* Vol. 1. Winnipeg: Dept. of Urban Affairs, Province of Manitoba with the co-operation of the Dept. of Political Studies, University of Manitoba, 1973.

Yellis, Kenneth A. "Prosperity's Child: Some Thoughts on the Flapper." *American Quarterly* 21, no. 1 (1969): 44–64.

Index